DATE DUE

THE WILDER SHORE

By Stephen Longstreet

Fiction

THE PEDLOCKS
PEDLOCK & SONS
THE LION AT MORNING
MAN OF MONTMARTRE
REMEMBER WILLIAM KITE?
EAGLES WHERE I WALK
A FEW PAINTED FEATHERS
WAR IN THE GOLDEN WEATHER
MASTS TO SPEAR THE STARS

Non-fiction

THE BOY IN THE MODEL-T
THE REAL JAZZ OLD AND NEW
TREASURY OF THE WORLD'S GREAT PRINTS
SPORTIN' HOUSE
THE WILDER SHORE

Travel

THE LAST MAN AROUND THE WORLD
LAST MAN COMES HOME
THE WORLD REVISITED

Plays

HIGH BUTTON SHOES

1. *Fleeing the San Francisco fire of 1906.*

THE WILDER SHORE

A GALA SOCIAL HISTORY OF SAN FRANCISCO'S
SINNERS AND SPENDERS

1849 – 1906

TEXT AND DRAWINGS BY

Stephen Longstreet

"The great pleasure in life is
doing what people say you cannot do."

WALTER BAGEHOT – 1869

DOUBLEDAY & COMPANY, INC.

GARDEN CITY, NEW YORK

1968

Library of Congress Catalog Card Number 68–18100
Copyright © 1968 by Stephen Longstreet
All Rights Reserved
Printed in the United States of America
First Edition

To the Memory of the Friend

WILLIAM FAULKNER

And his years on the West Coast
When he suggested there could be
this kind of book . . .

2. *The time of whisky and guns.*

Look history over and you will see. The missionary comes after the whiskey—I mean, he arrives after the whiskey has arrived. Next comes the poor immigrant with ax and hoe and rifle; next, the trader, next the miscellaneous rush; next the gambler, the desperado, the highwayman, and all their kindred in sin of both sexes; and next the smart chap who has bought up an old grant that covers all the land; this brings in the lawyer tribe; the vigilance committee brings the undertaker. All these interests bring the newspaper; the newspaper starts up politics and a railroad; all hands turn to and build a church and a jail —and behold, civilization is established forever in the land.

Mark Twain

I believe the power to make money is a gift of God . . . to be developed and used to the best of our ability for the good of mankind. Having been endowed with the gift I possess, I believe it is my duty to make money and still more money, and to use the money I make for the good of my fellow man according to the dictates of my conscience.

19th century multimillionaire

America is the land of the self-made man—the empire of the parvenu. Here it is felt that the accident of birth is of trifling consequence; here there is no "blood" that is to be coveted save the red blood which every masterful man distills in his own arteries; and here the name of parvenu is the only and all-sufficient title of nobility.

Henry Clews

CONTENTS

3. The Golden Gate before they built the bridge.

BY WAY OF INTRODUCTION

"The only history worth reading is that written
at the time of which it treats, the history of
what was done and seen, heard out of the mouths
of the men who did and saw . . ."

John Ruskin

The erudite Mr. Ruskin did not have such a book as this in mind,
but his credo fits this informal social history of an era of sinners
and spenders and some remarkable men and women. Some were
good, others bad, charming or greedy; all were hot to live, eager
to enjoy; while building a city in no anxious insulation, or for
that matter patriarchal rigidity.

I have gone to original documents, unpublished letters, journals,
daybooks, yellowing newspapers, forgotten reports, rather than to the
modern popularizers of the times for what I set down here. It
was all amazing, from the cry of "Gold! Gold in Californee!" to
the shouts of "San Francisco is burning" on the quivering morning

of an April in 1906, as the tremors of the great earthquake shook down and charred the old city, perhaps as a lesson that nature— as one critic put it—is our voracious and inescapable executioner.

I have found two major original sources, unpublished, that give an intimate close-up of both ends of the scale of living in the city in those days. The person identified as R.J. in the text was a distant relative of my mother; he was an active wine merchant in San Francisco from 1859 to 1910, in the gay bachelor tradition. He mixed with the best people to present his imported champagne and wines. He knew rich miners, silver kings, railroad builders, boodle grabbing political rascals and their ladies, doxies and casual friends. He diligently kept a series of daybooks, in which he recorded his business contacts, his social appointments, and with crisp frankness wrote out some of the gossip, details of parties and dramas of which he was aware. Descendents of relatives of his still live on the West Coast, so he will remain identified here simply as R.J. Like most of us he, too, searched for the sufficient self. In an old letter he wrote: "We can permit ourselves remorse—but never regrets."

The second document I used was sections of the unpublished memoirs of a madam—Nell Kimball—who ran a sporting house in New Orleans until 1917, but who from 1898 to 1901, because of a scandal in her place involving a prominent family, was told by friends on the police force of that Southern city to get out of town for a few years "till things cooled off." She came to San Francisco and there ran a high class brothel for some years before returning to New Orleans. I have touched on some of her experiences before, in writing of the birth of jazz music in Storeyville, but the San Francisco portion of her memoirs is here printed for the first time. I acquired the Kimball MS in the early thirties, a time when conditions did not permit the publication of the details she wrote of in her life as a sporting house madam.

Two vital sources of events and details were *The Annals of San Francisco*, by Frank Soulé, John H. Gihon, James Nisbet, 1855, and *History of the San Francisco Bay Region*, by Millard Bailey, 1924.

There are also about four hundred volumes of memoirs, histories, confessions, police reports and privately printed texts that it would be very impressive to list, but not here. A historic gold mine or rather series of mines were the loud and gaudy newspapers of the period; shouting at the top of their voices they told of the happenings, social events, crimes, political pilfering, passions and personalities of the city from the gold discovery of 1849 to the loss of the old city in 1906. I have had to check with care, for newspapermen *and* Mark Twain, Bret Harte, Jack London, Frank Norris and others wrote with imagination at times and often turned away a bit from the truth. But in the main what I have used after careful sifting appears to fit the facts as later historians have used them. I had the run of almost the complete files of the newspapers of the region: *Times, Call, Herald, Alta California, Globe, Examiner, Chronicle, Bulletin* and *Call-Bulletin.* For this and other aid I thank the Library of Congress, Washington; the Huntington Library, California; the New York Public Library; the Bancroft Library at Berkeley, California; the State Library of California at Sacramento.

The material as a social history urgently needed graphic illustration. The woodcuts and engravings of the period were lively enough, but remote and rather over-romantic. The old photographs unless used in great number were inadequate. And the intimate stance I wanted of the people I had set down did not exist. So I decided to draw from life actual Californians of today, *but* in the costumes I found in a rare set of old fashion plates showing the proper tailor's touch, the mode, the cut, the tilt of the tall plug hats, the high button shoes, and the very settings of plush and red velvet, even bric-a-brac of Victorian and Edwardian grace. A smug pride was evident, and the vulgarity, too, of gold spittoons and the odor of the best horses. Clothes and menus, programs and carriages are often a form of psychological introspection, smelling of scent and a good white wine.

No man writes alone of a visit to a period. His knowledge has limits; so I want to thank Margaret Cousins, my editor at Doubleday, who saw merit in this project and nursed it through its birth pains; Helen Wurdemann, whose knowledge of historic women's fashions and styles of the past (some of her collection is now in the Los Angeles County Museum of Art) helped so much with the drawings: Lorser Feitelson, artist, teacher and friend, who encouraged me as a draftsman during a long period of time. And all those who helped with a press clipping, an old picture, a bit of scandal, gossip, details of mining, railroad building, sporting life, the great dinners, the splendid age of the horse and tiara.

If I have any personal idea about this kind of book, I advocate more history on the human level, free of the usual clatter of historic dates, battles, kings, horrors, crusades, pogroms, bigotry and power drives to deadly wars, murderously fought for peace, *always* peace. I admire an older historian of San Francisco, Ambrose Bierce, inditing formal historical writing: "History: An account mostly false, of events mostly unimportant, which are brought about by rulers mostly knaves, and soldiers mostly fools."

This is not that kind of history.

Miradero Road, California.   *Stephen Longstreet*

THE WILDER SHORE

Book One

DIGGING FOR GOOD FORTUNE

1

FIRST WAS THE LAND

Bee It Knowne Vunto All Men By These Presents
Ivne 17 1579
By The Grace Of God And In The Name Of Herr
Maiesty Qveen Elizabeth Of England And Herr
Svccesors Forever I Take Possession Of This
Kingdom Whos King and People Freely Resigne
Their Right And Title In The Whole
Land Vnto Her Maiesties Keepeing Now
Name By Mee An To Bee Knowne Vnto All Men
As Nova Albion

Francis Drake

So reads a brass plate bearing this inscribed message found on the north shore of San Francisco Bay between San Rafael and Corte Madera Creek during the summer of 1936. It is five by eight inches in size, roughly engraved with a sharp tool, most likely on board Sir Francis Drake's famous vessel the *Golden Hinde*. The record shows he set down in his log that around Latitude 38° he found a "faire and good baye with a goode winde to enter same." It now seems likely he entered the Golden Gate and set his sea hawk's eye on the hills on which San Francisco now stands and was the first non-native to discover the place under the scudding clouds, the guttural gawk of its sea gulls.

However, is the brass plate for real? an actual historic item? Turned over to metallurgical experts it was tested chemically, its patina checked, the famous Carbon 14 dating technique applied.

By these tests the plate went back to the Elizabethan era. The professors went to work on the actual text, the I for J, the V for U, and the free wheeling spelling. Here, too, they agreed the plate was the real and true thing. The University of California's Herbert E. Bolton formally announced it as a genuine plate, thus setting up Sir Francis Drake as the European discoverer of San Francisco's site.

In England, it seems, the discovery of merely more "savage land" wasn't very important. Spain was strong and closer to the Golden Gate; so nothing ensued from the English discovery. The gore and thunder, the splendid rhetoric of Shakespeare's Elizabethan age also made for an instability of temperament—and there were just *too* many discoveries all over the place.

Today the official guidebooks are bland and give only niggardly details: "San Francisco is on the central coast of California, on a peninsula bounded by the Pacific Ocean on the west, Golden Gate on the north, San Francisco Bay on the east. New York City is 3,012 miles east, Miami 3,162 miles southeast, Los Angeles 405 miles south. Juan Cabrillo, a Portuguese explorer in the service of Spain, sighted the bay in the early 16th century and Sir Francis Drake sailed by it in 1579. Don Gaspar de Portolá arrived in 1769. In 1776 the Spanish established the mission and presidio of San Dolores.

"Built on hills, between the mountains and the sea, San Francisco has one of the most beautiful settings of any American city. Its inhabitants are inclined to resent the Easterner's description of their city as a 'little New York.' Everyone agrees San Francisco is a sophisticated town filled with well-dressed people, a financial and business area of prime importance, and a cosmopolitan, colorful, interesting place to visit. Many of its streets have steep grades and the weather is often damp, but the loyalty of San Franciscans remains steadfast."

No hint here of its wild, brutal, rich past or its harlots, social battles, new rich society in the days of gold dust and champagne corks and six horse coaches.

"It never gets either terribly hot or terribly cold—not for long;

4. When San Francisco was a sporting town.

the weather may be described as mild. Unlike other American cities, San Francisco's warmest months are September and October. Rainfall is slight from May through September, but fairly heavy during the winter months. Humidity is San Francisco's weather problem—the annual average is 73%. Most days are moist; there are also heavy sea fogs that roll over the city in the early evening and burn away in the morning sun."

An early issue of the San Francisco *Herald* gives us a truer picture of the early town: "There are certain spots in our city infested by the most abandoned men and women . . . The upper part of Pacific Street, after dark, is crowded by thieves, gamblers, low women, drunken sailors, and similar characters, who resort to the groggeries that line the street, and there spend the night in the most hideous orgies. Every grog shop is provided with a fiddle, from which some half-drunken creature tortures execrable sounds, called by way of compliment, music. Shortly after dark the dancing commences, and is kept up unceasingly to the sound of the fiddle, until broke up by a row or the exhaustion of those engaged in it. These ruffian resorts are the hot beds of drunkenness, and the scenes of unnumbered crimes. Unsuspecting sailors and miners are entrapped by the dexterous thieves and swindlers that are always on the lookout, into these dens, where they are filled with liquor—drugged if necessary, until insensibility coming upon them, they fall an easy victim to their tempters. In this way many robberies are committed, which are not brought to light through shame on the part of the victim. When the habitués of this quarter have reason to believe a man has money, they follow him up for days, and employ every device to get him into their clutches . . ."

As for the social scene—we find in the unpublished daybook of R.J., the wine merchant and man about town, such items as these: "Fine afternoon, chat with Mike DeYoung at bar of Bank Exchange. Both drinking Duncan Nichoil's good version of Pisco Punch. Mike turning to me, banging a gold double eagle on the bar: Damn it, take a look at it. Those mint marks say it's from the San Francisco mint. We make our own coins here. Nick, two more Piscos.

"Went this morning with John McKay and party to see the

sending off as an American exhibit of his solid silver dinner service to the Paris World's Fair [1873]. Took twelve husky porters to get it loaded—McKay saying it was made for him by Shreve and Co. from his own Comstock Lode silver, dug from his own mines. Went up then to Wells-Fargo on Montgomery Street to see the gold bullion still in its wooden cases come down from the Mother Lode. Lunched at M's—*Gigot d'agneau en croute, Crêpes Baumanière*. Sold an order for sixteen dozen of the Burgundy, four of the Preussische Staatsdomane.

"Serviced some of the 1,000 magnums of champagne at Virginia City (International Hotel) for dinner John McKay gave for Duke of Sutherland. Strange mixture of full evening attire, tails and white ties and cowboy boots.

"Stocked Zek Kendall, who was in the big strikes at Tonopah and Goldfield, with a cellar full of Madeira, Dom Perignon champagne, Steinberger Kabinett."

Going back in time to explorers in rusted iron from the Gulf of Tehuantepec, to an age of rancheros, serapes, vaqueros, tales of fandangos and deadly grizzlies, how does it all lead to the city at the headlands of the Golden Gate, the vigilance committees, the glitter and vice of the Barbary Coast?

The calm and peace and brotherly love of the early mission culture around San Francisco and down the coast to Mexico have become too encrusted with rosy legends and myths. It was actually, historians show, a land grab and enslavement of the Indians in most cases, beginning with Father Junipero and his Franciscan priests, who had the Indians labor at building twenty-one missions on land taken from them. The missions may have been picturesque, sanctified in origin, but in truth the holy fathers in sandals and flapping robes created the first California real estate boom. Vast acreages of land were seized for the Church, the Indians rounded up for forced labor. The California Indian was never a proud and valid fighter for his rights. He was baptized and converted without his being aware of the significance of it, and he was put to work from sunup to sundown at hard manual labor, paid merely in a thin miserable wine. He had to provide his own corn as food. It was the

5. *California Indian—the true Native Son.*

same thing that happened in the Sandwich Islands, later called Hawaii, but this time it was the Protestant missionaries who came to assess the natives' souls and land. And as Mark Twain was to put it: "In the end the missionaries had the land and the natives had the bible."

The California missions were amazingly wealthy. Even as early as 1834 the San Gabriel Mission alone was worth eighty million dollars, comprising seventeen vast ranchos, holding huge herds of sheep, steers, horses, and serviced by three thousand miserable Indian slaves living in adobe huts. Of their condition a later report states they were "slave laborers and slaves . . . seldom permitted to live as families. Those who tried to escape felt the full force of raiding parties who brought them back dead or alive." It is good to know, however, that dead or alive their souls were usually saved. It had been planned to have the Franciscans turn the mission lands, after ten years, back to the civil authorities, but of course such plans were not followed, and the government was reported as slack, lazy, dishonest and indifferent, imbedded in a moral insufficiency and ornate Spanish manners.

When Mexico broke with Spain it got rid of the unpopular, disliked Spanish priests in power and a series of degrees secularized the missions and their wealth. On paper the land was to go to the Indians, the rest was presented as grants to high caste civilians, soldiers and Mexican and Spanish political fat cats. The padres did their best to avoid and delay the decrees, and when the division was over the Indian had almost nothing, and the most sly and aggressive of the dons had seized unbelievable empires of land from horizon to horizon. Power as usual had been created by an attentuated and intricate web of politics. Grandees of land, kings of beef, barons of vineyards made their own laws, held their own courts (one was held on horseback) and fiestas complete with executions and floggings.

These mordant joys didn't last. Falling markets in cattle hides and tallow, dry spells that made the land dust bowls, an arrogant and lunatic love of vice, remarkable epics in whoring and gambling and money borrowing: all this with the dictated Peace of Hidalgo in 1848 (when the United States took over the whole hog) ruined the vast land grant empires. The hostile U.S. courts, complete with land-shark lawyers and carpetbagging con men, asked the land-owners to prove clear title to their ranchos. Lacking money, the dons paid off in land to Yankee lawyers and the legal sharpers they hired to defend their rights.

In the end it was the same game as in Hawaii all over again. The lawyers and their political partners got the land, the dons remained with dusty memories of past glory. An average land grant case manipulated through the courts took from seventeen to eighteen years to adjudicate, and hardly ever came out in favor of the Spanish or Mexican holder. There were more than five hundred original big grants; of these the U.S. courts, complete with spittoons and flatulent legal jargon, upheld only about seventy.

The schemes to strip the dons were many; the crude methods might vary, but the end result was shocking. Take the Rancho de los Alamitos; it was twenty-six thousand fine acres, yet it went to a Yankee with pull for $152 in "delinquent taxes."

There is a shell of myths about California and the West thick as a turtle's. Study the life of the real "Captain" Sutter. This flashy, not too respectable ego-maniac, the self-appointed "Captain" John A. Sutter, runaway Swiss bankrupt, was trying to start a personal empire in the Sacramento Valley, complete with Hawaiian and Indian concubines and semi-slave Indian retainers. Here in 1848 someone found the yellow crumbs of gold. Though Sutter called his place New Helvetia, California, it did not stir men's imaginations any more than Zanzibar or Iceland, *before* the talk of gold.

What was to be San Francisco was little more than fifty or so adobe shacks, faded tents and lopsided slab-log sheds, set along half of Yerba Buena (Good Herb) Cove. The Hudsons Bay Company had failed to make a settlement here some time before. Often a Nantucket whaler drifted in, weathered and shaggy after two or three years in the Japanese Sea or the semi-Arctic, hunting the giant sperm whale. For the most part Yerba Buena's three or four hundred citizens—no one really kept records—scratched the native flea, lived their placid lives, ruled in theory once by far off Mexico

City, which place in turn nodded for indolent orders from the direction of Madrid, from the imbecile rulers with the drooling chin. The settlement's thoughts on human nature were mostly a lazy self-knowledge.

Franciscan monks in pious zeal had built a mission below Yerba Buena, which was still a long way from becoming San Francisco. That was in 1776 when the Gringos along the eastern shore of the continent were signing a Declaration of Independence, and fighting their Hanoverian king, George III, another beef-faced Gringo. The Mexican soldiers up at Yerba Buena's Presidio (or fort), near what was to be named the Golden Gate, found it a wild place, for beyond them were only the gulls and the hill rats and some rabbits. In 1835 the harbor master, oddly enough an American, W. A. Richards, set up a tent made of old ship's sail on a lot that was to be included in the future city.

In 1846 the Americans seized the city and six months later, in 1847, the alcalde, or mayor, decided to call the place San Francisco, after someone's favorite saint, St. Francis, who, we are told, talked to birds; perhaps it was later hinted the sea gulls had gotten to the alcalde when the Gringos made him eat umbrage like cake. So that was the town's new name. In the fashion of the times, unencumbered by need for excuses, or the legal pretext of modern armed peace missions, the sloop-of-war *Portsmouth*, USN, commanded by a Captain Montgomery, simply marched a detachment of sailors up to the Plaza and raised the American flag, to the natives' apparent indifference. Time was to see the Plaza renamed Portsmouth Square and the waterfront street called Montgomery. Nearly two years later, records show, there was a population of seven hundred whites, half *Americanos* or native stock, the rest Mexican-Spanish, Negroes, Sandwich Islanders (as Hawaiians were then called before the missionaries swapped their Bibles for the land). There were a few Indians. The full count of standing structures, taken by someone with a country sense of humor, listed two hundred buildings, including the barns, tents *and* outhouses, single seaters and doubles.

In 1846 the Mormons, not knowing of the seizure of the town a few days before, and being run out of Nauvoo, Illinois, by a traditionally American lynch mob, sent a feisty Elder of the Latter-day Saints, Samuel Brannan, with a company of immigrants to the Pacific Coast, where the United States' anti-polygamists had no gentile jurisdiction over their begetting and begetting. The Elder Brannan, seeing the American stars and stripes over the Presidio, in rage danced on his hat and shouted, "There is that damn goddamned rag again!" (In theory Mormons were against profanity, drink and tobacco, but both Joseph Smith and Brigham Young, two founding fathers of the sect, like other backsliders, boozed, chawed tobacco, and were known to curse.)

Elder Brannan, ecclesiastical and greedy, set up a general store at Sutter's Fort and urged Brigham Young to bring the whole flock of Elders and their harems to San Francisco rather than to the dismal Salt Lake Valley. But Brigham, a wiser man, decided the wilderness was the place for his virile sons of Abraham. So San Francisco just missed being the heartland of polygamy. The early Mormons had resources uniquely their own.

Elder Brannan in anger refused to pay his share and his flock's share of their wealth into the mother church in Salt Lake City, and Brigham Young sent out his pious gunmen to San Francisco, the Destroying Angels, also known as the Danites, to lean on Elder Brannan, using muscle or lead. Elder Brannan had his own hired gunslingers, called the Exterminators, who went out to meet the Destroying Angels of Brigham Young in the dry desert lands before they could get to the city. It was a kind of gang warfare, and some saloon wit later called it "the first East West sports contest."

It was said: "Sam Brannan was so far sighted he wiped his arse before he shat." In any case he became rich, a prosperous big spender in San Francisco's gay world, and resigning from the Church of Latter-day Saints, replaced it with the first vigilance committee, another lynch mob dedicated to his version of law and order by rope and Colt. Sam Brannan, lost to Mormonism in time, took to the bottle, found many easy ways to spend his fortune, drifted to Mexico to die there lonely and in rags, an object lesson to the duality of the world.

To backtrack in our history to the gold rush: Captain Sutter was a large landowner, cattle raiser, land sower, trader, a master stud to Indian girls and Hawaiian *vahines*. But he was a careless man about business. His habit was to buy supplies on vast credits, owe much for years and hardly ever pay up. Land rich, a sultan of the Sacramento, he lived like an Asian potentate, building and expanding his estates, always short of cash, always a bad credit risk but full of pleasure in his livestock *and* handmaidens.

In January of 1848 he had plans for building a sawmill on the American River, sixty miles east of what was to be the capital city of Sacramento. The captain hired James A. Marshall, a drifting handyman, to build the mill, and he, while cutting a tailrace in the stream bed, saw and picked up some shiny particles he hoped were gold.

One of the mill carpenters was a Mormon who kept a journal: "January 24. This day some kind of metal that looks like gold was found in tail race."

Marshall showed Sutter his find. Sutter tested it and agreed it was gold but said to keep it a secret. Marshall, a loose-tongued fellow, soon spilled the fact and the gold rush of history was on, not fast and bursting seams as in the films, but slowly at first, as people decided there *might* be something to it. It was April before people in San Francisco began to desert their shacks and move up over Sutter's land, stealing his cattle, cutting up his fields, destroying him forever as a rich man. Soon two thousand men and a few women were hunting gold with a licentious energy.

Some of the Mexican-Spanish Californians moved out along with the gold hunters, but most of them stayed with their own placid lives, smoking corn husk cigarettes, eating the Arroz Mexicano (Mexican rice), which retained a flavor twice removed *a la española*. The *Yanqui* adopted some of their life in the west, especially food like chili or enchiladas with black beans, raw avocado purée, *sopa del pan* (bread soup) and the native olives, frijoles and tortillas. The Americans liked the *salchichón* (salami) and the Spanish *aguardiente* (brandy).

Those that joined the gold hunters in their relentlessly hard tasks panned for gold by sloshing dirt in a pan of water and floating off the lighter material, hoping for a few gleams of gold specks to pick up. But this soon gave way to a more back-breaking method. The wife of a doctor in a mining camp at Indian Bar described the bleak realities of the process in a letter home: "In many places the surface soil, or in mining phrase, the top dirt, pays when worked in a Long-Tom. This is a trough about twenty feet in length and eight inches in depth, formed of wood, with the exception of six feet at one end, called the 'riddle,' which is made of sheet-iron perforated with holes about the size of a large marble. Underneath this colander-like portion of the Long-Tom is placed another trough, about ten feet long, the sides six inches in height, which, divided through the middle by a slender slat, is called the riffle-box. It takes several persons to manage properly a Long-Tom. Three or four men station themselves with spades at the head of the machine, while at the foot of it stands an individual armed 'wid de shovel an' de hoe.' The spadesmen throw in large quantities of the precious dirt, which is washed down to the riddle by a stream of water leading into the Long-Tom through wooden gutter or sluices. When the soil reaches the riddle, it is kept constantly in motion by the man with the hoe. Of course, by this means all the dirt and gold escapes through the perforations into the riffle-box below, one compartment of which is placed just beyond the riddle. Most of the dirt washes over the sides of the riffle-box, but the gold, being so astonishingly heavy, remains safely at the bottom of it. When the machine gets too full of stones to be worked easily, the man whose business it is to attend to them throws them out with his shovel, looking carefully among them as he does so for any pieces of gold which may have been too large to pass through the holes of the riddle. I am sorry to say he generally loses his labor. At night they pan out the gold, which has been collected in the riffle-box during the day. Many of the miners decline washing the top dirt at all, but try to reach as quickly as possible the bed-rock, where are found the richest deposits of gold."

She adds sadly: "A man may work in a claim for many months

6. *Two miners—one found gold, the other didn't.*

and be poorer at the end of the time than when he commenced, or he may take out thousands in a few hours. It is a mere matter of chance. A friend of ours . . . told us that after working a claim for six months he had taken out but six ounces."

The real easy work was stealing Spanish land grants. All this stealing was behind opaque and usually dishonest procedures. The Rancho Rodeo de las Aguas was swindled over to new-won owners for only $450 in cash and $800 in promises. Today it's known as Beverly Hills, the most expensive real estate in the world. It is on record that one proud Spanish owner killed himself at the sheriff's sale of his property. But mostly the dons quietly slipped into poverty, shrugging their shoulders at Yankee greed. The Indians must have smiled (for they do smile) as they repeated folklore and tribal legends of when the land was theirs before the padres, the grandees, the white men who spoke with the forked tongue. A great-great-grandson of Don Julio Verdugo (the Verdugo Hills are still on the map) became a hot tamale peddler.

Following the land grabs came the railroad builders. The land was there but too few people to use the rails, so they began to lure people west, with promises on brightly printed broadsides, to a land of milk and honey where there were Gila monsters and rattlesnakes. The Santa Fe and the Southern Pacific began a rate war for passenger business. Both for a time were hauling passengers west at one dollar a head! A local bribed newspaper blessed it all calling it, "The greatest mass movement in history of good, plain, middle-class, God-fearing men and women."

Railroad agents toured Europe, and even covered Ireland, selling lots and land to the amazed immigrants, even before they had packed or booked passage. In wait for the new pioneers were shyster lawyers, townsite sharks, deed swindlers, interest defaulting bankers, costly land surveys, county services in the pay of boomers and early wheeler dealers. Methods explaining syndicates, subdivision of tracts, mining properties, ranch land, grazing and water rights, mineral assets caused one businessman, Harris Marks, to exclaim of these early hustling Californians: "Two thirds of our population were, in a sense, more insane than sane."

Every town was a boom town, every scheme a fortune. Hotel clerks and bellboys sold land and whores with the ice water. Ministers were known to keep their Bibles interspersed with land deeds which they offered to the parishioners as bargain gates to wealth. Amen, *Amen!* Already in the town the human vultures—sports, harlots and shady lawyers and land grabbers—were beginning to set up their nets.

Sang an early California poet:

> Mad'moiselle, I love you well,
> I fain would kiss your toe.
> Ah! *oui*, Monsieur, my cheeks are near,
> You need not stoop so low.

Anticipatory dreams loomed large in the town's image of itself. The first big gold strikes were hardly out of the bed stream before certain citizens, like Sam Brannan, peddlers and shopkeepers like Collis P. Huntington, saw this was the chance of a lifetime. Buildings were the things to erect; anything that could shelter, offer love at a price, hold a deck of cards or a wheel of chance, serve something hot ("If you bite through it, it's food."), something potent to warm the gizzard of the gold hunter.

Meals of baked pumpkin and bear meat, a piggin of soaked corn hominy and a bit of chili would give way to dishes by a French chef, if one had the where-with-all gold or coins made of it. Marquetry cabinets would replace a dirty shirt rolled in a muddy blanket.

If the miners were victims of malignant bilious fevers, stiff joints and illnesses ("the miseries") found only in *materia medica* and not known to the mule doctor who usually serviced most camps, there was always the idea that enough of the soft yellow metal could bring true the dreams of taffeta petticoats, wasp waists and whisky in cut glass tumblers.

The *Annals* remarked in its survey of 1849: "Every immigrant on landing at San Francisco became a new man in his own estimation, and was prepared to undertake anything or any piece of business whatever . . . The great recognized orders of society were tumbled topsy-turvy. Doctors and dentists became draymen . . . lawyers, brokers and clerks turned waiters or auctioneers.

"At the close of 1849 the population of the town numbered at least twenty (thousand) and probably nearly twenty-five thousand souls. A very small proportion were females—a still smaller one, children of either sex; while the vast majority were adult males in the very prime of manhood . . . There was no such thing as a *home* to be found. Both dwellings and places of business were either common canvas tents, or small rough board shanties, or frame buildings of one story. Only the great gambling saloons, the hotels, restaurants, and a few public building and stores had any pretensions to size, comfort or elegance."

Business went on as usual, and if supplies were scarce, the shopkeepers didn't mind putting fancy labels on damaged goods. A newspaper listed the method: "A large quantity of damaged ginger, mixed with sawdust, has been put up in new cases, neatly labeled and sold for the genuine article—as also a large quantity of damaged saleratus, damaged oysters, damaged peaches, stinking butter in genuine firkins, marked with the favorite brand of Hope & Co., bogus yeast powders with the mark of Preston U. Merrill on them. The peaches were bought at a low figure and put in new boxes made to imitate genuine Chile peaches, as they sell for a higher price; these . . . as also on cream of tartar, which is very scarce and high priced now."

Upper class crimes of passion delighted the town. An eyewitness describes a husband who had just discovered his wife's lover: "Graham brought a double-barreled shotgun and informed me what he intended doing when Lemon came down the usual way to his place of business. I said to him, 'Will, don't do that. Go out and meet him on equal terms.' He left the gun and instead took a Colt's revolver and met him (Lemon) on the south side of Merchant street opposite the plaza. Lemon's shot staggered Graham, who retreated backwards and tripped and fell on the steps of the Union Hotel. . . . Lemon, while he [Graham] was down . . . placed the muzzle of the pistol in his mouth and fired, carrying away several teeth. My brother, not being conversant with the customs of this kind of fight, interfered and took Lemon away, who still had another load in his pistol, and it no doubt saved Graham's life."

2

INSIDE THE GOLDEN GATE

Energies, embroilments, turmoil beyond count along with lots of whisky and beans went into the Sacramento Valley with the men who came to dig for gold. Mexicans and South Americans came along too, the first of many outsiders to dream of bonanzas of instantaneous fulfillment. Gold seemed to be everywhere, and the mobs fanned out to the Yuka and the Feather rivers, up the gulches, ravines and the icy cold rushing brooks of the Sierras.

Marshall, the discoverer, did better than Sutter. He got rid of his share of the mill for two thousand dollars, boasted he knew of better gold fields, and so the miners got a rope ready to hoist him to heaven unless he told. He ran for it and the mob tore the mill to bits, and so no commemorative plaque sits on the right spot.

In time the East heard of the gold discovery through slow mails and slower ships. In September 1848, the Baltimore *Sun* published the news, based on the report sent by a former American consul on the coast to the Secretary of State, James Buchanan (later president). Apparently there was the usual Washington news leak, and other big city papers copied the story. In the Middle West freighters and fur men brought the news; so the autumn of 1848 saw the first overland gold hunters on their way, packs on their backs, rifles over shoulders, and usually picks and shovels too. "I'm goin' to Californiee, my banjo on mah knee!"

The shipping lines beat most of the wagon trains in. In February 1849, the steamship *California*, with a cargo of chafing Eastern and

7. *Trouble at the mines.*

Southern gold seekers, cast her anchor into the mud of Yerba Buena Cove. In a year's time fifty thousand men were coming through the Golden Gate headed for the diggings, and wagon trains were bringing thousands more. San Francisco Bay soon looked like the Dead Sea Graveyard of All Ships. Thousands of vessels and ships of all sizes and tonnage were deserted by their crews and officers, left to rot, while the men departed up the Sacramento where the talk was, you just "shook gold nuggets right out of the grass roots."

Wrote an eyewitness: "Sailors were the most unrestrainable in their determination to go to the diggings; and it was there a common saying that sailors, niggers and Dutchmen were the luckiest men in the mines; a very drunken old salt was always particularly lucky." At least before he got back to town to face the wild women, the deadly whisky and the nimble-fingered gambler.

The city soon had fifty thousand residents, mostly men, mostly in their teens, twenties and thirties. Only half of the wealth seekers dug; those with strong backs and simple minds. The rest sold tools, supplies, set up shops, sporting houses, gambling hells. Others shoed horses and mules, sold lots, dealt in mines, or became plain highway men, claim jumpers, bullion thieves, drunkards and loafers. Even the law was greedy. Said a judge at an inquest of a killing: "I find the corpse fifty dollars for carrying a concealed weapon."

The ships, deserted and empty, rotted and sank at their anchors. Some were dragged up on the beach and converted into hotels, grog shops, whore houses, and in time the city grew up around them as the cove was filled in. Today the hulls of New England clippers and Bristol rigged schooners still lie under the filled shore; are under some of the city's streets. The clipper *Niantic* came ashore at Clay and Sansome streets, and on its timbers rose the well-known Niantic Hotel; spacious, with a splendid bar and rumors of indoor plumbing.

Attempts were made to cut streets up the steep hills, and the pounding of mules and horses, drays and supply convoys soon made the grandest mud puddles on the coast. Some of the crossings were said to be bottomless; there are legends of animals and drunks being drowned in the local quagmires. Horse litter, brush, packing cases were tossed in to fill the puddles, but all that resulted was a deadly black smelly mess. Animals failed at times to pull their loads through it. Someone put up a sign:

STREET IMPASSABLE
NOT EVEN JACKASSABLE

Building plans were simple, for there was a demanding over-abundance of customers and a dismal lack of shelter from fog, rain and cold. Tents, shacks, shelters made from broken up shippings were hard to find. Springless mattressless bunks in barracks cost as high as fifteen dollars the night. A nabob who demanded a "private room" could shell out three hundred dollars a month,

8. *The ships came and stayed to rot, and the crews went to the gold fields.*

cash in advance. If the room had a wooden floor, a rug, or glass in the windows, the going could be a thousand a month.

A smart owner leased the chairs, benches and tables, including the billiard table, for as high as ten dollars for an eight hour sleep. A rocking chair often came to fifty dollars for the night. Usually the guest furnished his own bedding. But the proper landlords, letters home reported, charged nothing for the lice, fleas, other insects native or imported; gray ship's rats came ashore and native mice moved indoors. Signs warned: GUESTS WILL COVER THEIR HEADS AGAINST ATTACKS OF RATS. There were many persons bitten; chunks of noses and ears being lost. Queasiness in a gold hunter was a disaster.

Everything had to be paid for in gold or silver; fantastic prices were the rule. A few gin-soaked old biddies put out signs: CLOTHES REFRESHED (one could hardly call it a proper laundering). In time the simplest thing was to ship one's dirty shirts and linens to Honolulu, or to Canton in China, by clipper ship and get them back snowy white, starched and folded. The trip took six months.

The town cooking was usually bad. It consisted of singed salt beef, rancid barreled pork, burned beans and frost-spoiled potatoes. The miners who had struck it rich bid up the services of the few true cooks available. From New Orleans in 1850 came Mammy Pleasant, huge, black and with a reputation as a great chef with spider skillet and spices. The bidding for her services started at the wharf and she was won at five hundred dollars a month in solid money, with the added guarantee, "No washin' no dish-washin' at all."

Even with pay at three dollars a day for hand labor the cost of food kept many a man belly-rattling hungry, for although some smart former farmers began to set up gardens and farms near the city, the prices remained sky high. You could get eggs at fifty dollars a dozen, fair apples for three dollars each, tea and coffee were four hundred dollars a barrel, flour, pork in brine, forty dollars the barrel.

By the individual portion the price of a boiled egg, fried or poached (and most likely gamy) was a dollar each, a small nickel loaf of bread cost seventy-five cents in the Far West. The rich ate terrines of foie gras, the rest burped on empty stomachs.

A man could stay hungry, chew weeds and curse the beans, but he had to have tools to dig for gold. And most hadn't brought tools, or in time the tools wore out. The bright-eyed merchants, hair sleek with Rowland's Macassar Oil, had supplies. One of the Studebaker brothers—John—of the famous Studebaker wagons and later auto cars, settled down in Hangtown (later Placerville) and beat out picks and shovels. When he went back home to Pennsylvania, he carried several thousand dollars in gold around his waist with which he started his wagon business in earnest. Philip Armour, the founding father of the meat-packing empire, began in California as a butcher, selling meat, wild and pickled, from bear to native tough steers.

Necessities sold like luxuries as to cost. A kitchen knife was thirty dollars, a washbowl or a pan could go for five dollars. A pair of boots that would, maybe, keep out water cost a cool hundred dollars, and all in gold or silver. "None of that yere paper money." Building was going on like on a mad Tower of Babel—one miserly plank set you back twenty dollars.

The price of gold was set at sixteen dollars the ounce, and a pound of tacks cost a pound of gold. Horses, donkeys and mules, called jackasses, jenny mules and tom mules, were as costly at times as the finest blooded racing stock. The going was rough up into the creek beds and up the mountain trails and a pack hoss or jackass could carry a mighty load. And was also "danged good company." You could trust and love a critter when lonely, unless you had a balky cement-headed, mean-mouthed mule.

It was an unsanitary time, destructive to body, mind and spirit. Aches and pains were plentiful, followed by epidemics of smallpox, yellow jack, big casino (syphilis), and other uncontrolled and strange diseases abounded. Any kind of pill, even if mere sugar dust, any sort of medicine, even if only caramel-colored water, cost ten dollars. Pain killers like laudanum (dissolved opium) cost a dollar a drop, and men were happy to pay it. If you were well heeled with a poke full of gold, a doctor would write you a prescription in dog Latin for one hundred dollars. Snake oil doctors reaped rich harvests. The best medicine, everyone with hoss sense said, was a swig of *forty rod*, also called *mountain dew* and *leadmine whisky, red eye*, and *Injun pizin*; all names for alcohol in various forms. Americans preferred rye with branch water or corn pressings in the form of alcohol firewater, too strong even for Indians, it usually being diluted, doctored with chewing tobacco and pepper, at thirty dollars a quart. O pioneers—strong stomachs opened the West.

The Mormon gunmen who came overland were called Sons of Dan, Brothers of Gideon, also Danites, after a passage in Genesis: "Dan shall be a serpent by the way, an adder in the path that biteth the horses' heels so that his rider shall fall backward . . ."

Many others came by sea. A New Yorker, Bayard Taylor, who took the Panama route in 1849, gives an account of the journey to San Francisco by sea: "Among our company of two hundred and fifty there were, of course, many gentlemen of marked refinement and intelligence from various parts of the Union—enough, probably, to leaven the large lump of selfishness and blackguardism into which we were thrown. I believe the controlling portion of the California emigration is intelligent, orderly and peaceable; yet I never witnessed so many disgusting exhibitions of the lowest passions of humanity as during the voyage.

"Fifty-one days have elapsed since leaving New York, in which time we have, in a manner, coasted both sides of the North-American continent, from the parallel of 40 N. to its termination within a few degrees of the Equator, over seas once plowed by the keels of Columbus and Balboa, of Grijalva and Sabastian Viscaino. All is excitement on board; the Captain has just taken his noon observation. We are running along the shore, within six or eight miles distance; the hills are bare and sandy, but loom up finely through the deep blue haze. A brig bound to San Francisco, but fallen off to the leeward of the harbor, is making a new tack on our left to come up again. The coast trends somewhat more to the westward, and a notch or gap is at last visible in its lofty outline.

"An hour later we are in front of the entrance to San Francisco Bay. The mountains on the northern side are 3,000 feet in height, and come boldly down to the sea. As the view opens through the splendid strait, three or four miles in width, the island rock of Alcatraz appears, gleaming white in the distance. An inward-bound ship follows close on our wake, urged on by wind and tide. There is a small fort perched among the trees on our right where the strait is narrowest, and a glance at the formation of the hills shows this pass might be made impregnable as Gibraltar. The town is still concealed behind the promontory around which the Bay turns to the southward, but between Alcatraz and the island of Yerba Buena, now coming into sight, I can see vessels at anchor. High through the vapor in front, and thirty miles distant, rises the peak of Monte Diablo, which overlooks everything between the Sierra Nevada and the Ocean. On our left opens the bight of Sausalito, where the U.S. propeller Massachusetts and several other vessels are at anchor.

"At last we are through the Golden Gate—fit name for such a magnificent portal to the commerce of the Pacific! Yerba Buena Island is in front; southward and westward opens the renowned harbor, crowded with the shipping of the world, mast behind mast and vessel behind vessel, the flags of all nations fluttering in the breeze. Around the curving shore of the Bay and upon the sides of three hills which rise steeply from the water, the middle one receding so as to form a bold amphitheatre, the town is planted and seems scarcely yet to have taken root, for tents, canvas, plank, mud and adobe houses are mingled together with the least apparent attempt at order and durability. But I am not yet on shore. The gun of the Panama has just announced our arrival to the people on land. We glide on with the tide, past the U.S. ship Ohio and opposite the main landing, outside of the forest of masts. A dozen boats are creeping out to us over the water; the signal is given— the anchor drops—our voyage is over."

The country behind San Francisco was no rose garden, and the farther one got from the Pacific the rougher it became. One Alonzo Delano wrote in his journal for September 17, 1849:

"On reaching the encampments below, and seeing the hundreds of white tents and wagons, with multitudes of cattle cropping the grass . . . all uneasy sensations vanished. I met many traveling acquaintances, and was soon invited to share the hospitality of friends for the night. Lawson's was on the opposite side of the creek, and a little before evening I went over and found two or three small adobe buildings, one of which was called by courtesy a store, having a little flour, whisky, and a few groceries for sale. Around the trading post were lounging gangs of naked Indians of both sexes, drunken Mexicans, and weary emigrants, enjoying respite from excessive fatigue in the flowing bowl; and take it all in all, it did not give me a very flattering impression of the morals of the citizens. My first act was to provide for the creature comfort; and purchasing a little beef, bread, sugar and cheese, I returned to the camp to enjoy a feast . . ."

It was a strange mixture of Calvinistic grimness of purpose, Mormon optimistic, basic beliefs, middle class Yankee agrarian hope and camp meeting minds crying out in the straw pen; such as the bellow of randy Presbyterian preachers insisting a man must learn to forgive himself even while mad for the hunt for gold.

Ships brought a host of gold seekers around the Horn. The clipper *Memnon*, one thousand tons, made it from Castle Garden in New York to the Golden Gate in 120 days. Coming into the Bay without lights and buoys was a difficult job. The Golden Gate itself is thirty-five miles wide at first, narrowing to three miles, then to one mile as the town comes in sight. It has four daily cycles of tough tides to worry about and fight against. The caravels of the Conquistadores, lateen-rigged, and the English ship of Drake, heavy rumped in the poop, treated the Bay with respect and awe. Seamen got to know North Beach, Telegraph Hill and Meiggs Wharf (one thousand feet long and one of the first); Point Lobos and Lands End were also welcome sights. Seal Rock House was built in 1858 for the city sports and diners, for real ladies and fancy ladies to come and see the sea as they dined high up. The place burned down in '61 and Cliff House was built, a sinner's

9. *Rich miners in all their glory ready for fun.*

haven with private dining rooms, low glowing lights, satin sofas, discreet waiters, couches and ornate door bolts.

Adolph Sutro, on land self-named Sutro Heights, built Sutro Baths and Gardens. In that combustible age they too burned down several times and were rebuilt. Once a schooner loaded with dynamite for miners came ashore and blew up a corner of Sutro's. The gardens remain today open to a public that now has houses with private bathtubs of their own.

The whiskered millionaires, the caped spenders, the sudden rich, would arrive at Seal House in a hired hansom or their own carriage with the lady, or tart, properly veiled, and be shown into a private room of blood-red drapes, yellow burning lights, the damask tablecloth set for an intimate dinner for two. "The rooms gave off," (R.J. reports) "a smell of sin and scent, body powder, good Havana leaf, the tang of red lobster shells and spilled wine." Soft-spoken words, a sudden laugh, a nod to the wine steward, a polite withdrawal of waiters, the champagne bubbling in crystal glasses.

The sexual duet could be played out in leisure in an age which did not hurry itself or need the aid of hi-fi, stereo, drugs or fear an invasion of privacy. Only the far-off strings of a violin, or a husband, armed, banging at the door.

3

MADAMES AND MINERS

When a miner with his boots greased or tarred came to town with gold in his poke (a poke was a small deerskin bag tightly sewed to hold gold dust and nuggets), what he wanted was a drink, a hot bath, a haircut, a shave; clean clothes if he was fussy. Then he wanted more whisky, sex, gambling, a place to hoot and holler, merry as a grig. San Francisco, eager for mercantile gain, almost at once began to cater to his desire for comforts and vice. It all paid off well.

The Park House, a two story hotel, cost a mere $30,000 to build, rented for $120,000 a year, half of which came from gamblers who had their dice tables, faro setups, card games on the second floor. Not so fancy a setup was a canvas tent, fifteen by twenty-five feet, at Washington and Kearny streets that served as a gambling saloon with a rental of $40,000 a year. Even the U.S.A. was taken, paying a rental for the Customs Office, a mere board shed, of $7,000 a month. Life was dangerous, often short, bereavement and alienation daily fare—only luck seemed at hand.

Gambling joints in the early days of San Francisco ran into at least a thousand in numbers. Not until 1855 were they licensed by the city with a bit extra for graft to the political fat cats. An anti-gambling law was passed by the Legislature in 1854, but the payoff protected most places and they ran wide open. And justice was mainly an unrealized potential. Though a crooked Tuolumne faro dealer was convicted by law for cheating, there was usually only a quick hanging with a borrowed rope. The anti-gambling law itself was repealed five years later, the gamblers and property owners buying off the lawmakers. Dice, roulette and cards remain even up to today part of the scene. ("When you lose your shirt, cover your ass with your hand.")

Most of the games were fairly honest, a braced (rigged) game was deadly to the swindler. Any sort of game was on hand: faro, monte, rouge et noir, vingt-et-un, rondo. Oddly enough poker was not very popular as "it took too much time fer the action."

Portsmouth Square, the old Plaza, was the gamy, articulate place to find gamblers, voluptuousness in women and games. Everything on the Square was for gambling. Even the eating places, saloons and hotels had tables for play. An early observer put it this way: "As there was no comfort at their sleeping quarters, men spent money freely at different places of riotous excess, and were indeed forced to pass their hours of leisure or recreation at drinking bars, billiard rooms and gambling saloons. Such places were accordingly crowded with a motley crew, who drank, swore, and gamed to their hearts' content. *Everybody did so*; and that circumstance was a sufficient excuse, if one were needed, to the neophyte in debauchery. But of all their haunts, the gambling saloons were the most notorious and the best patronized. Gambling was *the* amusement, *the* grand occupation of many classes, apparently the life and soul of the place. The extensive saloons, in each of which a dozen tables might be placed, were continually crowded, and around the tables themselves the players often stood in lines three or four deep, every one vying with his neighbors for the privilege of reaching the board, and staking his money as fast as the wheel and ball could be rolled or the card turned. Judges and clergymen, physicians and advocates, merchants and clerks, tradesmen, mechanics, laborers, miners and farmers, all adventurers in their kind—everyone elbowed his way to the gaming table."

It was a twenty-four hour show; no time for delicate trepidation, no period out even for Sunday prayers. When there was sunlight, the chuckaluck, monte and faro games were played out in the open air. On rainy, cold days whatever gave shelter, canvas roof, some planks or a shed, assisted the gambling to go on.

Wilson Flint, who landed in December 1849, and later became a state Senator, gives us a picture of an ordinary Sunday morning. "I wended my way with the throng to Portsmouth Square, this being at the time the great resort of the denizens of this rising metropolis. Three sides of the square were mostly occupied by buildings which served the double purpose of hotels and gambling houses, the latter calling being regarded at the time as a very respectable profession. On the fourth and upper side of the square was an adobe building, from the steps of which some were discoursing from the text: 'The way of the transgressor is hard.' It was a scene I shall never forget. On all sides of you were gambling houses, each with its band of music in full blast. Crowds were going in and coming out; fortunes were being lost and won; terrible imprecations and blasphemies rose amid the horrid wail."

The first place opened for gambling after the gold discovery was the El Dorado. It began as a canvas tent, but became in time a big box-like affair with a few private rooms hung with cloth curtains where whores worked at their trade under erotic pictures, all described as "costly oil paintings by world famous artists." The furniture was modeled on the decor of a Paris brothel by someone who had never been there. There was a banner and flag-draped stage, an active and noisy band (the sort Oscar Wilde on his American tour said he saw playing under a sign reading: *Don't shoot the piano player—he's doing the best he can*). A bar ran the full length of a wall backed by cut glass mirrors, crystal glass bowls and bottles with colored alcoholic content. Presiding over the bar was Professor Harry Thomas, who admitted to being "the world's greatest bartender." He was the author of *The Bon Vivant's Companion, or, How to Mix Drinks*.

In his daybook, the wine merchant R.J. notes: "Professor Thomas, inventor of Blue Blazer and Tom and Jerry. Fine looking fellow. Good head of hair and clear features. Stands up behind the bar pouring contents of a Blue Blazer from glass to glass. Splendid sight. People stop their play at gambling tables over piles of gold dust, gold coins, silver cartwheels and nuggets to watch professor at his trade. Dealer and croupiers twitch a bit, not permitted to indulge in drink while at work. They look pale, thin in black and white, with string tie, cheroot in one corner of mouth. Rumor is they are desperate men in last stages of galloping consumption. Can well believe this, each with a derringer in shirt front, Colt in pocket and a Bowie knife maybe in boot. Must get recipe for the Blue Blazer . . ."

The gambling places had exotic names. There was the Mazourka, Varsouvienne, Alhambra, Verandah, Aguila de Ore. And just folksy American places like Bill Briggs', Steve Whipple's, Dennison's Exchange, Ward House. All were about alike in style and purpose, some fancy, some plain; all active in gambling games; all encouraging the hustlers, the shills, and always the tarts, many working for the house.

R.J.'s daybook contains a great deal of information on gambling games.

"Faro most popular game of all. Even a small mining town like Columbia has 135 games going. To play Faro there is a set-up called a Faro Bank. Faro played with standard 52 card deck playing cards. Deck shuffled, cut, placed face up in open-top dealing box. Faro dealer removes top card, laying it face up to start pile on which winning cards will be added. Dealer removes another card from top of deck, placing it by side of dealing box. Third card in deck exposed and identified. Second and third cards, unknown when full deck was placed in box, form the first *turn*, or cards on which betting is done. 25 pairs are taken from deck; card that remains in dealing box following action on each turn is *winner*. First active card withdrawn from box is the *loser*. Special names for top and bottom cards in deck, both are discarded. The first is *soda*; final one *hock*." (As can be seen from R.J.'s notes the game is very complex and therefore not popular today.)

"Layout on which betting is done is one card of each denomination in deck, an enlarged print of card on table. For Faro you wager that card on which you bet will either be winner or loser when it appears. A straight bet is a bet it will be a winner. *Coppering* your bet (a six-sided black chip on top) is a no bet; you want the card a loser. You can bet high card on layout in front of dealer. A straight bet is winner to be higher card than loser. A coppered bet is loser to be high card. Aces are low value in deck.

"Armed hired hand called *lookout* or observer sits on high chair, keeps eye on game and players. Sees all bets and payoffs are correct, that case keeper records the cards as used, settles disputes that arise. Undivided attention on game. Lookout and dealer trade jobs with one another. Some dealers have been shot—lookouts have killed players who pulled a hogleg [pistol]."

The best close-up we have of the professional gambler (the ones presented in Bret Harte's fiction are too romantic) comes from the pioneer historian Hubert Howe Bancroft's *California Inter Pocula*. "His temperament is mercurial but non-volatilized. Supreme self-command is his cardinal quality; yet, except when immersed in the intricacies of a game, his actions appear to be governed only by impulse and fancy. On the other hand his swiftest vengeance and cruellest butchery seem rather the result of policy than passion. He is never known to steal except at cards; and if caught cheating, he either fights or blandly smiles his sin away, suffers the stakes to be raked down without a murmur, treats good-humoredly, and resumes the game unruffled. United with the coolest cunning is the coolest courage. He is as ready with his pistol as with his toothpick, but he never uses it unless he is right; then, he will kill a man as mercilessly as he would brush a fly from his immaculate linen. He accustoms himself to do without sleep, and if necessary can go for several days and nights without rest. He deals his game with the most perfect sang froid, and when undergoing the heaviest losses there is no trembling of fingers or change of expression."

They had to be able to handle the loungers and brawlers, the half-breed Kickapoo, Choctaw and Chickasaw that wandered all over the West. Men were mean or chuckleheaded at the gambling tables, full of salt-pork-fed dyspepsia, raw-edged in their rheumatic joints gotten from working in wet diggings. The gamblers had to encourage their interest in the games and not let them be too roused up by their losses. A man could get tolerable mean after losing his months of hard work just at the toss of a pair of dice or the turn of a card; leaving with his britches pocket empty. About all that was left for him was to get a grubstake—a backing of food and tools for percentages—and while waiting for that listen to the street preachers harangue the crowd:

> The earth is Yahweh's and its fullness,
>   the world and those who dwell therein.
> For he based it upon the seas,
>   established it upon the ocean currents.

Sexual allure—warm pockets of pleasure—was usually combined with gambling. In 1850 the Bella Union imported Mme. Simone Jules, a lady gambler, beautiful, a very French treat, with huge glowing eyes, black hair. She was to handle a roulette wheel, and there was a land rush to play with her. The other gambling places had to bring in women with the rustle of taffeta—all handsome, all quick with the cards, wheel or the dice. There were also women harp and piano players, and as long as they exhibited plenty of ankle and bosom, the music lovers were pleased with female froufrou and furbelows. The girl violinist—French, real or claimed—at the Alhambra received her pay of thirty-two dollars an evening in the form of two ounces of gold dust. The Bella Union, "always the innovator," imported a Mexican group of two guitars, two harps and a flute to the half querulous hostility of the crowd.

The tune "Aloha" from the Sandwich Islands was sung at the Bella Union to the enervating words of "You Never Miss Your Sainted Mother Till She's Dead and Gone to Heaven." For all its crude and hard way of life it was a more sentimental era. Even the whores wept into their bergamot-scented hankies.

Betting was done at a wild pace and the bigger places would often handle $200,000 a day in play. Quick and impulsive one shot bets could run high. A rich drunken digger once bet $20,000 on one card in a game. Another time raw gold valued at $16,000 was placed as a bet at the Bella Union, a house which got the biggest play and the top sports. Long deadly serious games were often played out like a World Series. Jim Rynders, a professional gambler playing at Steve Whipple's joint, sat in a three day faro game and

10. *All that money can buy in the shape of popular size.*

came out $89,000 ahead. The record loss may well be that of Ed Moses, who asked, "Kin all house limits be lifted in faro?" His arbitrary wish was agreed to. He won and lost, won and lost, then lost *lost*, and his last IOU was signed for $60,000 on the turn of one card. His entire loss for the session was $200,000. Return to the gold diggins for a loser was a sort of rite of purification.

R.J. in his daybook writes of the last of the great faro dealers, Bill Briggs. "Always good to see Bill come out of the Ward House, four, five o'clock in the morn, pockets loaded with what he calls 'chicken feed'; pint of small coins. 'Come along, sport, watch me feed the kids.' He has maybe fifty, sixty dollars in small change and we sashay along down to the fruit and vegetable market, night flares burning, a dozen kids there, collecting garbage for their pigs and goats. Maybe to take home and eat. Bill starts tossing coins by fistfulls, laughing till his face is red, kids diving for coins and turning cartwheels, crying out, 'More, more, Colonel Briggs.' Which is flattery as he's never been a colonel. He always says the title was too easy to come by. With a last flick of two bits or four bits, he takes my arm. 'How about cutting the morning slimes with a touch of bourbon and branch water?' Does this almost every night, tossing away half a hundred dollars, just to see the market kids scramble for it. . . . A fellow impenetrable and harassed by some secret agitation. . . ."

Briggs' partner, Colonel J. J. Bryant, wanted to be the first elected sheriff of San Francisco. He saw nothing wrong in a pro- fessional gambler holding public office as a law keeper. His rival was the Texas Ranger Colonel Jack Hayes. ("Almost any white man who didn't work with his hands could be called Colonel.") The colonel from Texas outdid the free lunch and free booze of his rival by staging what must have been the first Western rodeo of tricky and fancy dressed riders in the streets of the town.

The *Annals of San Francisco* called it the "finest specimens of horsemanship ever witnessed. The sight of the hero took the people by surprise and called forth the admiration and patriotism of the vast multitude of spectators. Men crowded around him on every hand, some seizing the bridle, others clinging to his clothing and stirrups, and each anxious to obtain a grasp of his hand. The noise and tumult terrified the spirited beast he strode, which reared and plunged amid the enthusiastic crowd, though so admirably managed as to do injury to none; when at length his rider giving him the rein, he dashed into and along the adjoining street, followed and greeted by loud huzzas. . . ."

(Of course Colonel Hayes won the election—the mob in California always likes a good show and a handsome front rather than mind and matter in politics. The rise of the modern horse-riding actor Ronald Reagan to political popularity shows that even today show business is all.)

Speculation, not hard work, was the way to wealth for many. The thousands of *veara* of new built land were made by covering and burying ships rotting at their anchorage. (A *veara*, the Spanish yard, was 33-and-a-half inches.) So began the great American game of land selling and land buying, often on little cash. Bankers, shark-minded characters with carpetbags full of greenbacks—called shin plasters—and gold coins, would lend at a rate of from eight to fifteen percent, always with interest payable in advance. Loans were usually by the month; for who knew what anyone would be doing beyond a month; if alive. The old lazy Spanish times when a lot would bring fifteen dollars were gone, and you had to pony up thirty, forty thousand dollars if the scrap of earth lay in the right part of town. Real estate, gambling, brothel-keeping and merchandising were the early and late roads to wealth. But it was raw new gold that fed it all; gold grubbers and gold strikes in the dirty little camps on the mountain streams made it tick; there among the woodbine, red oak, men dug and built Long Toms and cradles to shake the gold loose from the grass roots and the prehistoric gravel.

The lies were great, the naiveté boundless. There was talk of a lone man taking out ten thousand dollars of gold in a day, of a miner who found a thirteen pound nugget worth thirty-five thousand dollars. There were rare lucky strikes. Two enterprising miners found a huge nugget and carried it off back East to exhibit at fifty cents a peep.

In real value it has been figured that forty million dollars worth of gold came out of the squalor and sweat and rheumatism-producing toil of the early digging. In the end the trollops, barkeeps, gamblers and merchants got most of it. Few miners went home with loaded buckskin pokes under their shirts. Some who tried were murdered up a lonely trail, or shot from ambush in sinister games called *dry gulching* and *bushwacking*. More often when he made a strike the miner hurried to San Francisco to fulfill the promiscuous dreams of all those months when the pay dirt was just trickling in. As Bret Harte was to write:

> I know thy cunning and thy greed,
> Thy high hand lust and wilful deed . . .

Gold-loaded miners took to dollar cigars, fruit out of season, outfits for the harlots, fine tailored suits of black broadcloth, starched shirts, top hats glossy as sin. All were tried on, paid for by hard gotten gold dust along with a handsome tip. When sober the miners dreamed of more fun; drunk they were robbed, rolled, stripped and often drugged and shanghaied on some dismal ship with a bully mate, bound for India, Peru or remote seas that only the whalers knew.

Teeth of pure gold seemed an item of social status, as today the newly rich California dupes go in for collecting what is sold as *avant garde* art. Many a miner pulled out a good tooth to have a new one made for him of his own gold. Henry Cogswell was the first dentist ashore in 1849—right after the three card monte games. He opened his "painless" dentist parlor on California Street to pry out good teeth for replacement with gold ones. His records show there were miners who had *all* their own teeth extracted and plates of pure gold put in. Dr. Cogswell (the title "Doctor" like "Colonel" was often an honorary one in early casual medical practice) ended up with a fortune of two million dollars. He didn't waste his money on soft women or red eye whisky. Dr. Cogswell was a hater of Demon Rum and as a prohibitionist fought the bars and saloons. He ordered twenty drinking fountains, each topped by a statue of himself. None have survived so we don't know if his statue held a replica of a gold tooth in one hand and a pair of the pliers of his trade in the other.

If the newly rich in their gaucherie didn't go for gold teeth, finger rings, stickpins, then to their silky Dundreary whiskers they added butter-gold watches (big as turnips) anchored with massive chains. One eyewitness reported that miners "fastened their coarse, dirty shirts with a cluster of diamonds the size of a shilling, wore colossal gold rings on their fingers, and displayed massive gold seals and chains from their watch pockets; while hardly a man of any consequence returned to the Atlantic states without receiving from some one of his friends a huge gold-headed cane."

4

DANCE TILL THE SUN COME UP

> Hang up yer coat
> And kick the wall,
> Choose yer partners
> And promenade all!

The miners, merchants, the gamblers and the lawyer-sharpers who really made it big preferred for their most intimate moments strictly private parties in the sporting houses. Here exhibits of erotic shows, the meeting of new arrivals, or the greeting of old favorites could be carried on behind ornate drapes in rooms where the furnishings were at least from New Orleans if not from Paris. The scent of body powder and flushed cheeks was here, of whale oil lamps or the new coal gas jets, spilled wine and the salt wind from the Golden Gate. All gave the madam's home away from home an atmosphere that kindled sparks in the memories of old Native Sons when their power of enjoyment was banked. Nostalgia and faint far-off strains of old music engendered great lies.

One finds a detailed study of a sporting house gala in the *Annals of San Francisco.* "It is a *soiree* night. The 'lady' of the establishment has sent most polite invitations, got up on the finest and most beautifully embossed note paper, to all the principal gentlemen of the city, including collector of the port, mayor, aldermen, judges of the county, and members of the legislature. A splendid band of music is in attendance. Away over the Turkey or Brussels carpet whirls the politician with some sparkling beauty, as fair as frail; and the judge joins in and enjoys the dance in company with the beautiful but lost beings, whom tomorrow he may send to the house of correction. Everything is conducted with the utmost propriety. Not an unbecoming word is heard, not an objectionable action seen. The girls are on their good behavior, and are proud once more to move and act and appear as ladies. Did you not know, you would not suspect that you were in one of those dreadful places so vividly described by Solomon. . . . Everything within the bounds of the market and the skill of the cook and confectioner is before you. Opposite and by your side, that which nor cook nor confectioner's skill have made what they are —cheeks where the ravages of dissipation have been skilfully hidden, and eyes with pristine brilliancy undimmed, even heightened by the spirit of the recent champagne. And here the illusion fades. The champagne alone is paid for. The soiree has cost the mistress one thousand dollars, and at the supper and during the night she sells twelve dozen of champagne at ten dollars a bottle! . . . No loafers present, but the male *ton*; vice hides itself for the occasion, and staid dignity bends from its position . . ."

Somehow it was still so Victorian in its attitude toward secret vice—yet so far from the Queen in Buckingham Palace. Amoral diversion was aware that vice tasted better if a bit of the sense of sin remained.

"Following the pioneer came not law and order but first the harlot," Ambrose Bierce said, standing at the bar of the Palace Hotel. "Then the jack-leg lawyers, and corruption of governing bodies by the boodle grabbers" (as R.J. quotes him in his daybook .

Certainly the harlot heard the call to San Francisco when the first big gold strikes were hardly out of the ground. At the start of the rush there were fifteen women listed as *white* in the town; rather unfair as Mexican-Spanish descendants were not counted. By the end of the year there were three hundred women entertaining lucky gold seekers. Two-thirds were, according to a white historian, whores from Mexico, Chile and other points in South America, known fondly as *Chilenos*, and unfondly as *Greasers*. The frenzied animation of a Walpurgis Night set the tone of the town's early history.

11. *Always back an ace with a gun.*

The tarts' prowling grounds and bedding grounds were at Clark's Point, in clapboard shacks and tents. Pallets and cots served for the trade in concupiscence. Gambling was combined with living off whores and by the first half of 1850 two thousand prostitutes had come ashore. Ships were unloading them from every point of the compass. France, Italy and Germany furnished a goodly number; New York and New Orleans were major shipping points of "fancy goods." San Francisco quickly developed one of the largest red light districts in the nation. One house bragged that the district could produce a whore from *any* nation on earth. *The Pacific News* carried among its social notes the item that nine hundred of the *demi monde* from Paris and Marseilles, carefully processed for skill, beauty and friendliness, were on their way. The first fifty women were escorted by their *macquereaux*, or macks (pimps). These imported courtesans, the newspaper daintily pointed out, were for city consumption, adding that at the mines Indian girls were "available at reasonable prices." Journalism had a freedom of expression in those days that it later lost in sponsoring art museums and music centers.

The stews of Telegraph Hill welcomed the French invasion forces, and no one bothered to listen to the sea captain who quoted: "*Souvent femme varie. Est qui s'y fie.*" The waterfront was a scene of much action in the sexual sense. The smartest and more beautiful sluts went into the ornate sporting houses off Portsmouth Square, and with practical French sense saved their money, often married rich and prominent husbands. Some even became social queens. R.J.'s daybook later in the seventies contains an item on the subject. "Fine women hostesses this Christmas evening. Nob Hill mansions all ablaze with lights, wassail drunk in every ball room. More diamonds and feathers than ever. Hard to believe half of these grand dames were spreading their legs for trade twenty years ago on the Barbary Coast, taking on sailors, being beaten by their macks to spit out the gold coins kept hidden in their mouths. Great deal of truth in the bawdy ditty about the Native Sons."

12. An import to the gold country—who mined the miners.

The ditty R.J. refers to is still heard among the beatniks and those disrespectful of the San Francisco Establishment. The most presentable version is:

> The miners came in forty-nine,
> The whores in fifty-one;
> And when they got together
> They produced the Native Son.

R.J. continues: "As a youth I remember many of the ladies from the bagnios, even then socially active at fancy dress shindigs, going to the masquerades, fetes. Screaming in the carriages, carrying on in the private rooms, drinking and singing in the suites with railroad, lumber men, the true hoi poloi. On party nights the gambling palaces advertised by poster and newspaper. Tables pushed to one side while cards and chips still flew; the center of the floor all a mass of dancers and high flingers. Wild but not dangerous; the warning sign reading: *NO WEAPONS INSIDE,* showing a touching interest for rule and order."

The *Annals of San Francisco* also takes notice of the women from the Portsmouth Square sporting houses at the public balls as "lewd girls freed from the necessity of all moral restraint." The innate coarseness of social contact was, however, attempting a veneer of refinement. The men were still searched for pistols, knives and saps or brass knuckles at the doors. The gambling house bands and orchestras played loudly, and it was the rare night that someone didn't lead mass singing to the tune of Stephen Foster's "Oh Susannah," which, with "My Darling Clementine," was one of the gold rush top hits. The words sometimes got changed from "Oh Susannah."

> I˙ came from Quakerdelphia,
>   With my washbowl on my knee;
> I'm going to California,
>   The gold dust for to see.
> It rained all night the day I left,
>   The weather it was dry;
> The sun so hot I froze to death,
>   Oh, Anna, don't you cry.

In the yellow gleam of gas lamps the ladies often went at each other with fingernails and teeth, and the gents, too, went in for some roughhouse, known on the frontier as "gougin' and kneein'." But burly bouncers were there to keep order, and they did it with fist, cut down pool cues, bung starter, or an oak bat used to crush ice.

> Oh, Ann Eliza!
> Don't you cry for me.
> I'm goin' to California
> With my washbowl on my knee.

These public jamborees of booted Silenuses and imported whores were well attended, and the meeting of the miners and the tarts in a more sentimental mood did often result, as R.J. wrote, in the beginnings of later socially prominent families who hardly knew the words of the wild old song.

> I soon shall be in Frisco,
> And then I'll look around;
> And when I see the gold lumps there
> I'll pick 'em off the ground.
> I'll scrape the mountains clean, old girl;
> I'll drain the rivers dry;
> A pocketful of rocks bring back,
> So, Anna, don't you cry.

But the main preoccupation was the hunt for gold, and it was mean, hard, tragic. For all the gallant legends and lies of movies and TV shows, there was a lot of modern bigotry in the town and at the gold fields. General Persifer F. Smith, on his way to California in 1849, issued a statement: "Only native Americans [meaning no Latin types or Indians] would be permitted to dig for gold," and he would use force to drive all others from the field—a threat he lacked troops to enforce. The Know Nothing, or Native American Party, an early version of the Birch Society, American-Nazis and Klan, was winning elections in the East by being anti-Catholic, anti-Jewish, anti-intellectual, anti-foreign. They stood ready—like some modern fanatics—to seize the government for the far right. They promised that all immigrants who got here later than 1812 were to be deported. However the Know Nothings didn't gain that much power, and the general never could enforce his WASP ideas in California.

Spanish, Mexican and South Americans, being on the ground or near it, had in many cases staked legal claims to the best gold bearing sands. They soon were in trouble. As Greasers (the term came to mean the dealers in hides and tallow—Mexicans—who sold their greasy and smelly product in the early days to Yankee ship captains) and Spanish-speaking miners were liable to lynch law. ("Give 'em a fair trial and then hang 'em!") California, as was said of much of the West, "was fine for men and dogs, and hell on foreigners, women and horses."

The most active stars and stripes patriots were a criminal gang of thieves, pimps and skull crackers, at first called the Hounds, later the San Francisco Society of Regulators; most of them had come out as volunteer soldiers from New York. They beat and murdered Chileno miners and practiced the protection racket. They would tolerate Greasers for payment of money and gold dust. The historian Bancroft wrote:

"The Hounds asserted their determination to protect American citizens against Spanish-speaking foreigners, and sometimes claimed to have instructions from the Alcalde to extirpate the Mexicans and Chileans." The alcalde was, of course, by this time a Yankee.

As recorded in the *Annals of San Francisco:* "Without provocation and in cold blood they barbarously beat with sticks and stones, and cuffed and kicked the offending foreigners. Not content with that, they repeatedly and wantonly fired among the injured people, and amid the shrieks of terrified women and the groans of wounded men, recklessly continued their terrible course in different quarters, wherever in fact malice or thirst for plunder led them. There were no individuals brave or foolhardy enough to resist the progress of such a savage mob."

Sam Brannan and others proclaimed a meeting in Portsmouth Square and called on the alcalde, one Doc Leavenworth, for "Law and Order." Two hundred deputies volunteered and oiled and loaded their pistols and rifles. The Hounds took it on the lam, but twenty were captured in fair condition. At their trial two of their leaders were found guilty of "riot, conspiracy, robbery, assault with intent to kill." They were sentenced to ten years in prison, but it was only for the records. The Know Nothing political fat cats had the Hounds—great vote collectors and ballot box stuffers—out of jail in a few days, and they drifted out of town.

Action, of course, caused reaction, and the Latin Americans, in fear of their lives, produced an outlaw hero, Joaquin Murieta, born Joaquin Carillo. His sidekick was Three Finger Jack, also known as Manuel Garcia. Joaquin, born in Sonora, Mexico, had drifted north in his teens with a circus, together with his wife, Rosita Felex (who, of course, also had another name, Antonia Molinera). Joaquin had staked a rich claim in Stanislaus County with his brother, but American miners, resentful and itchy, raped his wife and beat him up. His brother was murdered. Joaquin was also accused of stealing his own horse, for which he was stripped and promptly flogged until he passed out in agony.

From then on Joaquin and Rosita became outlaws. Dressed in men's clothes, her hair cut short, Rosita was handy with a pistol. Their career lasted three years. Joaquin could at times command as many as seventy to eighty riders, all of whom hated the Gringos because all of them had been outraged, beaten and robbed by the Yankees. Joaquin is said to have hunted down all those who had raped his wife, lynched his brother or flogged him over the horse he already owned.

The Murieta gang were the first major stagecoach robbers of the era. They murdered travelers, boldly attacked and captured camps and mining towns in the manner of Pancho Villa. Murieta, who was sometimes called the Robin Hood of the Sierras, often shared his loot with abused Latin Americans. But he was no hero actually, or noble or even sensible. He avenged things done to him or his family and was as bad as the Americans who had hurt him and whom he hated. He saw only a bleak compulsive reality and no hope. When he captured any of the men who had made him an outlaw, he dragged them at the end of a rope attached to his horse

13. *The Mexican-Americans had a hard time of it—they rarely got justice.*

until they were ground to bits on the rocky mountain trails. He was no protector of minorities; for some obscure traumatic reason he hated the Chinese ("those damn yellow foreigners"). His favorite game was to tie a half dozen Chinese together by their queues and cut their throats. He boldly demanded supplies, drink and clothing from the camps and was rarely refused, for he would burn and slaughter if turned away.

In 1852 the State Legislature put up posters announcing *Five Thousand Dollars Reward* for Murieta's capture DEAD OR ALIVE. The outlaw rode boldly into Stockton just as a sheriff's officer was nailing the notice to a tree before a large crowd. Murieta elbowed his way to the poster and lettered in on the bottom of the notice: I WILL PAY $1,000 MYSELF. J. MURIETA

No one stopped him as he wrote—neither the law nor the citizens—and he rode off. He was betrayed later by a gambler friend named William Burns, who led a posse of twenty-five men to the outlaw's camp at Tulare Lake. They opened fire on the sleeping men by the light of the campfire. Three Finger Jack was cut down. Murieta managed to get to his horse and weapons, but a fusillade of lead plunked a half dozen slugs into him. Dying, Murieta dropped his rifle and said, "No more shooting. You done your work."

The reward money, six thousand dollars by that time, was given to the posse under a Captain Love. William Burns, the betrayer, was later gunned down by Murieta's friends. Murieta's head, and Three Fingers' hacked-off hand were displayed, pickled in a large jar of whisky, in San Francisco. As the press proudly announced: JOAQUIN'S HEAD is to be seen at King's, Corner of Halleck and Sansome streets. ADMISSION ONE DOLLAR.

There was some doubt that the head (which continued, some said, to grow hair and so became a holy relic among superstitious Latins) actually had belonged to Murieta, aged twenty-one, three years an outlaw. James Marshall, who started the gold rush, and who knew the outlaw, said it was not Murieta. So did Rosita, Murieta's wife. She said he had made it away to Mexico with large herds of horses and gold worth fifty thousand dollars. True or not, the Robin Hood of the Sierras was never heard from again.

As the early California poet Judge Edward McGowan, also a battler against the deadly Vigilante lynch mob, wrote in a parody of Pope's lines:

> A little stealing is a dangerous thing,
> But stealing greatly is a noble art.
> It's mean to rob a hen roost of a hen,
> But stealing millions makes us a gentleman . . .

Or a railroad king, as we shall see.

5

THE ONE AND ONLY KING

The Grizzly Bear is huge and wild;
He has devoured the infant child.
The infant child is not aware
It has been eaten by the bear.

It was only proper and fitting, some barroom wits felt, that San Francisco should be picked as his residence and capital by the Emperor of the United States and Protector of Mexico, Norton I. He was not a king by any hereditary rights or by victory in battle in San Francisco in the middle of the 1850s. He was self-annointed, a chubby, short, stocky fellow with a Napoleon III moustache and beard, escorted around town by his two dogs, Bummer and Lazarus. The Emperor wore a self-designed uniform, combining the best features of the American Navy and the Army; full dress, royal regalia. On his head was tilted a high beaver hat with a shiny brass clasp holding up three highly colored feathers. The Emperor Norton, as befits an absolute monarch, issued his own kind of money; a friendly printer running off cash certificates of different denomination, all bearing the title: "NORTON I, EMPEROR OF THE UNITED STATES AND PROTECTOR OF MEXICO." The San Francisco merchants, bartenders and cabbies accepted this kind of funny money with a smile. There is no record that in those easier, less power-mad days the government of the United States ever took any action either against his claims to the American throne or the issuance of cash certificates in competition with the U. S. Mint. Washington had a sense of humor then, not publicity-made despots.

The self-proclaimed Emperor was born Jewish Joshua Abraham A. Norton in England in 1815. He was of a non-royal line. He never claimed any connection with the ruling House of Hanover (which later, ashamed of its Hun origin, called itself Windsor). In 1848 he was plain Mr. Norton in San Francisco, perhaps as a younger son sent out to the colonies to make his own way. He is supposed to have started business with $40,000, (no one knows whose money it was) and he put up a sign board reading: J. A. NORTON, MERCHANT. This sum of money hardly seems likely. Nor does it appear possible he was ever worth $250,000 before he was ruined by bad luck and bad business procedures. As Norton, the merchant, he is said to have paid back all his losses. It's not likely his first fortune or his losses were ever as big as reported.

What is known is that following his business failure J. A. Norton disappeared from the streets of San Francisco. When he reappeared in 1857, telling no one where he had been, he was no longer J. A. Norton, merchant, but Norton I, Monarch. It would be unkind to think he was a dangerous lunatic. His bearing was calm, proud and as perfectly regal as Mike Romanoff's, a later saloon keeper of Los Angeles and "heir" to all the Russias. He remained a kindly, cheerful, chubby figure, democratic, gossipy, interested in his city and his kingdom—a sort of non-sensual Edwardian king. One of his first actions was to present a check for three million dollars to the president of the city's biggest bank, "to build a bridge over San Francisco Bay." That proved he was nutty, people said smiling—imagine a Bay bridge! The idea seemed wild, and so the check drawn on the royal treasury was never cashed. The bridge came along years later.

Norton I lived twenty-seven years in San Francisco—a delightful reign—most of them happy royal years, he and his court, the two dogs. His own money satisfied his simple needs. He was a people's monarch. His script as payment was rarely refused; once for railroad transportation, to attend a session of the bribed and dishonest Legislature at Sacramento. The Emperor was in the habit of giving the tainted lawmakers his honest advice on matters of running the state. He sat in a special chair held for him in the Visitors' Gallery.

Once a railroad car waiter refused his currency; the Emperor became angry and threatened to "revoke the railroad franchise," (obtained by fraud and bribery as usual). The train conductor came forward to beg the Emperor's royal pardon, and the next day Norton I was issued a perpetual traveling pass, good on all trains of the Central Pacific.

So that the Emperor could keep neat and dry-cleaned and maintain his uniforms properly in order, the city's Board of Supervisors voted him at taxpayers' expense thirty dollars a year, for life. Norton I fed handsomely at the Free Lunch counters in the better saloons and bars, tossing a tidbit now and then to his faithful retainers, the dogs. He took it upon himself—for he was a working king—to inspect the wharfs and markets, nod approvingly on his subjects' fish and fresh tomatoes. He expected to be bowed to on the streets and usually was. Audiences rose when he entered (on the cuff) a local theater. He never abused his privileges or took a royal mistress.

Norton I held his royal duties seriously, for he was no playboy monarch. He spent days with pen and paper producing documents, issuing proclamations as impressive and empty as the documents issuing from the royal courts of Europe in those days. The Emperor was a modern diplomat, using telegrams and cables to keep in contact with other royal heads of state, Queen Victoria of England, the German Kaiser, the Tzar of all the Russias. In fact Norton I always felt that his counsel helped to settle the Franco-Prussian War. He was generous with his advice, offering it freely in the saloons and bars, fish stands and parks (to the whole world).

He was firm with President Lincoln, wiring him that it was his duty as President to marry the Widow of Windsor, Queen Victoria, "in order to maintain Western civilization by promoting mutual understanding between the two great English-speaking nations." Lincoln's secretary replied that the President would "give careful consideration to the command."

The Emperor went on doing his duty by his city and his realm until 1880, when one day while passing old St. Mary's Church, he was called to a higher kingdom and gave up his mortal rights,

14. *Citizens of Emperor Norton's kingdom.*

(to enter, we hope, heaven) leaving no heirs. The body was laid out in a royal rosewood casket, in state, at Lockhart and Porters' Funeral Parlor—all expenses borne by the Pacific Club—laid out on O'Farrell Street, where ten thousand people passed the casket, and thirty thousand subjects of the dead Emperor followed his funeral cortege. All over the city flags flew at half mast. Years later in 1936 when progress moved his grave, hundreds of wreaths were placed for Norton I. Dirges came from the San Francisco Municipal Band and an infantry battalion fired a three volley salute. So ended the memory of the only happy kingdom on record, to the Death March from the opera *Saul*.

It was a tribute to the wit and kindness of certain parts of the city and its citizens that the Emperor was treated with continued respect and human good nature. The eccentric was never a stranger to San Francisco; most likely the city was aware it had been built and made prosperous by many other strange men and women.

The nearest the town ever came to a formal nobility was "Lord" Charley Fairfax, reject from a good Virginia family, who claimed to be next in line to succession to the Fairfax barony in England. In San Francisco he was a plain drunk and a moocher really, never worked, always accepted a free drink. With some cynical grand joke and political power at play he was elected clerk of the Supreme Court of California. "Lord" Fairfax also married a rich and beautiful woman. He was involved in a few sword and fist fights, was even wounded and not expected to live—but did; alcohol, his friends claimed, being a great defense against infection and early Western medicine. He actually survived until 1869. The California town of Fairfax is named after him.

The town of San Francisco was to remain for a long time divided into two extremes. While the low mob, the shiploads of *filles de joie* rioted along the shore, the new rich, the promoters, learned how to address a maître d'hôtel when ordering glacéed pheasant, poisson in aspic, and a bottle of Cordon Rouge. Darius Ogden Mills promoted himself to being the richest banker in the West with his Bank of California, and he didn't care if his gaucheries showed. He bought fifteen hundred acres of the old Spanish land grant of Buri Rancho, including eight thousand steers, one thousand horses. And soon he had a château called Millbrae erected seventeen miles south of the Golden Gate. Mills had a fat controlling interest in the great Comstock Lode, had water rights, timber cuttings, freighting and coaching interests. He cut massive timbers in the high Sierras, floated them down his own sluice to his own slashing mills, shipped the lumber on his own railroad, the Virginia and Truckee, and sold it to his own mines. He even made Virginia City buy his water, piped down from the snowcaps.

There was nothing left for Mills to do, desire and own except the final status symbol of the Gilded Age: his own railroad car as the Grand Monarch of a frontier Versailles. It was built with the loving care of a yacht, of gleaming silver and teak and other rare woods, built by the firm of Jackson and Sharp, in Wilmington, Delaware (already a state where distant corporations hid assets from prying official eyes and vulgar envy).

Civilizing of the new rich was merely begun, on the top, by the importing of a grandiose chef, a winner of, say, the *Médaille d'Or de la Société Culinaire*, whose *côtelette de veau Provençale* and *filet de sole Colbert* was to be eaten by men and women who only a few years before had swallowed cold beans from a rusty pan; folk who once changed their flannel shirts at rare intervals of time. Ambrose Bierce, standing in his favorite bar, remarked: "A leap from the trees to a town house in one generation. Don't they know Sophocles? 'O you death-journeying men, what do your lives mean except they move to nothing?'" Bierce, the witty angel of gloom of San Francisco, loved to point out the overt symbolism of despair.

The dangerous part of town, away from the first mansions on Nob Hill and the glitter of new money (and plenty of it), was what was to be called the Barbary Coast. Here the whores and their macks and the thieves lived in jerry-built huts and unpainted houses along the waterfront bounded by Broadway, Pacific Street, the steep climb up Telegraph Hill. The Chilenos were thick here, and with them the smell of garlic, chili, outhouses and whisky flavored with Latin curses, which gave it all a color that later, much later, was called glamorous. To this district came all the human trash, the sea outlaws, the brutes, sadists, adventurers, black sheep, mountain men, exiles, escaped or uncaptured murderers, younger sons and wayward daughters; all drifters to the Pacific shore who scented spenders and sinners, victims and violence.

The Mexican government in the past had wisely made laws to keep out the Australians: convicts, branded hoodlums, ticket-of-leave men. These warped criminals saw in San Francisco a new theater of operation and easy living. The British penal colonies were made up of hard cases, the scum of English jails; some were Irish political rebels, but most were cruel and cunning types that did not want to stay in the bush Down Under in the back country and become sheep-herding larkins in dusty stations. They came from Sydney in New South Wales, from Van Diemen's-land, later called Tasmania.

The only sure thing about them was they were criminals, all hungry, all penniless, deep in privation and squalor. And felons by their very look—some branded on cheek or thumb. They were called Sydney Coves or Sydney Ducks, "cracklin' in the pond." So to San Francisco came this English cockney, Liverpool, Whitechapel invasion of thugs and trollops—into the Coast's dance halls, shady hotels, grog shops, sailors' hangouts, whorehouses. Street signs took an English turn in the lower town, spelled out words like Noggin of Ale, Bobby Burns, Hilo Jack, Johnny's, Jolly Waterman. They all drank, they fornicated like a mink pond. They were naturally lewd, greedy and mean. Few worked. They seemed merely to stand in the daytime, usually in doorways, or at tables drinking rum is some slow dissolution.

The name of the district became Sydney Town. The rich miners and the well-off merchants and enterprisers would go slumming in Sydney Town, to visit the harbor tarts working for the Sydney Ducks, to watch strange games in obscene shows in which the Australians specialized, at fifty cents to five dollars a gamy performance of oddly paired groups.

Visitors, unless well protected by bodyguards or the bribed law, found it easy to get their heads bashed in and their pockets emptied.

15. A *Sydney duck*—*one of the many Australian convicts on the town.*

The whisky was raw at the Boar's Head, where the showstopper was a ceremony marrying a woman to a boar. At another place, the Fierce Grizzly, there was a live grizzly bear chained out front. Some said he preferred fish and chips and kippers as food.

The Ducks were a sinister power over the vice and slum areas. The English-speaking bullies acted, while the law was slow to take over. It took two years just to get around to changing from the Mexican to American system of procedures for the courts, judges and codes of civil and criminal law. The American military caste (we have quoted one general's ideas) insisted for some time in running civil affairs with "spit and polish." Everybody who was not an outlaw was busy mining or trying to get rich, so there was not much interest in civilizing the town. There was a dilemma as to how to keep order but there was very little progress.

The ayuntamiento (town council) was supposed to run all affairs. But whether in time of change or not, to political minds the only interest was dipping into the public till. The local politicians did so gleefully, and soon they were bankrupting San Francisco, leaving it short two million dollars. The city cheerfully repudiated the debt, pleasing everyone except the people who owned the money. The ballot box grabbers were on hand.

The court, such as it was, was run by the alcalde, or mayor. For all his Spanish title he was a Yankee, and this one named Meade was a Know Nothing. He had a hatred of Mexicans and tobacco; he was a bigot with clean habits. When a Chileno was brought before him, one merely suspected of horse stealing, this is one version of the conversation:

"You smoke cigarettes?"

"Sí, señor."

"Blow the smoke through your nose?"

"Sí, señor."

"Guilty as charged, may God have mercy on your soul! Constable, take this fellow out, hang the sonofabitch! He stole the hoss sure enough!"

In those preposterous fast-moving times rope solved a great many problems.

The first mayor honored under the full American system was

John W. Geary, and the first thing he bought was a jail, or rather the brig *Euphemia,* deserted by her crew lighting out for the gold fields. This floating or beached hoosegow (a Mexican term) served as a lockup for some years. But only for those who loved prison and failed to escape.

There was an ordinance requiring the closing of Sydney Town at midnight. This merely meant a demand for honest graft and extra payoffs for the police force, which was run by a former Tammany boy and New York saloon keeper. They continued to protect vice and crime and to rob the city till. The gay spots grew wilder. The *Annals* reports: "There were usually two murders a day. Arson was common, prostitution and its earnings a way of life, robbery a spectator sport." All protection came from City Hall, and although in the early days San Francisco had a population of about forty thousand, someone proudly remarked it had enough crime for a city four or five times its size.

Fires set on purpose, or by accident, swept the town six times in the first years of the gold rush. Four of the fires were created by arsonists for insurance and looting. When the two ringleaders were tried in court, they were freed by fixes arranged by the political bosses. Sydney Town was as dangerous as a nest of rattle-snakes. The *Annals* report: "Even the police hardly dared enter there; and if they attempted to apprehend some known individuals, it was always in a numerous, strongly-armed company. The lawless inhabitants of the place united to save their luckless brothers, and generally managed to drive the assailant away. . . .

"When the different fires took place . . . bands of plunderers issued from this great haunt of dissipation, to help themselves to whatever money or valuables lay in their way, or which they could possibly secure. With these they retreated to their dens, and defied detection or apprehension. Many of these fires were believed to have been raised by incendiaries, solely for looting. . . . Criminals left no doubt of the fact, that not only had frequent attempts been made to fire the city, but that some of these had un- fortunately been successful. Fire, however, was only one means of attaining their ends.

"The most daring burglaries were committed, and houses and

persons rifled of their valuables. Where resistance was made, the bowie-knife or the revolver settled matters, and left the robber unmolested. Midnight assaults ending in murder were common. And not only were these deeds perpetrated under the shade of night, but even in daylight in the highways and byways of the country, in the streets of the town, in crowded bars, gambling saloons and lodging houses, crimes of an equally glaring character were of constant occurrence. People at that period generally carried during all hours and wherever they happened to be loaded firearms about their persons; but these weapons availed nothing against the sudden stroke of the 'slung shot,' the plunge and rip of the knife, or the secret aiming of the pistol. No decent man was in safety to walk the streets after dark; while at all hours, both of night and day, his property was jeopardized by incendiarism and burglary. . . .

"Bail was readily accepted in the most serious cases, where the security tendered was absolutely worthless, and where whenever necessary, both principal and cautioner quietly disappeared. The prisons likewise were small and insecure; and though filled to overflowing, could no longer contain the crowds of apprehended offenders. When these were ultimately brought to trial, seldom could a conviction be obtained. From technical errors on the part of the prosecutors, laws ill understood and worse applied, false swearing of the witnesses for the prisoners, absence often of the chief evidence for the prosecution, dishonesty of jurors, incapacity, weakness, or venality of the judge, and from many other causes, the cases generally broke down, the prisoners were freed. *Not one criminal had yet been executed.* Yet it was notorious that, at this period, at least one hundred murders had been committed within the space of a few months; while innumerable were the instances of arson, and of theft, robbery, burglary, and assault with intent to kill. It was evident that the offenders defied and laughed at all the puny efforts of the authorities to control them."

The idiosyncrasy of playing with lucifer matches saw new San Francisco rise on older burned-out versions. People became visibly nervous at the sound of bells on a windy night.

Book Two

TIMES ROUGH, TOUGH AND TENDER

6

NO LAW AND LESS ORDER

> Sister, did you bring me silver?
> Sister, did you bring me gold?
> Did you bring me anything
> To keep me from the gallows pole?

Violence usually comes to a new place overcrowded by lonely men far from their roots. The violence and mob rule that took over for some years in San Francisco was strangely enough a kind of American frontier mystic force—special in some ways to itself, and yet native American in its roots. The first serious historian to try to define it became famous. He was Frederick Jackson Turner, whose paper, "The Significance of the Frontier in American History," created a furor when delivered before the American Historical Association in 1893. Turner saw beyond the flapdoodle of frontier rapscallions acting like chuckleheads or merely working off high spirits in horseplay.

He said: "The wilderness masters the colonist. It finds him a European in dress, industries, tools, modes of travel and thought. . . . It strips off the garments of civilization and arrays him in the hunting shirt and the moccasin. It puts him in the log cabin. . . . In short, at the frontier the environment is at first too strong for the man. He must accept the conditions which it furnishes or perish. . . . Little by little he transforms the wilderness, but the outcome is not the old Europe. . . . The fact is, that here is a new product that is American."

Turner saw beyond the simple violence a kind of open-air philosophy of naked power, keyed to the demands of a hard life, and he moved past that surface reading to something special and different in those Yanqui mountain men, pelt hunters, army bullies, who had first seen California and pushed against the Mexican-Spanish culture. He saw the steady, never relaxing power of the gold hungry, the land grabbers, the city builders, the strength of a wide awake way of life to which softness would not come for a long time, and whose basic physical core still today strains our culture and way of life. It persisted even when the green frontiers were no longer there, or the need to fight varmints, hostiles, to ax big trees and dig ore by merely staking a claim or driving off a rival with a shotgun and a gizzard full of birdshot.

"As has been indicated the frontier is productive of individualism. Complex society is precipitated by the wilderness into a kind of primitive organization. . . . The tendency is anti-social. It produces antipathy to control, and particularly to any direct control. The tax gatherer is viewed as a representative of oppression. . . . The result is that to the frontier the American intellect owes its striking characteristics. That coarseness and strength combined with acuteness and inquisitiveness; that practical inventive turn of mind, quick to find expedients; that masterful grasp of material things, lacking in the artistic but powerful to effect great ends; that restless, nervous energy; that dominant individualism, working for good and for evil, and withal that buoyancy and exuberance which comes with freedom—these are traits of the frontier. . . ."

Let us take a look at the mountain men who were to become Californians and join the San Francisco violence. After the Spaniards the first Americans to penetrate the West were the beaver hunters in the beginning of the nineteenth century, who went West for Mr. Astor and others to furnish the raw material for a new fashion; the tall beaver hat made from the hair of the busy animal living in mountain streams. Everybody wanted a beaver hat, and the hairy mountain men in greasy buckskins went out with their Kentucky or Hawkins rifles as the first explorers of the headwaters of the Gila, the Big Muddy, the Colorado and the mountain ranges

16. Violence on the American frontier—fruit of the lynching tree.

leading to California, to set traps, marry squaws, fight off Cheyennes, Snakes, Utes, Gros Ventres, and to try to hold on to their own long hair.

They were hard and mean and strong, out of Jackson Hole and Fort Laramie, and almost indestructible. They had to be to survive the bad water and worse whisky, the Indian arrows on the Spanish Fork and Seedskedee Crossing, hand-to-hand battles with grizzly bears, and the lonely life when they were snowed up in a brush lean-to. They dressed, played and sang in their own way, and when they came back they were shaggy as goats, and wild, but loaded with wedge-presses of pelt from their caches. They ate anything when hungry, including, legend says, each other. ("Meat's meat," said one survivor of a two party group who showed up in the spring all alone.)

With the passing of the tall beaver hat and the coming into fashion of the silk and ordinary felt hat and the iron derby, the mountain men faced West and many joined the Gold Rush and went wild on the Golden Gate. As they said in San Francisco, "Tearin' up the town was enough to make a cow laugh."

Since both the police and the city government were corrupt, law and order was a personal matter most of the time. A group, or gang, or social class, decided what was best for its own way of life. This could only lead to private vengeance and mob rule. Vigilance committees were spawned by men with gravel in their craw and a disrespect for formal culture.

The first great sampling of mob rule began on a February night in 1851. Two men knocked out the senior partner of Jansen, Bond & Co. with a blackjack and got away with two thousand dollars in gold. Two of the Sydney Ducks were arrested and taken to City Hall, where a mob of loafers, miners in for a spree, wheelwrights, horseleeches and others, numbering five thousand, began howling for a double hanging. The beaten businessman identified his attackers, but it was soon clear that the politicians and the gang lawyers with a Spencerian flourish of a pen would have the prisoners out of jail in a matter of hours. The trial would be a mockery. (As Turner wrote: "Individualism in America has allowed a laxity in regard to government affairs which has rendered possible the spoils system and all the manifest evils that follow from the lack of a highly developed civic spirit.")

Sam Brannan, the defrocked Morman, was suspected of printing and circulating a sockdolager of an inflammatory handbill:

CITIZENS OF SAN FRANCISCO:

The series of murders and robberies that have been committed in this city seems to leave us entirely in a state of anarchy. 'When thieves are left without control to rob and kill, then doth the honest traveller fear each bush a thief.' Law, it appears, is but a nonentity to be scoffed at; redress can be had for aggression but through the never failing remedy so admirably laid down in the code of Judge Lynch. Not that we should admire this process of redress, but that it seems to be inevitably necessary. Are we to be robbed and assassinated in our domiciles, and the law to let our aggressors perambulate the streets because they have furnished straw bail? If so, 'let each man be his own executioner. Fie upon your laws.' They have no force. All those who would rid our city of its robbers and murderers will assemble on Sunday at two o'clock on the plaza.

It was too good to miss—and the law, crooked and lazy—was too pert and uppish. The citizens were taking care of things in their own way. A mob of hundreds attacked the courthouse where the prisoners were held; but it was withstood by another private group of moral defenders, a volunteer military group, the Washington Guard. It resulted in black eyes being handed out for everybody while the prisoners were locked up more securely in cells in the cellar. The mob came back at nightfall, fortified with spoon victuals and primed with whisky, and demanded that the prisoners should not be released on bail. Some citizens spoke to the mob on ways to get a proper trial, not a mockery, with a quick release of the Sydney Ducks.

Sam Brannan was on hand and ready to talk out as usual: "We are the Mayor and the recorder, the hangman and the laws. The law and the courts never yet hung a man in California, and every morning we are reading fresh accounts of murders and robberies. I want *no* technicalities. Such things . . . shield the guilty."

While this was true, the people—not really settled down—made little effort to see behind the filthy politics, the venal police. They were all for direct action as they chomped on their chaws of *niggerhead*—a natural leaf twist tobacco which disfigured the jaw and resulted in a flow of juice—to be discarded—that made it unsafe for women in gingham gowns and percale bonnets to pass too close. The idea of a lynching made the chewers move their loaded jaws even faster. Despite all the hard toil and the dangers of disease, accidents, the risks of mining and sailing, life was most of the time actually dull. So the ultimate thrill was to see a human being twitching and turning at the end of a rope; a perverse pleasure that has not yet—modern historians tell us—been tamed· and discarded. The cruelty of the frontier was not deeply felt; no more than tying a tin can to a dog's tail and turning him loose with a volley of stones.

Americans drank potent whisky—"fairly make your hair rise when toting a load. A jug of forty rod sure rousted Old Scratch out of a man." So there was screechy laughter and cheers when Sam Brannan was for a lynching at once. Cooler heads suggested it would be just as fitting to observe a hanging later. Next day the leaders of the vigilance groups—everybody seemed to be a great talker—addressed a crowd of nearly ten thousand people in the Square, demanding an immediate trial. A jury was quickly picked, a judge hurried into court, and the case presented at record speed. By evening the jury was trying to come to a verdict. The score stood nine for guilty, three undecided. Hearing this the mob outside howled: "Hang 'em. *Majority* rules!" Several crowds tried to storm the jail but were pushed back. For a week the bullyragged prisoners sat and worried as cries of the mob rang around the jail.

A new fully prepared trial then took place and the Sydney Ducks were found guilty of "assault and robbery" and sentenced to fourteen years.

Sam Brannan was not happy at any sentence less than hemp stretching. (He still remembered the old Mormon prayer: "I do pray for my enemies—I pray they all go to hell.") As one early observer put it: "In ridding San Francisco of the thieves, gamblers and desperadoes that infested it, none were more active, outspoken and fearless than Brannan; and he lashed the malefactors and their official supporters with a vigor of vituperation that has rarely been equalled."

All the Sydney Ducks—full on execrable booze—were also angry at the verdict. They began to spread the word they were going to burn the town. There had been great fires already, suspected as set by looters. The new rumors were no mere talk. Near midnight on May 4, 1851, a Sydney Duck was seen coming from a paint store on the Square where he didn't belong, and in a moment it was a mass of flames. Other set fires blazed up in various parts of San Francisco, mostly in the business sections where stores and warehouses bulged with rich gear and supplies. Soon two thousand buildings were flaring torches. Twenty blocks of the town went up like dry hay. A whole area nearly a mile by a third of a mile in size was destroyed. At first it seemed that even ships and their cargoes would catch fire; rigging and sails burned well. But by hasty work in tearing down the docks and wharves a fire gap over the water saved the ships and their contents. As in all early fires there was a shortage of water. The DeWitt & Harrison warehouse on Commercial Street was saved by pouring eighty thousand gallons of vinegar on it! One wonders how bad the food of cabbage and side pork, liver pudding, must have been at the time to need so *much* vinegar.

The looting was grand; satin, figured velvets, casks of beef, fancy furniture, liquor, guns. The Sydney Ducks and their followers danced in glee in the light of the fires as bales and bundles were carried off. Some citizens armed themselves to protect their property and a few looters were shot. An innocent bystander got it between the eyes as he tried to light his pipe with a burning stick. A major part of the city, three-fourths of it, lay in sooty ruin and smoke and the smells of burning remained for days. Yet for all the cursing and indignant talk it was no time for mourning or regrets, and in little more than a week the charred remains of timbers and cargoes and merchandise had been hauled off and lumber schooners were unloading fresh rosin-sticky timbers from the mills to start building afresh.

It was clear now to businessmen that the Sydney Ducks had to be contained and if possible rooted out of their dives. Property damage hurt. A meeting of solid citizens in broadcloth was held at Sam Brannan's place of business at Battery and Pine streets. A really tough new vigilance committee was organized. Part of the document, called its constitution, had teeth, even though its text was written in dog-lawyer terms. The Sydney Ducks had passed into the zone of fatality. The businessmen were as jumpy as a fiddler's foot, and the mob of mud-eaters, loafers, passing miners could be primed for anything deadly.

Whereas, it has become apparent to the citizens of San Francisco, that there is no security for life and property, either under the regulations of society as it at present exists, or under the law as now administered:

Therefore, the citizens, whose names are hereunto attached, do unite themselves into an association for the maintenance of the peace and good order of society, and the preservation of the lives and property of the citizens of San Francisco, and do bind themselves each unto the other, to do and perform every lawful act for the maintenance of law and order, and to sustain the laws when faithfully and properly administered; but we are determined that no thief, burglar, incendiary or assassin, shall escape punishment, either by the quibbles of the law, the insecurity of prisons, the carelessness or corruption of the police, or a laxity of those who pretend to administer justice. And to secure the objects of this association we do hereby agree:

That the name and style of the association shall be the COMMITTEE OF VIGILANCE, for the protection of the lives and property of the citizens and residents of the city of San Francisco.

That there shall be a room selected for the meeting and deliberation of the committee, at which there shall be one or more members of the committee appointed for that purpose, in constant attendance, at all hours of the day and night, to receive the report of any member of the association, or of any other person or persons whatsoever, of any act of violence done to the person or property of any citizen of San Francisco; and if in the judgment of the member or members of the committee present, it be such an act that justifies the interference of the committee, either in aiding in the execution

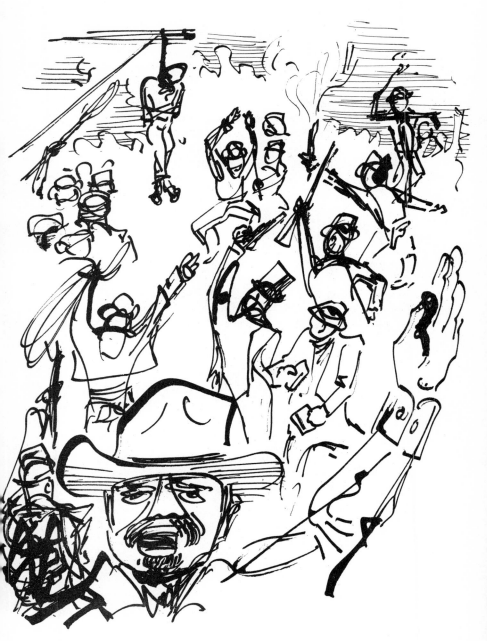

17. *The Committee of Vigilance turns to law and order.*

of the laws, or the prompt and summary punishment of the offender, the committee shall be at once assembled for the purpose of taking such action as a majority of the committee when assembled shall determine upon. . . .

That when the committee have assembled for action, the decision of a majority present shall be binding upon the whole committee, and that those members of the committee whose names are hereunto attached, do pledge their honor, and hereby bind themselves to defend and sustain each other in carrying out the determined action of this committee at the hazard of their lives and their fortunes."

A priority of hate, need for excitement, was clearly taking over. A local poet wrote:

A hundred fierce avengers arose and faced about,
And following their leader like mad, avenging fates,
Paused not until they gathered before the prison gates . . .
"Too slow," the leader muttered. Quick then his pistol flashed,
And swift in imitation, a dozen bullets crashed
Straight through the struggling robber. Then all was strangely still,
The while they contemplated the victim of their will.
Then spake the stern-souled leader: "Let's look upon his face,
And mark the robber's features, this demon of disgrace."

How smug are the righteous, some saint has said.

7

JUDGE LYNCH RIDES HIGH

There is a well-loved old folk song, now forgotten, that captures
the color and cry of the frontier mob; it's called "Judge Lynch."

Up sprang the sturdy miner, whose locks were streaked with gray,
With eyes which flashed their sentence, "Come, boys, there's work
    today,
They say the law is shuffling, that justice yet may fail,
While over there the horse-thief is resting safe in jail.
Let those with baby spirits stay here or weakly flee,
But men of nerve and courage will rise and follow me!"
A hundred sturdy miners responded with a shout . . .
On rushed the fierce-eyed leader; they followed with a yell,
On heavy doors and barriers their sturdy weapons fell,
And out they dragged the prisoner with features scared and white,
With eyes which shone like embers, and limbs which shook with
    fright.
With speechless lips which mumbled, or vainly strove to pray,
The while his eyes watched wildly their leader grim and gray.
No faltering in purpose, no prisoner's chance for hope.
The gray old miner knotted and looped the fatal rope;
Then springing off as tigers spring fiercely from their lair,
The trembling wretch, uplifted, was struggling in the air.
He fought in desperation for every labored breath—
Around him in a circle the ministers of death.

With crude resourcefulness the vigilance committee was again at
work. John Jenkins, an Australian convict, known as the Miscreant,

had carried off, in full sight of people, a small cast-iron safe from a shipping office on Long Wharf. Chased, he dropped it into the Bay, and it was recovered. Ringing of the firebell of the Monumental Firefighting Engine Company announced Jenkins' capture. A quick "trial" held by the vigilance group was followed by Sam Brannan's pronouncement to the crowd: "Jenkins is guilty. He'll hang in two hours."

It was two o'clock in the morning. With ceremony the committee, carrying pistols, shotguns, Bowie-knives, escorted the tied-up prisoner, with a hangman's noose around his neck, as they marched to an old house on the west side of the Square. A strong oak beam was handy to toss the rope over. The police showed up then and mildly asked for the prisoner. Someone, most likely Brannan, a natural-born spokesman, said, "If you try to interfere with this hanging, we'll use our weapons." Meanwhile the prisoner calmly chewed on a large wad of gift tobacco, sure that the Sydney Ducks would rescue him.

The police at once turned on their heels and were off, and the prisoner was seized by his bound arms and placed under the high beam. With a shout a group of men grabbed the free end of the rope and rushing backward hoisted the prisoner high in the air. Here he slowly strangled, for these hasty ill-designed hangings did not break the neck as a professional job would, and the prisoner expired in agony.

As he hung there a solemn ritual was observed. *Each* member of the vigilance committee had to hold the taut rope for a few moments so everyone would be part of the group sport, and *also* would be implicated in the lynching. There was no prayer for the reverence of the prisoner's Maker, or a hope for his providence.

The coroner did a brave thing. In his report he indicated the dead man "came to his death at the hands of, and in pursuance of a preconcerted action on the part of an association of citizens, styling themselves the 'Committe of Vigilance.'"

Samuel Brannan and eight members of the committee were named. The committee boldly admitted its part, took all the honors for hanging Jenkins, and then published its membership list of nearly two hundred of the town's most respectable, rich and prominent citizens who led the mob. All criminals were ordered to leave town and death warnings were sent out. Incoming ships were boarded at the Golden Gate so that the vigilance committee could look over the passengers for "criminal types"—whatever that meant. If they had no proof they were "decent and honorable," the newcomers were shipped out to point of origin, echoing the modern bigot's cry: "Go back to where you came from." Seize and search action, against which citizens were protected by the Constitution, was ignored; the new rule was "if they don't look right—git."

There was a great exodus of petty thieves and unimportant felons, but the powerful criminals who delivered votes knew the politicians would take care of them. And to show they were still tough, the Sydney Ducks set afire an empty house at Powell Street and Pacific Avenue. Again a good part of the town went up in flames. Eighteen blocks were burned out. No action was taken.

The next month a famous Sydney Duck leader called English Jim black-jacked a ship's captain and his wife on their ship. The wife managed to hold English Jim until the sailors came and worked on him before turning him over to the committee. The membership—now four hundred—was all present to hear English Jim's confession of his crimes, and he, seeming proud of appearing before such a huge audience, presented them in gory detail. He stood at last in heavy irons, saying: "This is a goddamned tiresome business. Let's get it the hell over with."

English Jim was marched out at the head of a parade of vigilance members, with cheers all the way. Everybody who could get out followed along to the grand site picked for the execution. No mere beam seemed proper now for hanging. A special crane or derrick had been erected on the wharf at Market Street. As they neared the site, English Jim felt his courage seep from him and he fell to the ground. The last block or so he was held erect by some strong-backed members of the party.

The hanging was quickly done. About two dozen honorary officers pulled on the rope, and English Jim, one of the most hard-nosed of the Sydney Ducks (and by some thought to be their leader) spun slowly in the night mist and sea fog as the last torch went out or was tossed into the Bay, where spectators in small boats rested on their oars.

A special Grand Jury happily endorsed the work of the vigilance committee. Two more Sydney Ducks were sentenced to hang. By this time the governor, John MacDougal, came awake and spoke out strongly against the despotic "control of a self-constituted association, unknown and acting in defiance of the laws."

In answer the committee tried the game of the Big Lie, accusing the governor of having approved of the committee's way of life and death. The newspapers carried an item they provided and many members signed.

"We, the undersigned, do hereby aver that the present Governor, MacDougal, asked to be introduced to the Executive Committee of the Committee of Vigilance, which was allowed, and an hour fixed. The Governor, upon being introduced, stated that he approved of the acts of the Committee, and that much good had taken place. He hoped that they would go on, and endeavor to act in concert with the authorities, and in case any judge was guilty of maladministration, to hang him, and he would appoint others . . ."

The governor, now aware of the full suffocating pressure of mob and lynch rule, got the police to seize on a writ of *habeas corpus* the two Sydney Ducks held by the committee and waiting hanging. The prisoners were taken to the city jail under the City Hall to await a legal trial. Two days later nearly forty vigilance bullies "overpowered" the sheriff's guards and grabbed off the two Sydney Ducks, rushing them to a full committee meeting at the headquarters to be judged in a fog of rhetoric for a conformity of guilt.

In twenty minutes the two prisoners were hanging from redwood beams that stuck out of the front windows of the meeting room. The mob gathered outside for the fun, and greeted the dying dangling men with cheers. As usual Sam Brannan made a speech while the bodies still hung over the street, stating that the governor had better stand clear of the committee as nothing he could do would stop the work of hanging with ruthless impartiality every criminal who stayed in San Francisco.

The coroner's office returned the now formula verdict, and the governor made no move. Most of the thieves, con artists, arsonists and other criminals left town. As one observer put it, the remaining dance halls, saloons, gambling halls and whorehouses "were run in strict obeying of the law." Diverse elements were becoming a significant whole. It looked as if, legally or not, street and indoor crime had been frightened out of San Francisco except for licensed gambling and its marked cards here and there, and an extra ace up a sleeve; or the confidence men in the shape of gold brick sellers, creators of salted mines and land sales; or the madams and tarts who paid up honestly to City Hall for their protection. The politicians remained venal and were busy emptying the city till.

One of the town's biggest boosters was Alderman Meiggs, who had built the two thousand foot pier at North Beach, financed, alas, by the forging of thousands of city warrants for cash worth— only on paper—eight hundred thousand dollars to those dupes who bought marked warrants. A bank had trouble, a depression set in; and the city would have gone bankrupt if some bright mind had not solved it all by the repudiation of municipal bonds and warrants on some incomprehensible principle of city government.

A city of fifty thousand had about two million dollars' worth of debts it couldn't meet. The big thief in power was David C. Broderick, the saloon keeper and Tammany ward heeler from New York. Before he was killed in a duel, he became a U. S. Senator. He was the city's boss politician, beholden to none, milking away at every city teat that would pour out graft.

R.J. in his daybook writes: "They still talk of the old days when Senator Broderick ran S.F. as 'tight as a bull's vent in flytime.'" No jobs, no appointments, no nominations for public office were filled unless Broderick said so. What boodle there was in any public job had to be shared with Broderick, half and half. He cut it high on the hog and didn't even wear the demeanor of decorum. He is remembered as an impartial destroyer.

18. *High living in high fashions even in times of turmoil.*

Broderick's graft take was said to be in the hundreds of thousands a year, and when the newspapers attacked him, he did not sue for libel but warned editors his strong arm boys would go into action. He had brought out with him Bowery sluggers, ballot box stuffers, murderous hoodlums from New York's Five Points. This band, a sort of private Old Guard, was always ready to carry out his orders. His right arm was Dutch Charlie, born Charles P. Duane, whom a contemporary text describes as a "notorious politician . . . he has one thousand votes at his command, to be disposed of at elections by the simple plan of having his adherents vote three times in different sections of the city. Although he has no visible means of support, he lives regally on credit . . ."

Broderick operated out in the open, and even those who admired him did not hide the facts of his barefaced stealing. Writing of him, Jeremiah Lynch says in his book, *A Senator of the Fifties:* "He introduced a modification of the same organization in San Francisco with which Tammany has controlled New York for lo! these many years. It was briefly this. At a forthcoming election a number of offices were to be filled; those of sheriff, district attorney, alderman, and places in the legislature. Several of these positions were very lucrative, notably that of the sheriff, tax-collector and assessor. The incumbents received no specified salaries, but were entitled to all or a certain proportion of the fees. These fees occasionally exceeded $50,000 per annum. Broderick would say to the most popular or the most desirable aspirant: 'This office is worth $50,000 a year. Keep half and give me the other half, which I require to keep up our organization in the state. Without intelligent, systematic discipline, neither you nor I can win, and our opponents will conquer, unless I have money enough to pay the men whom I may find necessary. If you agree to that arrangement, I will have you nominated when the convention assembles, and then we will all pull together until after the election.' Possibly this candidate dissented, but then someone else consented, and as the town was hugely Democratic, his selections were usually victorious. . . . When he came there was chaos, and he created order. There was no party system in the town, and he created one."

The last two sentences may be ironic, but they sound full of admiration. And there were few Jeremiahs and Savonarolas to point him out as a calamity for evil.

It would be futile to repeat on these pages the full details of the second vigilance committee that sprang into action when a popular citizen died of wounds inflicted by another. One of the men who was lynched for this had engraved on his tombstone the words: MAY GOD FORGIVE MY PERSECUTORS. Open terror, well armed, walked the streets. The governor issued a proclamation declaring San Francisco in a State of Insurrection, demanding that the vigilantes turn in their weapons and go out of business. Instead the vigilantes declared a full state of war against the state.

Bold and eager for battle they set up an armed camp and fort near the waterfront, put up American flags, raised ten foot walls of earth and sandbags, and placed two field guns on the roof supplied with powder and cannonballs. This was Bunker Hill again. With monomaniacal glee the mob called it Fort Gunnysack, but the committee named it honorably Fort Vigilance. They had the only artillery in town, though there were guns in the federal army and navy camps at the Presidio and on Mare Island. The governor requested these heavy arms to put down the rebellion. The army and navy personnel merely sneered, passed the buck, saying they had to have direct orders from the War Department in Washington. The President of the United States washed his hands of the situation, saying: no help, no arms for the governor. (States' rights were solemn in those days, come rape, fire or battle.)

Major General William T. Sherman, in command of the State Militia, refused to march against the insurgents (Georgia would be different) and only about ninety men showed up to aid the governor. The governor ordered shipments of arms and supplies down from Sacramento by boat. The vigilantes seized the boats and cargoes and thus added to their arms in Fort Gunnysack. They took over the Armory and every other important building. They held the city captive in their full power, against all law and order groups. No shots were fired, but some knifing was done. A judge of the Supreme Court was put on "trial" and asked to resign. Four men were hanged and twenty-six sent into exile. The vigilance committee held the city and Fort Gunnysack until August of 1856. Victorious, it went out of business, turning over the rule to what was termed a "duly elected city rule of the people."

The whole of San Francisco turned out to see the big victory parade of the vigilante army. It was an impressive sight, eight thousand men, all well armed with captured supplies. They stepped out to the blare of bands, marched to Fort Gunnysack and lay down their arms like heroes. Flags were soon furled, the breastworks dissolved or pulled down. All gunpowder, cannonballs, rifles, pistols and cutlasses seized or captured were given to the governor. That worthy politely recalled his Proclamation of Insurrection against the Sovereign State of California (and indirectly against the United States of America).

No matter how one romanticized the event, it was civil war against the state and the nation, and the lynching of four men without proper legal trial or by a jury of their peers, or—naturally— without any right of appeal to legal or higher courts. As a modern Historian, John Meyers Myers, put it in his book, *San Francisco's Reign of Terror:* "None of the founders of Europe's police states had been so much as born when the San Francisco Committee of Vigilance patented the whole bag of totalitarian tricks. There were public strutting and secret courts, the unleashing of dog soldiers with unlimited powers of search and seizure; and a mob schooled by a bought press to rough up any who wouldn't cheer viciousness. There was even the picture of an eye—posted to let serfs know that their masters were ever on watch—which George Orwell thought he had coined when lashing at statism in *Nineteen-Eighty-Four.*"

Californians have always taken pride in being first in most kooky actions, with a kind of cheerful perverse pomposity in their prejudices and the Yahoos they elect to high office.

Violence leads to an imbalance, an insufficiency, as has been recently discovered in the matter of the Mafia. No criminal group can operate without a corrupt political system and tainted courts of justice. As San Francisco continued to be looted, the top poli-

19. *The law was all in the gun—and dishonest city fathers didn't care.*

ticians saw they needed an army of thieves, pimps and brothel owners as a protective shell, and also as an added source of income.
Slowly the Sydney Ducks began creeping back to San Francisco,
and in the next two or three years the town was wide open again,
a roaring wild city. Debauchery which had previously to seek farther
afield could now be bought by the yard (or body), and swindlers
and killers, gamblers and whores swung cheerfully with the times.
It was the usual cycle that Lincoln Steffens was to observe in his
muck-raking book, *The Shame of the Cities.* A reforming clean
sweep of crooked politics had no lasting power. Sometimes the
reformers became corrupt in office; or the citizens, bored with
goodness, shouted "Throw the rascals *in.*" So reform ended in
vice, and vice in time brought on reform, and that again went
into its dance of crime. Today we no longer vacillate; we accept
the crime syndicate as a second government.

An early exposé volume, under the lurid title *Metropolitan Life
Unveiled, or the Mysteries and Miseries of American Great Cities,*
gives a wild picture of San Francisco after the first bursts of action
of the vigilance movement. "Masked men appeared openly in
the streets and garrotted citizens, apparently defying law or resistance; the rough element had apparently banded together for the
purpose of preying upon the wealth held by honest hands. . . .
Politics was in fact accountable for this chaotic condition of city
affairs. . . . Society was sore diseased. Villainy wielded the balance
of power, and honesty was at a discount. 'The law's delay, the
insolence of office' became the chafing cause of much discomfort.
Honest voters on election day felt that it was but ill-spent time
to cast a vote. Ballot box stuffing, not *vox populi,* placed men in
office. In short, the town was ruled by gamblers, rowdies and state-
prison convicts."

And the street preacher in hope of converts shouted outside the
Bella Union: "Babylon is fallen, is fallen, that great city because
she made all nations drink of the wine of the wrath of her fornication—*cecidit, cecidit, Babylonia illa magna.*"

8

GAMBLERS, MERCHANTS AND HIGH FASHION

Her bed was the brown turf
And her house was out of doors . . .
Meg Merrilies

The Hangtown parvenus rode softest in their imported carriages. Even the miners still waiting for a strike, the loafers, hungry sharpers, had their guitar and banjo hoe-downs and cut their pigeon-wing steps in broken boots. It was a strange assortment of peoples from every place. Runaway clerks and sailors, farriers, bone setters, hog-gelders, sluts of all kinds, bedraggled wives. Life was a drop of rum, some self-deprecating humor and a bit of soaked corn to make hominy. Hogs could be heard screaming under the killing maul from farms on the outskirts of the city, where Indian women leached ashes to lye and gathered yarbs. It was not a healthy place, this land of muck and mire, cold rains, fogs, and sanitation not even in sight. The "miseries" got them, the cholera infantum, lung tubules; people worried more over horse croup or mule botts than a man dying alone in a muddy alley. Ten grains of calomel and jalop didn't cure everything.

But money could buy bear hams and deer venison, baked pumpkin, geese and ducks once flying south, and the biggest frogs alive from the river swamps.

Eccentric, capricious, self-infatuated; that was San Francisco. Wild oaks, sea hawks and gourd fiddles, and a hanging to the "Rogue's

March" on a tin flute. There were clay-and-stick chimneys and lots of gold-headed canes. There was palsy and yellow fever, too. And greedy girls existed in long stockings that led to mercury ointment. Gold coins spun across teak tables ("Druther spend it fast, knowin' there's moren up some place in the hills").

A state of dishabille began to create an American image, fill a native need; and one was made, innocently, by Levi Strauss. He was born in Bavaria in 1829, and lived in San Francisco until 1902. His youth was spent in Bad Ocheim in the Bavarian Alps. His family were small town clerks and officials. There was no reason for them to go to America. The family made ends meet, felt no poverty, had been set for generations in their mountains. But there was talk of the gold discovery in California, and Levi's two brothers, Willy and Jacob, were already in New York City, writing letters home (not fully true) about how easy the living was in the new land. Levi started off for the gold fields by getting to Hamburg, where over a million people in time were to board the Hamburg-American Line ships. He got on after living for days or weeks in barracks in the town on herring, pretzels, knockwurst and beer. The ship Levi boarded was packed, the trip rough. Levi was dismally seasick. But at last the Golden Land rimmed the horizon, Castle Garden where the immigrants landed. His brothers, Willy and Jacob, met him—not in fur coats and top hats; no solid gold watches and chains in sight, but *still* his brothers.

They were not bankers, not landowners. They were, they admitted to Levi, "Peddlers." Such a shame to the official clerking dynasties of pen-pushing Strausses! *Gott im himmel!* They were the lowest of the low—pack peddlers, selling needles, thread, pots, pans, ribbons, yarn, scissors, buttons of pearl, bone and brass to village wives, farm girls, backwoods yokels. This peddler's load, Levi learned, was put into two packs, one of a hundred pounds on his back and to balance it one of eighty pounds in front, all held by leather straps to distribute the weight. Levi found it heavy. But soon he was in the wilds of New Jersey, with his dozen words of English, peddling. In three months, free of debt to his brothers, he decided California and the gold lands were ready for him. Willy lamented, Jacob swore. But Levi said needles and thread, cloth, were what miners would need, and some little luxuries such as scissors, thimbles and several rolls of a special canvas cloth, imported from the French town of Nîmes, and labeled *Serge de Nîmes*. The New York peddlers called it De-Nîmes, and soon actually denim. Levi hoped it would sell as material to make tents against the wet and cold miasma of the gold fields.

It was the winter of 1851 before Levi Strauss and his bundles went downriver to the Narrows of New York Bay and to the Atlantic with the tide, to touch at Charleston, Rio de Janeiro, Lima, coming with the spring of 1852 to San Francisco. The ship dropped anchor and Levi, sea-sprung and dizzy, looked out at the crude roaring town, with its shanties, the sound of gunshots, laughter, cries of anger. The shore line look was muddy. Even from the ship it seemed mired thick and gamy. The Barbary Coast in view was explained to Levi as the place for the whorehouses and gambling palaces. Behind it he saw the steep hills, and mountains as green as his mother's salad had been. Many small boats came out to the ship, and soon the travelers were opening bundles and selling what they had brought around the Horn. Trade was brisk, and Levi soon sold what he had, all but the rolls of denim which were still in the hold. Everyone talked of wealth with a flamboyant plausibility ("Nuggets bigger'n your thumb").

Once on shore it was clear to Levi that he had sold out too cheaply. He found himself in a place where living was high; five dollars for a night's buggy bed, poor meals at the cost of a German state banquet. No wonder so many men looked hungry and so many slept in blankets out in the open along the wharf, while a few feet away the houris and odalisques drank whisky from cut glass tumblers.

An egg cost Levi a dollar (a mule and a mere pick and shovel were priced at two hundred dollars). And all he had to live on were some rolls of denim which he couldn't sell. People told him it wasn't the right stuff for tenting. He got a two-wheeled cart for fifty dollars of his small capital, and loading his rolls of cloth, went pushing it through muddy streets that seemed to have no bottom. His quest for a living seemed doomed to frustration by its absurdity.

20. *Moving in wearing the first pair of Levi's ever invented in San Francisco.*

He had a product for which there was no demand. Beans, yes, flour, of course, pans, skillets, axes, shotguns, pistols, boots, even Noah Webster's *Spellers*. But no need for his *Serge de Nîmes*.

The Yanqui pitchmen—seasoned peddlers with their medicine shows—did well. They sold Carboline for the hair, Wizard Neuralgia Oil, Electric Linament. "Good for man, good for hoss, palsy, morbid acrimonies, yellar fever."

Levi studied the market, the chaotic shopping, the look of curiosity and greed on the faces of seller and buyer. The shops carried *Blanc de Perle* body powder for the ladies of the Barbary Coast in their Rainy Daisy skirts (short to keep the hem out of the mud), but even they in their ruffled jackets passed by Levi Strauss, cloth seller. They wanted silks, taffetas, froufrous of lace, cut velvets, batiste gored corsets. Levi cursed himself for not stocking ornamental hatpins, black lace cotton stockings, aigrette plumes.

He had a problem. The hand cart was getting no place in the deep mud of the town. Even the few respectable women in their percale bonnets passed him by. On the edge of town Levi Strauss appealed to some miners, rough fellows, all whiskers and tattered shirts. These were for-sure real miners down from the diggings with their mules splashing by. A miner on a lean horse asked Levi what he was selling

"Tenting," said Levi Strauss.

The man shook his head, said he didn't need no tenting, but he damn well needed pants. He certainly did, Levi saw. The miner's pants, what was left of them, were patched, and here and there soiled miner's skin showed through the gaps.

Levi spoke. "I can make you pants." He went on to say he could make the pants of a material that would last *and* last. He fingered the denim and the miner said he'd take a pair, but he needed them right away. He asked how much? Levi guessed at a price. "Six dollars."

The miner said he'd pay in gold dust and gave Levi a good pinch of gold. Levi measured the man's girth and length of leg with a bit of string; he had no tape measure. He told the miner he'd deliver, and he pushed his hand cart to a tailor's shop and made a desperate deal to have his *entire* denim cloth cut up into pants! He paid with the gold dust the miner had given him. Levi's senses were dizzy as he mopped his worried brow.

So began an American success story, in San Francisco, dear to the hearts of business moralists. Levi Strauss's denim pants peddled from his hand cart were a sensation. For while a miner could buy fancy duds in town, no one had seen the need for work pants, or just loafing round pants, pants for farming, ranching and doing things out of doors. Pants as easy to take as sorghum molasses on Indian mush.

Levi Strauss opened a store to sell his denim work pants made of cloth shipped by his brothers from New York around the Horn, and the pants became the uniform of the miners in the tamarisk and mesquite of ranch workers, farmers cutting piñon pine, or just town folk who lifted bales and carried things.

The first denim pants were crude but wearable. The newer batches were better-fitting. Men liked them tight around the hips with big pockets where they could put mine specimens of quartz or carbonates, a railroad handkerchief of red or blue, a chaw of *niggertwist* eatin' tobacco, stray nails, pipe, petrified chestnut for luck, or Barlow knives, a pistol or two, silver dollars, even an Episcopal or Mormon prayer book. One miner whose pockets carried too much so that they tore had rivets made of blacksmith's nails to reenforce the pockets. Levi liked the idea and used copper rivets at all points of strain in his pants, so they remained firm no matter how much red eye gravy and ham, liver pudding savored with onion and sage a man ate.

Pants became *Levis* in the West. Cowboys, miners, ranchers, lumberjacks came to the shop to be fitted with *Levis* (the capital letter came early).

Denim Levis are still worn. They are even fashionable, chic, the mod mode; part of a tradition of the West that began in San Francisco. Warehouses in Europe now stock Levis, women wear them proudly (whereas the pioneer wives pulled them on with a sense of shame at wearing their husband's castoffs).

Once a twenty dollar saddle, a ten dollar Stetson and a pair of four dollar Levis together with a shirt and boots started many a man in life; often a grubstake backed on shares from the shop dealers started a galoot on the road to fortune, or merely dreams. It was not only the Conestoga wagon, freighting, saddlery, wheelwrighting and tanning that a man needed in a trade. He needed a pair of pants that wouldn't expose him to weather, ridicule and the horse laugh. Levi Strauss gave him that protection, copper-riveted. The Levis were a sort of uniform.

Levi Strauss was a simple man. He always could see the logic of the Emperor Vespasian taxing privies. "Money doesn't stink."

As De Tecqueville wrote: "The passions which agitate the Americans are not their political but their commercial passions; or, rather, they introduce the habits of business into their political life. They love order, without which affairs do not prosper; and they set an artificial value upon regular conduct, which is the foundation of solid business."

21. *Barbary Coast saloon—waiting for sailors.*

9

DELILAHS AND JEZEBELS

"For love," R.J. records Ambrose Bierce as saying, "a flat surface is best. A woman should be taken like wine, at room temperature. . . ."

The most notorious and inflammatory of nineteenth century Delilahs and Jezebels to hit San Francisco was Lola Montez, who came in the early fifties. A newspaper reports her as being a big, bold, handsome woman "with fine bad eyes and a determined bearing . . . dressed ostentatiously in perfect male attire, with shirt collar turned down over a lapeled coat, richly worked shirt front, black hat, French unmentionables [how did he know?] and natty polished boots with spurs. She carried in her hand a riding whip. . . . Someone once took hold of the tails of her long coat and as a lesson received a cut across his face that must have marked him for many a day."

She had a reputation of liaisons and adulteries as the mistress of kings and geniuses, world shakers in Europe. After landing in San Francisco she used her past to put on a play about King Ludwig (once her royal lover), *Lola Montez in Bavaria*. Although she had some pitiful claim as a dancer, she was poor on her feet, and if her audience didn't care to see her dance, she was willing to shake the hand of any citizen for one dollar. Meanwhile, whip in hand, she walked Telegraph Hill, Nob Hill, the waterfront.

Lola saw America as a brave new land and she married an American named Hull. She went with him to Grass Valley, where she said—a girl of no reticences—she tamed a grizzly bear with her voice and her whip so that it would follow her like a dog. This hardly seems possible to anyone who knows about grizzlies. The miners in the gold camps—those muddy Sodom and Gomorrahs —liked the sexual nuances of her dances. Her special number was "Lola's Spider Dance." Dressed in tights, she shook out rubber spiders from her short skirt with many a wriggle and twist in an early version of belly and hip-gyrating, bumps and grinds. Then she would stomp on the spiders with her high-heeled slippers. The randy miners in beards and red flannel shirts loved it all and would shout, "Lola, gal, look up-aways! 'Nother spider further up!"

Lola in her preposterous exuberance was one of the sights of San Francisco and the gold camps, with her whip and exotic costumes, and claiming herself one of the most famous women of history; impulsive, capricious, vehement, and stomping on rubber spiders. Californians, new to the upper class demi-monde, accustomed only to the drabs of the Barbary Coast, listened to her.

Her own story, as she told it to the nabobs of San Francisco or to some rich miner in the diggings, grew better with each telling. Her name, Montez, came from her father, the great toreador Montes, hero of the Spanish bullrings. Her mother, at times, was Queen Maria Christina. At another time she remarked that the white collar she wore was in remembrance of her father, Lord Byron, who produced her with the help of a Scots laundry woman. Then, too, she was of noble birth, stolen away by the gypsies of Seville, who cruelly but skillfully trained her to become a dancer (hardly true if one saw her dance). She claimed to speak nine languages, not over-looking the Hindustani. To the local Venus and mining camp Bacchus she was glamor. "Pioneers," Robert Louis Stevenson said while in San Francisco, "never copulate sadly."

She was beautiful, a *jolie femme*; perhaps by our modern standards a bit plump, her jawline too firm and square, her teeth so strong-looking that she could have been an actual man-eater, a complaisant carnivore. Yet for all the bewildering diversity of her

22. *In the parlor houses all the girls admired Lola Montez.*

claims to noble birth, she was actually shanty and lace-curtain Irish. Her mother was a disreputable Dublin milliner, her father a low grade officer in the British East Indian Army. Lola was born into a sanguinary world two months after her parents were married. She was christened with a big name for a small baby: Maria Dolores Eliza Rosanna Gilbert. Sent home to England from India as a child for an education, she got little of that and grew into adolescence with wonder but no awe. When her mother attempted to marry her off to a rich sixty-year-old lecher, Lola eloped with her mother's own lover, a very young Lieutenant James. The marriage failed—he was not her idea of *l'homme moyen sensuel*. Lola went on the stage and her mother sent out black-bordered cards announcing that her daughter was dead. It was a fun family, but a bit on the mad, distraught side.

When he saw her on the stage in Warsaw, a very old man, the Paskevitch (viceroy of Poland) fell in love with Lola and offered her estates, diamonds, all the luxury available. She turned him down, and in anger he gave orders that she was to be hissed from the stage. The Polish patriots took her side and there were street riots. Orders went out for her arrest, and she sat in her locked hotel suite with a loaded pistol in her hand. The French consul gallantly claimed her as a French citizen.

Of course this is *her* own version of her early life. Is there a residue, a sediment of truth in it? The ungallant historians of the period claim she was hissed off the stage in Warsaw for being a poor dancer with no ear for keeping time to music. Moving on to Prussia—there is a bewildering diversity to her travels—she attended on horseback a review of the Army for the royal guest Tzar Nicholas I. Lola, her horse excited by the military music, saw a chance for a quick bit of publicity. She cruelly spurred the animal right toward the two Kings and was poised to leap into the arms of either William IV or the Tzar, fainting properly as a lady should. However, a royal guard grabbed the reins of Lola's horse in time and had his face cut by her whip in recompense. She was the talk of Prussia for this exploit. Moving on to Dresden she batted her eyes at the piano genius and Don Juan of the 88 keys, Franz Liszt. His reputation in bed at this time blotted out his fabulous skill at the piano. The two sex maniacs traveled together as lovers, and he wrote a sonata which he dedicated to her; two egotists full of jealousies and disreputable animosities.

At Bonn were Queen Victoria and her saintly and humorless husband, Prince Albert, come to unveil a statue to Beethoven. At the gala state banquet Lola jumped up on the table, and kicking over dishes and silver, went into her dance (most likely an early version of the "Spider Dance," as seen later in the gold camps). Liszt left her on the run, but Lola's fame and her whip got her to Paris. ("Let's see if her feet are as light as her hand.") She flopped opening night, was hissed; but boldly advancing to the gas jet footlights, she lifted a very fine leg, and pulling off a garter, flung it with a kiss toward the audience. The author, Théophile Gautier, serving as a theater critic, wrote: "We sense that Mlle. Lola should do better on horseback than on a stage."

Lola merely smiled at the scurrilous press and said, "I am subject to my whims and sensations alone." She became the darling of the Bohemian literary set of Paris. Dumas *père* and she had a fling at each other's sensualities on a visit to his house. But he said of her, "She has the evil eye and will bring bad luck to whoever's destiny is linked with her." Dumas had the indiscreteness of a buffoon, and they posed for a photograph together, he weighing in at near three hundred pounds.

Lola tried to shoot one of her lovers, ran another into debt, and a man named Dujarier died in a duel for her. From the witness box at the trial, over the duel, Lola said with tears in her eyes, "I myself handle a pistol better than poor dear Dujarier. If he wanted satisfaction, I would have been happy to take on M. de Beauvallon myself."

There is no record around San Francisco of her as a dead-eye shot with pistol, rifle or shotgun.

She was twenty-seven then and broke. Just in time she latched onto Prince Henry of Reuss, a postage-stamp-sized principality in Thuringia. Being a neat man, he threw her out when one day she walked across his flower beds.

Lola wandered over Europe with no money and dancing badly as ever, till she drove a little madder the addled king, Ludwig I of Bavaria, who became infatuated with her and introduced her to his court and the Jesuit advisers of his Catholic country. "I have the honor to present to you my best friend, Fraulein Lola Montez. You are to see you accord her *every* respect."

Ludwig ordered her to dance at a command performance, which his claques made a howling joy. Proudly she announced it was her last appearance as a dancer. The Jesuits, aware of the proclivities of kings, saw her as a barrier to their drive for power, and their leader shouted to Ludwig in private audience, "She is the King!" And Ludwig nodded, "Yes, she is the King."

Lola, now a countess, formed a new cabinet, which at times was called the *Lolaministerium*. She had become a European power, all in eight weeks' work (counting nights). Jewels, palaces, works of art, all were hers. An American observer of the scene noted she threw "a plate or a book, or attacked with a dagger, poker, broom or other deadly weapon." Some said she debauched the students. A Catholic divine, Johann Döllinger, wrote: "Lola Montez has formed a male harem . . . I must not pollute your ears . . . she is a second Messalina."

Her title was Donna Maria de Dolores Montez, Countess of Landsfeld, but she underestimated the potency of her political enemies.

In 1848 when gold was discovered in California, street riots in Bavaria over Lola's power reached their height. She was almost lynched by a mob, and the King sadly signed the order banishing her.

In the end she left for England where she married a cornet of the Life Guards, a very rich man. His relatives dragged her into court as a bigamist, she having forgotten James. The lovers escaped from England to live in Spain. Here Lola stabbed her cornet with considerable vehemence and he bowed out in his bloody shirtfront.

There was only America left now, with all that stirring talk of rich miners and businessmen in California. Whip, and past, packed in her

lean luggage, she sailed, as one writer put it, "in the full zenith of her
evil fame for California."

Her caprices seemed always her undoing, for no rich miner ever
fully attained her heart except for the unknown Mr. Hull. Her
"Spider Dance" was what kept them going for a while, but in the
end Mr. Hull (he seems to lack a first name in all reports about
him) irked her, and in a rage she threw his baggage out of the
hotel window and told him to make tracks. She took on as a lover
a gold-hunting German, Baron Adler. One day he went into the
mountains to hunt more gold and was never heard of again. Some
said Lola's grizzly bear had eaten him, title and all.

Lola left the cottage in Grass Valley (it is today a tourist's visiting
place), said her farewells to the sports, gamblers and friends of
San Francisco, and took a theater group to Australia. The whip went
along and she used it often. But in the mining hamlet of Ballarat
she got her comeuppance. As she was about to flog a male mocker,
the man's wife got hold of the whip and flogged Lola to a frazzle
until unconscious. On the return sea trip Lola is said to have pushed
her manager, and lover, overboard. In the end she went back to
King Ludwig, and recently discovered papers show that they were
married in 1857. She was thirty-seven and the deaf old King
seventy-one. His major wedding gift to her, medical men say,
was syphilis. He died, and on Lola's return to America the disease
began to destroy her. She lectured for a poor living as a "Demos-
thenes in Dimity," on the subject "Art of Beauty and Gallantry."
She died in a soiled peignoir in a cheap dirty room on a pile of rags
in a corner. Like many old whores she turned to the Bible, and
some cynics have said her favorite scene was of Jesus with a whip
flogging the money changers.

Social history must relate observation to experience, the street
songs to the cries of pain. Behind the fancy painted figures on the
murals of heroic miners and Spanish cowboys, hide hunters,
mountain men, greasy scouts, men in broken boots and highly
rouged dance hall girls, the true West Coast was created by
millionaires, who came poor and early, but wisely let others break
their backs with pick and shovel. The nabobs bribed whole cities,

bought territory and state officers, owned the legislators and boldly seized resources; they left their loot in the end as parks, universities and museums, badly designed monuments to their power and their ability to outsmart the other fellow in a horse trade, stock swop or land swindle.

Railroads, mines, stage coaching, timber cutting, fishing, stockbroking, law offices were as dangerous as pirate raiders. Banks demanding ten percent on loans were as deadly as machine guns. They all lived under tall black hats and traveled behind the best horses with coats polished like old loved furniture. Their mansions and French castles rose in the Pacific breezes, all as the true rewards for men who made the wilder shore.

After the Civil War you could point at the new millionaires and assess their wealth with pride. Leland Stanford of the Central Pacific Railroad was worth ten million to start with. He and his partners—the story is—had a pact for their rail company to be paid so much a mile for laying track on level ground and double that a mile on mountain right-of-ways. So Mr. Stanford and friends simply had new maps printed moving the Rockies sixty miles west. Laying level track at mountain prices! James Phelan was in whisky and real estate, worth a mere two and a half million; Michael Reese in land and a bit of a loan shark, two million. Lloyd Tevis, who owned part of Wells Fargo and Company, was valued at ten million. Ben Holladay's famous stage coaches earned him seven and a half million. The Bank of California's D. O. Mills had nearly four million to start with. Henry Miller made it big in cattle; James Lick combined piano selling and real estate. All were multi-millionaires. (And remember, this was before money was devaluated, and a million dollars then was like five to seven million today. Also this was solid gold currency money, not the inflated paper printing of today.)

Rich names come to us from the past, the Comstock Lode, the Central and Union Pacific, tales of trolley car line steals, highhanded acquisition of water rights, secret mines and fantastic stock schemes. Senator George Hearst had a boy who wanted to run a newspaper, and there was Lucky Baldwin, Charles Crocker, Mark Hopkins, Collis P. Huntington; all were to badger, steal, loot, build and hold on to vast fortunes. Mrs. William K. Garrison, wife of a mayor of the town, poured from a solid gold tea set. Jewelers like J. W. Tucker advertised "One Pound Solid Silver Watches." No miner would carry one that weighed less. Decline and dissolution would set in in three generations, but to begin with there was a sense of immediate urgency.

San Francisco had many whiskered, boiled-shirted Medicis, who ate ten course dinners, lived for the color of theater, and were ranked as game sports by the pimps, touts, men-around-town; solid citizens who could raise a glass of whisky. Among the strongest was William C. Ralston, a dreamer with hard fists and ideas of grandeur. He was raised on Midwestern native stone and fed on Mississippi steamboat food. He had been a hired hand on the side-wheelers as a young man, and was twenty-three in 1849 when the talk was all of gold in Californiee. He left the Gothic steamboats at New Orleans and got to Panama, a fever jungle of 'gators and murderous Indians. Ralston ended up on the Pacific side of the Isthmus as a boat agent in the momentous rush to the gold fields.

He was just at his prime, being six feet, two inches in his yarn socks, and already weighing two hundred pounds, most of it pure muscle meat. In 1852 West Coast shipping was going to sea with anything afloat, and Ralston took four hundred passengers out onto the angry Pacific from Panama to San Francisco in eighteen days on a side-wheeled Mississippi riverboat. He was a doer and liked the town and adopted it. By 1856 he owned mills and factories supplying the simple needs and the luxury items of the expanding place. He possessed boats, wineries, canneries, had solid shares in railroads, and was the owner of his own theater and his own bank.

He had come to a wild town that in its early days was said to "outdo in human vice, Cairo, Port Said, Marseilles and Hong Kong." Ralston gave the city social class. San Francisco saw him at his best when there were still only twenty-nine states and a national population of merely twenty-three million. He loved the hill city which stood on an earthquake fault. To its early crudity he added a patina of flashy, expensive taste.

Ralston decided he would build a great Palace Hotel, and with Promethean competence he planned 96,250 square feet of rococo

Victorian aesthetics crossed with the elaborate chic of Louis XV. It was solid, however, solid enough to cost him five millions of gold currency dollars. A fireplace in *every* room, and marble enough to make even Michelangelo drool with envy. Four hundred and thirty-nine bathrooms ("Is the man mad?") for only twelve hundred guests, which came to too many guests in every bathtub. The Palace rose on a full city block, with fat paunches of tiers of bay windows, miles of hissing steam pipes and their baroque cast iron radiators. There were parquet floors of golden oak, rare carpeting of capricious pile. The lobby itself was planned to be paved with silver dollars set in cement for people to walk on so as to get the feel of money from their feet up. Décolleté breasts and shoulders could be shown off here.

For the well-to-do it was a wider more comfortable time than ours. Men's habits were catered to then, unlike today when everything from the automobile to the wallpaper is designed for women. The Palace ordered 900 spittoons—also called cuspidors and gaboons—sent from New England to relieve the chewers of pungent cuds. England produced the toilet seats, 960 of them, and it was rumored some of them were Chippendale. Opulence and order were William C. Ralston's gods.

For pleasure he loaded his great English-built coach with guests and drove it behind four fine horses down to Belmont, his peninsula estate south of the city. Belmont cost Ralston three million dollars to build . . . the stables being as splendid as the house. He usually drove four matched bays and always raced the San Jose trains along the Camino Real, the Kings Highway, to Belmont (often crossing the tracks just ahead of the locomotive *San Jose*), entering Belmont through a huge portcullis, raised only at the moment the coach dashed for it. There could be two hundred guests for a weekend. The chef was a master, the wine cellar full. There was prodigious waltzing and other devil's steps, and to Ralston life was like a sum of money in a bank—one depleted it by expenditure, but expected redeposits.

There were games for the guests' amusement, bowling and croquet. And for the strong there was cut-throat poker or rondo

23. *A tycoon and his girl at the Palace Hotel.*

coolo, in the mist of heavy Havana cigars and decanters of the best Kentucky bourbon, while grotesque appetites sampled the chef's delicacies. Horses and light rigs were provided for lovers who wanted to find some bosky spot among forsythia blossoms by themselves. The rule at Belmont was that couples knew best their own relationship to each other, to their families, or to the local courtesans. Liberty Hall.

Meanwhile the Palace Hotel was nearly ready. It was a magnificent place and the town held its excitement back for the grand opening. All were waiting for the hotel to unlock its doors. But William C. Ralston, larger than life, was in trouble. There was a money panic on Wall Street in the East. Mine stock prices were dropping. Prodigious efforts failed. His bank was forced to close and as Ralston walked from his closed bank that bad day the great hotel loomed before his eyes, its interior still awaiting its first guests. With a sigh Ralston went to a bathhouse at the foot of Hyde Street, undressed, and went in swimming. The official story is that he had a heart attack in the water and died on the sand. He was only forty-nine when he renounced the world.

Ralston was mourned by the rich and the mighty, by the simple citizens, also by the Botany Bay convicts escaped from Australia, by Chinese slave girls, Japanese picture brides, mine crews in town for a tear. Barbary Coast whores wept, sailors off the lumber scows and sealing fleets joined vintners, silver kings, Jewish shopkeepers, ward heelers, railroad men, to bury the man.

By the ironic game of cynical moralities five weeks after William C. Ralston's death his bank reopened, and the great hotel unlocked its doors, showing transported glories and good-bad taste. Its builder would have been proud of that gala night as Golden Gate aristocracy and gin-bottle waterfront characters rubbed elbows in the crowd and stared at his success.

10

SINNERS AND SPENDERS

God is my father
The Devil is my brother
Between them I can't
Call my soul my own . . .

The sinners of San Francisco in the complexity and ambiguity of their life, the seekers of frisky entertainment, had little difficulty in finding the people and places that catered to their needs. Old Sydney Town, where the Australian convicts, the Ducks, had roosted in Hogarthian confusion, was changing in the sixties by the time the vigilance committee had done its work. It became the Barbary Coast, most likely because a randy seaman first called the waterfront section that in memory of the wild African shoreline where the dreams of sailors were often translated into a sinister reality. The American version lay rimmed on the east by the shoreline and East Street (now called the Embarcadero), in the south the district lines were Commercial and Clay streets. On the west Chinatown and Grant Street, on the north Broadway and sections of North Beach and Telegraph Hill.

Dance halls, brothels, pawnshops, groggeries, saloons made up the Coast, also sinister cafés, sailors' boardinghouses and crimping establishments (where sailors were drugged and shanghaied for long brutal sea trips). There were strange little shops, usually fronts for local Fagins, dealers in stolen loot, opium smoking, gambling in any form, vice in any combination or design. Drink, music, debauchery were at their height in a district roughly within the area made by the boundaries of Broadway, Washington, Montgomery and Stockton streets. ("Mon, if you kan't find it there, nobody is doin' it.")

In the alleys and dives and streets every way led to the sad dreams and loud pleasures of men. Later, much later, after the fire and earthquake of 1906, the Barbary Coast shrank to the block on Pacific Avenue between Montgomery and Kearny streets. But this was not the real high-flavored, acid-stinging Coast any more. It was just for the tourists palpably striving to thrill on a guide's misinformation.

Later, too, came the Uptown Tenderloin of gambling houses, dance halls, cabarets, brothels, saloons; all up along Larkin, Eddy, Powell and Mason streets, all meeting with Market Street.

An alley was a good place for a whore to service a customer in a hurry, or to conch (blackjack) a man flashing a wad (showing money), to push a chiv (knife) into an enemy, or smash the sauce (have a drinking party). The dank, dark alleys were paved with old cats, discarded garbage, a derelict or two living in an old barrel or packing case. Dead Mans Alley was notorious, so were China Alley, Murder Point, Bull Run Alley, Hinckley Alley. And some had names not for print. All had their tenements, their citizens and guides who often led victims to a *cul de sac* for plucking, loving or killing.

The Barbary Coast owes its fame, its public attention, to the local newspapers, who, when in need of color or a filler on a dull day would give their readers a jolt with a bit of detailed horror in the journalistic style of the period when it came to describing the Coast. "That mysterious region so much talked of, so seldom visited! Of which so much is heard, but little seen! That sink of moral pollution, whose reefs are strewn with human wrecks, and into whose vortex is constantly drifting barks of moral life, while swiftly down the whirlpool of death go the sinking hulks of the murdered and the suicide! The Barbary Coast! The stamping ground of the Ranger, the last resort of the *blasé* and ruined *nymphe du pavé*, the home of vice and harbor of destruction! The coast on which no gentle breezes blow, but where rages one wild sirocco of sin! . . .

Night is the time to visit the Coast. In the daytime it is dull and unattractive, seeming but a cesspool of rottenness, the air is impregnated with smells more pungent than polite; but when night lets fall its dusky curtain, the Coast brightens into life, and becomes the wild carnival of crime that has lain in lethargy during the sunny hours of the day; and now burst forth with energy scenes of wretchedness and pollution unparalleled on this side of the great mountains."

The death rate was high. Consistent hedonism is hard work. Life was amorphous and meaningless—money, flesh, alcohol, gambling was all.

Pacific Avenue and Davis Street got the Coast trade because it was the first bit of land the sailor and the traveler saw when landing from his ship. There were clothing stores and auction palaces more or less honest.

> My name is Solomon Levy,
> And I keep a clothing store
> Away up on Pacific Street—
> A hundred and fifty-four.

From there on to Kearny Street everything on the ground level was a dance hall, saloon or concert saloon (band, dancing and booze). *Deadalls* were places that sold a vile wine and a worse beer. Cellar joints were plentiful, and there was little decor except for a platform for shrill singing and prancing and shaking performers, a corner for a piano, perhaps a fiddle or a banjo, a brass horn of some kind. And, of course, a bar. *Melodeons* were places named after the dismal reed organ that furnished their music. They were *for men only* except for the singers, actresses and the hand-slapping waitresses. Entertainment consisted of obscene posing, bawdy lyrics, slapstick erotic acts and any dancing that revealed a well-shaped female.

Across from the city jail (as if to save time in arrests) were rows of Mexican fandango places full of guitar music, and the fandango stepped there was as hot as the native chili. The lure of the Coast was simple; a man wanted music, flesh and alcohol, a test of luck at a gambling game. And usually a bloody fight thrown in and a guaranteed hangover from the crush-skull whisky, of subterranean, illegally distilled badness.

Farmers, miners, sailors came, mixed with outlaws, pimps, arsonists, river pirates, horse thieves, gamblers and the usual scum of degenerates and perverts. *"La belle epoque,"* wrote one French madam, "was every day."

Records show that on the Coast there was an average of one murder a night and a dozen robberies and assaults. There were laws, of course, and police (always walking in pairs). The law said no woman or girl was to be in any cellar joint from 6 P.M. to 6 A.M. But bribes or a wink of the eye took care of that. The French *cancan* was the big popular number, the feature of all the places. *Oo la la,* with flashy white loose drawers, black stockings and the exotic final fling called *la split,* in which the whole troupe of dancers flung themselves rump first on the floor, extending one leg directly in front of them and one leg directly behind—all done with a *thump* and *bump* as if splitting themselves up the middle, showing stockings, garters and lacy frilly drawers, the girls batting their eyes rapidly and breathing hard from the effort of the dance.

Much later, in 1879, the newspapers started a crusade against "the evil French cancan" and a splitter named Mable Santry, of the Rentz Troupe, was jugged for indecent exposure. This must not be taken as meaning any flesh was shown. Her dance was called "immodest and indecent" because she failed to "keep her long skirts down over her ankles." Mable was found guilty, fined two hundred dollars, and that reform crusade was over. The Coast dancers of *La Cancan* went wilder than ever, and new forms of twisting, lifting the tail of the skirts to show the drawers, the most resounding new versions of the split were invented by *les artistes.*

The girls and women of the Coast ran the gamut of youth and beauty, beginning at fourteen and going on to old age raddled with disease and drink. There was a kind of Trade Union in women, and no matter what vices they practiced or how they looked, they were always referred to as PRETTY WAITRESS GIRLS. The costuming was often gay, even if in need of cleaning,

and cut to show off those charms men looked for in a night
on the town. The striptease already existed; it was a private affair,
and a customer for four bits (fifty cents) could strip and view a
waitress to his heart's content. The rite of fornication was a matter
of individual taste, at added cost.

24. Under steam—next stop, the Barbary Coast.

An enterprising owner of a fandango palace actually invented
the idea of the topless waitress nearly a century before San Francisco
revived it in the 1960s. The girls wore red slippers, black stockings,
rosebud garters, very short crimson jackets; the rest of the attire did
not exist. All innovations were called Parisien. (American vice was
merely "horsing around.") Oddly enough the topless waitress fashion failed because the girls in the Golden Bay area could not stand
the cold and damp. And customers came to pop their eyeballs

in such crowds that sales and reasonable order were impossible. ("Them tiddies put the eyeballs out on stems.")

A contemporary voice describes the Barbary Coast as "the haunt of the low and the vile of every kind. The petty thief, the house burglar, the tramp, the whoremonger, lewd women, cutthroats, murderers, all are found here. Dance halls and concert saloons, where blear-eyed men and faded women drink vile liquor, smoke offensive tobacco, engage in vulgar conduct, sing obscene songs and say and do everything to heap upon themselves more degradation, are numerous. Low gambling houses, thronged with riot-loving rowdies, in all stages of intoxication, are there. Opium dens, where heathen Chinese and God-forsaken men and women are sprawled in miscellaneous confusion, disgustingly drowsy or completely overcome, are there. Licentiousness, debauchery, pollution, loathsome disease, insanity from dissipation, misery, poverty, wealth, profanity, blasphemy and death are there. And Hell, yawning to receive the putrid mass, is there also."

Hell, and the Pretty Waitress Girls, paid about twenty dollars a week, with a twenty percent cut on the likker they got the *chump*, *mark* or *sucker* (all terms of contempt for customers) to buy. Of all whoring done during business hours and on the premises half of the take had to go to the house. A short dance cost from ten cents to half a dollar a twirl. The house took half of that too. (This all caused irreconcilable rancor between management and labor.)

The cabaret and concert saloon performers made about the same pay as the waitresses, no matter if *they* were billed as singers, dancers or actresses. After their stage turns they had to mingle with the customers and their behavior patterns and get the booze sold. Prostitution was their real trade, for few "concert artists" on the Coast had any real voices or skills on stage.

The visitors and habitués of the places gave the talent such endearing names as Dancing Heifer, Waddling Duck, Galloping Cow. One wonders where Lady Jane Gray came from. She was handsome but glum, a manifestation of an anxiety neurosis, no longer young but daffy on the subject of English aristocracy. Shaking her cardboard and glass-jeweled coronet she confessed to the buyers of drinks that she was the true illegitimate daughter of an earl—some high-binding British curmudgeon—no less, and of the best blue blood there was, and let no bastard present, goddamn it, say she wasn't!

Little Lost Chicken was a young girl, very matey, with sly servility, very small and looking very helpless as her leaky falsetto took on her one song:

> The boat lies high
> The boat lies low
> She lies high and dry
> On the Ohio!

With the word *Ohio* she would burst into tears—a victim of *globus hystericus*—to be comforted by any fatherly gentleman who wanted to hug her close and dry her eyes, and *she* meanwhile would expertly pick his pockets and gather in his watch and chain.

For the final physical act of love most places usually had a large room overhead, or in the cellar, cut up into stalls and small rooms, which contained for the worshipers at Venusberg and Pretty Waitress Girls, a cot, or a floor pallet, a basin of water and a candle. The time between dances was clocked at fifteen minutes, so no detailed and leisurely love could be made. The price, paid to the bartender (in advance), was fifty cents to a dollar, and two drinks to take along. The sophisticated customer might ask for an aphrodisiac to be put in the girl's glass, but no matter what he paid for, all the girl actually got was cold pure tea.

The true purpose of all saloons, clubs, cabarets, was not sex but robbery. While dancing the girl felt out her partner's pockets for wallets, noticed rings, watches and cuff links, probed for gold poke, or listened to the tinkle of double eagles and other gold coins. Safety for the prey, out alone, lay in buying drinks and drinking them. Once he wanted to disengage, he was invited to "have a few on the house." No matter what he drank, he was drugged with sulphate of morphine, snuff in his beer or tobacco juice in his whisky. The man who drank too little got the deadly *Mickey Finn*, which was a powerful cantharides or a bladder-destroying dust called *Spanish fly*. Some hearty men survived drugging and Mickeys and they were clubbed, robbed and rolled into the alley.

Two Mexican señoritas, sisters of twelve, had their own method of playing the game. When an amorous visitor went upstairs, both sisters went along, and while the first sister took the hasty lover in her arms, holding him very tightly, the other one banged him on the head with a blackjack, usually a limber leather club filled with birdshot. They picked his pockets with copious joy, removed watch and rings and then had him tossed outside. A few men were killed by the girls' hard blows on the head, but the waters of the bay took care of stray bodies.

No historians kept detailed figures, but some put the number of gambling houses, dance halls, various kinds of bars and concert saloons at nearly a thousand in the sixties.

The best remembered are the Coliseum, usually called the Big Dive, Canterbury Hall (most likely a holdover from Sydney Duck memories of Merrie Old England), the Lousiana, Dew Drop Inn (*not* a tearoom), Cock o' the Walk, Rosebud, Opera Comique, Occidental, Brooks' Melodeon, and the natively named Arizona and Montana. All were architecturally vague but there was lots of glass, tables, bars and noise.

Pigeon-toed Sal ran the Billy Goat at Pacific Avenue and Kearny Street. She was a mean, hard Irishwoman whose place got its name from its odor of spilled drink, stale food and bedding, and the unsanitary state of its patrons. Sal tended bar, acted as bouncer, carried a pistol and a wagon spoke or ax handle for keeping order. She was the poor sinners' friend, for her terrible whisky cost only five cents a mug, beer a dime, a huge schooner. On a mundane plane she catered to black despair.

The meanest hardest joint was the Hells Kitchen Dance Hall, also known as Bull Run, either as a pun, or in celebration of the Union's two defeats, at which its owner, Ned Allen, claimed to have been a soldier. It opened its bar to the town in 1868, and on its first Christmas night such a splendid fight took place that over a dozen men were seriously hurt by gouging, groin-stomping, finger-breaking and other forms of rough and rowdy catch-as-catch-can fighting. One witness, most likely exaggerating, said, "After the fight why eyeballs lay 'round like grapes."

Bull Run Allen was a sporty dresser, his costumes and fingers sugared with diamonds, his white-ruffled shirt setting off his huge unnaturally red nose. Allen felt ashamed of his strident bulbous nose and carried in a coat pocket a salt shaker full of flour with which he would dust his nose from time to time. He ran a three story place at Pacific Avenue and Sullivan's Alley; dancing and bars in cellar and first floor and hustlers' stalls and beds upstairs. Assignations made money and so did the hookers (girls named after General Joe Hooker, who spent so much time in the red light district of Washington during the Civil War, the neighborhood was called Hooker Division, and the whores hookers).

"Anything goes here," announced Allen, flouring his crimson proboscis. Fifty girls worked at the Bull Run, apprentices and old roundheels; depraved, sick, brazen, abandoned and cynical. Allen had a sort of crude frontier wit and gave real whisky to the girls, not cold tea as the other places, and he enjoyed their drunken caterwauling. He also served them huge glasses of beer and did not permit them to leave the tables for the privies. The Allen girls as a result wore diapers and no lacy drawers. Allen did not protect them from men when they were drunk and unconscious. Details of this are too gruesome and revolting to go into. But we can cheerfully report that Bull Run Allen went mad with drink one night and attacked his patrons with a large ivory weapon bought from some sea captain, and was stabbed to death by a Barlow knife owned by a Barbary Coast hoodlum, one Barlett Freel. There was always an incoherent psychological desire for murder on the Coast.

Murder Corner, also known as the Opera Comique, stood at Jackson and Kearny streets, and the Pretty Waitress Girls and entertainers were called "Spanish and French" and usually were. It was notorious for the most obscene shows and acts, and the best Nob Hill thrill hunters came there with their guests for a night on the town. The silver and railroad kings, the gold miners who hit it rich, the shipping magnates, the lumber and cattle barons and all greeted by the owner, Happy Jack Harrington, the "Fashion Plate of the Barbary Coast." He appeared in curled brown hair topped by a very high plug hat of glistening polish, a claw hammer-tailed frock coat, the usual gambler's white ruffled shirt with a neat bow tie. And the pride of Happy Jack; a most ornately worked silk waistcoat and his skintight trousers of pale lavender or cream yellow, which some said he didn't pull on "he just poured into 'em." Twirling his waxed snuff-colored moustache, long as a Chinese mandarin's, he'd see that the quality, the society guests got a good table, and no hanky panky or robbery or the Mickeys usually dealt out to the ordinary riffraff and sailors on a spree. Happy Jack's paramour was Big Louise (it was the age of large Rubens-type women, much later made fashionable by Lily Langtry and Lillian Russell, who graced the beds of millionaires and kings).

Besides clothes Happy Jack was enamoured of whisky—it had a cumulative effect on him, made him incoherent—and he drank himself into a fit of delirium tremens, that deadly last stage of the alcoholic, when hallucinations become real and reality becomes fearful visions of mad inferences. Happy Jack, pulling himself out of the hell of the D.T.s, fell plunk into the hands of the Praying Band, savers of souls on the Coast, who shouted, "Have you seen Jesus?" Happy Jack had seen fearfully colored elephants and man-eating mice, but at this point he preferred Jesus. So he got religion, sold off his place of sin, had a Bible presented to him by the Praying Band with his name in gold on it. He became the manager of one of those hole-in-the-wall eating places, usually called greasy spoons, up on California Street, where the smell and sound of the Coast couldn't reach him. He asked Big Louise, his large vociferous girl, to come along to salvation, but she gave him a cold no, married a rich miner and left town on the assumption a saved sinner was a poor lover.

However the reformed Happy Jack finally went back on the sauce and was found dead drunk one morning in the street, his Bible held firmly on his chest. For him it was a quick trip back to the Barbary Coast, back in the sin business at a new place at Pacific

Avenue and Sansome Street. In his revulsion for the Praying Band, he hired Platt's Hall, got a brass band, and announced he was talking on the subject: "The True Inwardness of the Gospel Temperance Movement, or, The Potato Peeled!" Only the press and a few bums showed up. Happy Jack lambasted the Christers, as luring a man alone into a cold world of honest folk where he was a fish out of water and could only reap the dregs. But he boasted he had pulled himself back to his own beloved disrespect "by cheating with marked cards!" If we can believe the newspaper reports Happy Jack became a mighty speaker against the Lord, and as he patted the Bowie knife he always wore under his left armpit, he shouted:

"Oh, King Alcohol! Great is thy sway! Thou makest meaner creatures, kings and the unfortunate fellow of the gutter forget his miseries for a while."

"Hooray! More wind to ya!" someone cried.

"I was proprietor of one of those popular places of amusement known as dives and all was serene and calm and I was happy. But they came down and took from me during the night my beautiful place where fortune and comfort in this life were to be mine. My beautiful soubrettes and Spanish dancers have gone, and when I look back on the scenic effects of those beautiful melodramas and the midnight dances with lighting effects, its no wonder that I stand before you as a frightful example of the destructive effects of temperance. But though crushed to earth, I will rise again!"

He was the hero of the self-immersed society of the Coast, with a voice like the tambourine and the bones banged on street corners.

Happy Jack was a hanger-on in Denney O'Brien's Saloon and dog pit. In the cellar were staged epic and savage battles of a revolting nature between dogs and rats, dogs and dogs. A good-sized wharf rat was sold to O'Brien for use in the pit fights for two bits. ("Two of them could lick a man.") A few weeks after escaping the Praying Band Happy Jack was at O'Brien's, where he took on a load of drink. He grew mean and went looking for trouble which he found in the shape of a prizefighter and barroom brawler named Billy Dwyer. As Billy brought his fists into position, Happy Jack stabbed him in the stomach with his Bowie knife, and Billy died. Happy Jack drew a verdict of manslaughter and a sentence to San Quentin. (As R.J. records: "The pioneer, it was said—as soon as he settled and built a privy had next to build a prison before a place could be called civilized.") No more of Happy Jack's history is known to us. Like so many, he proved adaptability is not essential to a short life.

Not everybody mined, not everybody murdered, or led a sinful life. Before the railroads came (and they were already being planned) there was the romantic figure of the Pony Express Rider, who didn't last long, but left much memory.

The editor of the *St. Joseph Free Democrat* almost shook himself apart writing of this wonderful fast carrier:

"Take down your map and trace the footprints of our quadrupedantic animal: From St. Joseph on the Missouri to San Francisco on the Golden Horn—two thousand miles—more than half the distance across our boundless continent; through Kansas, through Nebraska, by Fort Kearney, along the Platte, by Fort Laramie past the Buttes, over the Mountains, through the narrow passes and along the steep defiles, Utah, Fort Bridger, Salt Lake City, he witches Brigham with his swift pony-ship—through the valleys, along the grassy slopes, into the snow, into the sand, faster than Thor's Thialfi, away they go, rider and horse—did you see them? They are in California, leaping over its golden sands, treading its busy streets. The courser has unrolled to us the great American panorama, allowed us to glance at the home of one million people, and has put a girdle around the earth in forty minutes. Verily the riding is like the riding of Jehu, the son of Nimshi for he rideth furiously. Take out your Watch. We are eight days from New York, eighteen from London. The race is to the swift."

Book Three

ALIVE TODAY, DEAD TOMORROW

25. *California society rider—he helped bring in the railroad.*

11

THE MEN ON THE IRON HORSE

In eighteen hundred and forty-eight,
I learned to take my whisky straight.
It's an elegant drink and can't be beat
For working on the railway.
Fili-me oori-oori-ay.

San Francisco ached for the transcontinental railroads and got them.
The sound of the train whistle drowned out the war cries of Kiowas,
the Sioux and the Apache. It was a wide land ready for enterprise,
rape, profits and daring. As the historian Henry Adams said: "They
had no time for thought, save for that single fraction called a
railway system. The generation between 1865 and 1895 was already
mortgaged to the railways and no one knew it better than the
generation itself."

Thomas Benton told Congress: "Build the Pacific Railroad as a
national work, on a scale commensurate with its grandeur." In
1853 Stephen Douglas won a point; the Pacific Railroad to be built
all by private enterprise. Large sections of the public domain, Western territories to be turned over to the railroad builders for nothing.
It was grab and carry off—seize and hold—and lay track. In 1861
the railroads were land companies through grants for their promise
to build, and they did a business in farmlands and town sites. In
1862 the government passed the Pacific Railroad Bill. Two companies were given federal charters. The Union Pacific, building
west from the Missouri River, granted twelve million acres of land,
alternate sections ten miles deep, *and* twenty-seven million dollars

six percent, thirty-year government bonds as a first mortgage. The Central Pacific, going east to meet the Union Pacific, granted nine million acres of land, twenty-four million dollars in government bonds.

A Senator Wilson howled in pleasure: "I give no grudging vote in giving away either money or land. I would sink $100,000,000 to build the road and do it most cheerfully, and think I had done a great thing for my country. What are $75,000,000 or $100,000,000 in opening a railroad across regions of this continent, that shall connect the people of the Atlantic and the Pacific, and bind us together. . . . Nothing!"

A watch peddler turned California shopkeeper was also delighted; Collis P. Huntington and three partners were boys with eyes on the main chance and the Railroad Act was their quivering prey. Huntington sent a message to his partner, Leland Stanford: *We have drawn the Elephant.* (The railroad act.) East from San Francisco would go the rails to the rest of the world.

Collis Huntington ran a hardware store in Sacramento, a partner with Mark Hopkins. A pal was Leland Stanford, who had a store in San Francisco. Stanford was active in politics and was elected governor of California. They joined a peddler, ironworker and gold miner, Charles Crocker, to form the Pacific Associates. Huntington dominated; cool, bold, ruthless, untruthful, vindictive. Stanford, vain and extravagant, was hot for public honors, political influence. He was a Senator from California. "No she-lion defending her whelps or a bear her cubs will make a more savage fight than will Mr. Stanford in defense of his material interests." Hopkins, thin-lipped, took care of the books, of detail. Crocker, a politician, huge, weighing 265 pounds, took over the actual construction, "roaring up and down like a mad bull."

The Western Age had met its masters. Their unblunted belligerent drive, their lust for the aphrodisiac smell of money would give San Francisco a society, a society to rival the East's. And soon the dilettante, the colleges, the foundations, would feed on the robbers' bones for a century. Naive and imperceptive people found the Big Four magnificent—and often they were.

Huntington bribed people: "It has cost money to fix things . . . I believe with $200,000 we can pass our bill," he wrote from Washington. Communities and counties along the way were lined up. Soon San Francisco, Stockton, Sacramento and others were compelled to give rights-of-way, harbor sites, to make stock subscriptions from $150,000 to $1,000,000—the last San Francisco's share. Huntington wrote: "Central Pacific is out to get a lot of money from interested parties along the line between the Spadra and San Gregorio pass, if it would build the railroad." It worked, as one report showed: "They start out their railway track and survey their line near a thriving village. They go to the most prominent citizens of that village and say, 'If you will give us so many thousand dollars, we will run through here; if you do not, we will run by.' And in every instance where the subsidy was not granted this course was taken and the effect was just as they said, to kill off the little town. . . ."

Only in some nebulous future would the meek inherit the earth. Meanwhile San Francisco had a railroad to build.

It was raining over the Sacramento, a crowd including Chinese turned out, standing upon hay to keep feet dry. Flags waved, guns fired, a band made music, and Governor Stanford, a shovel in hand, dug the earth for the embankment. Crocker called for cheers. The Central Pacific Railroad had begun.

So for four years, three thousand Irishmen, ten thousand Chinese coolies worked in desert heat and mountain snow. The Chinese worked for a dollar a day, half the wages of white men. Huntington was a firm advocate of unrestricted Chinese immigration. The result was a San Francisco Chinatown that added color and legends to the city's history, some bloodshed, Chinese girl slaves, and often fine food.

Meanwhile the little towns and cities took their dance tunes from the "Big Four." Henry George writes in *Progress and Poverty*: "A railroad company approaches a small town as a highwayman approaches his victim. The threat, 'If you do not accede to our terms, we will leave your town two or three miles to one side!' is as efficacious as the 'Stand and deliver,' when backed by a cocked pistol. For the threat of the railroad company is not merely to deprive the town of the benefits which the railroad might give, it is to put it in a far worse position than if no railroad had been built. . . . And just as robbers unite to plunder in concert and divide the spoil, so do the trunk lines of railroads unite to raise rates and pool their earnings, or the Pacific roads form a combination with the Pacific Mail Steamship Company by which toll gates are virtually established on land and ocean."

But all this spoilsport talk was covered by the opulent razzle-dazzle of the railroad builder-kings, once three dry-goods merchants and a peddler. The iron rails moved northward out of Sacramento, Summit Valley, Truckee Lake in the Central Sierras, ascending 7,000 feet at 116 feet per mile, to the Washoe Mountains at Carson City, across Nevada, through Humboldt.

Oh, it was a wild coordination at vast costs, stealing *but* building. The Huntington Ring resorted to the corporate device of creating a separate construction company, "Credit & Finance Corporation," which had sole right to purchase material and building work for the road; solidly locked in with the Central Pacific. Huntington, Stanford, Crocker and Hopkins, sole directors and stockholders, received seventy-nine million dollars in bonds, stock and cash from the government and investors, paid over for building. Thirty-six million dollars was in excess of costs, not counting the frontage in river and coast cities which the associates got. The view from San Francisco was an awesomely extensive horizon ready for looting under its liver-colored clouds (as Buffalo Bill killed meat for the Irish work crews and drank whisky from a rusty tin cup).

> Fili-me oori-oori-ay
> Fili-me oori-oori-ay
> Fili-me oor-oor-ay
> To work upon the railway.

For the rails were going west to meet those being pushed east by the Chinese work gangs. The Union Pacific pushed forward winter and summer; engineers and tie and track layers, largely made up of Civil War veterans, went from the one-hundredth meridian westward through Cheyenne Pass, laying five miles of track a day. Central Pacific gangs worked at the same speed. At one time twenty thousand laborers were working on the railroad.

Samuel Morse had given them the telegraph, John Deere the steel plow, Charles Goodyear India rubber raingear. So "Dig ye terriers—dig ye gandy dancers!"

The directors of the Union Pacific had contracted with *themselves* at costs which were kited from $80,000 to $90,000 and $96,000 a mile, twice the maximum estimates. The total cost was $94,000,000. No one could ever figure why the railroad had cost more than $44,000,000 to build; $50,000,000 was unaccounted for save in the private pockets of the Big Four. Peter A. Dey estimated the cost of building the first hundred miles at $30,000 per mile; for the second hundred miles $27,000 per mile. A head of the company objected. Dey resigned. The contract was then given to a reasonable man who expended it to three times as much cash as called for.

Reclining between scrolled mahogany bed-ends in his San Francisco palace while a Golden Gate salt sea rain soughed on his French château slate roof, a railroad builder could feel he had the key to corruptibility of all mankind. He saw the world as ninny and poltroon, as rogue and dupe.

Collis P. Huntington was the master of the revels of high finance —long-nosed, with a cover of black beard hiding a part of his huge lined features. Some saw him as a Renaissance pope, full of strength and guile, cruel to punish, strong in words, clever and wary. And having a mean opinion of men less intelligent than himself, he had no respect for the politician no matter how high the post. He knew every man had his price. And Huntington would deal and pay. Congress took half a million dollars' graft a year from him. He wrote in anger: "I am fearful this damnation Congress will kill me. It costs so much money to fix things. . . . We should be very careful to get a U. S. Senator from California that will be disposed to use us fairly, and then have the power to help us. . . . X, I think, will be friendly, and there is no man in the Senate that can push a measure further than he can."

These bribings of Congress, commonwealths, judges, courts, were disbursements listed on company records as *General Expense, Legal Expense,* and when the going was tough, the cost painful, as *EXTRA Legal Expense.*

Huntington had a deep inner sense of guilt which no one ever saw. Yet once he tried to justify himself: "If you have to pay money to have the right thing done, it is only just and fair to do it. . . . If a man has the power to do great evil and won't do right unless he is bribed to do it, I think the time spent will be gained when it is a man's duty to go up and bribe the judge. A man that will cry out against them himself will also do these things himself. If there was none for it, I would not hesitate."

He wanted his letters destroyed. One can see why: "I saw Governor Axtell and he said he thought that if we would send him such a bill as we wanted to have passed into a law, he could get it passed with very little money; when, if we sent a man there, they would stick him for large amounts."

Today it is called publicity—payola—and the boodle may be TV cable monopolies worth millions, or a radio station, bank charters, airplane or missile contracts, or the contract for the erection of national stadiums or hospitals; the greedy, dishonest game remains the same.

Huntington was more direct than the ordinary briber of Congress. "I received your telegram that William B. Carr has had for his services $60,000 S.P. bonds, then asking how much more I think his services are worth for the future. . . . In view of the many things we have now before Congress it is very important that his friends in Washington should be with us, and if that could be brought about by paying Carr $10,000 to $20,000 per year, I think we could afford to do it, but of course, not until he had controlled his friends. I would like to have you get a written proposition from Carr, in which he would agree to control his friends for a fixed sum, then send it to me."

Huntington saw himself as the catalyst of already existing forces. In the end he himself became the victim of wet-lipped art dealers.

12

FUN AT THE BELLA UNION

The next time I saw darlin' Corey,
She was standin' ready for a spree;
She had a pistol strapped around her body,
And a banjo on her knee.

The San Francisco *Call* raised its prose in horror at the ladies of the town. "These females air themselves with offensive publicity and boldness. There is not an hour of the day or night when the vulgarity of the females . . . is not unveiled to everybody who happens to be going past. The wonder is that such exhibitions should have so long escaped the notice of those who ought to be able to suppress them, and have the authority to do so. . . . The inhabitants sun themselves at the doors of their dens and exchange Billingsgate. Drunkenness among these low creatures is common, and when they have imbibed too much liquor they are anxious to display their fighting tendencies on the thoroughfare, and their command of vituperative language. . . . For some reason the only occasion when police restraint is imposed on the female inhabitants of the quarter is when a brawl or fight has to be checked, or some noisy one has to be arrested."

There was a certain tenacious pride present. The proprietor of one place had a firm offer: "Five free drinks on the house if you find any of the pretty waiter gals wearin' underwear."

It wasn't only sex that drew the customers. Spanish Kitty ran the Strassburg Music Hall for years. Kitty, a bit sooty in color but very handsome with her big flashing eyes, was crowned the champion pool player of San Francisco. She had fine hands for skill with a chalked pool cue on the table, or over the head of a patron who got out of line in her magpie's nest of a joint.

Spanish Kitty's place had a rival in the notorious Eureka, large and bare as a cow barn, where everything went from bad hangovers to offers of bodies, games of chance, dances, music. Some of the girls married. The Fleet Sisters, no matter what their true names, married four chief petty officers of the Navy when the Great White Fleet was in the harbor. One of the husbands murdered three of the sisters; Little Josie, Dupree and Louise, then knocked himself off. No reason was given. The remaining sister, tenacious Dago May, preferred marrying whalers anyway. "They're less likely to show up. I guess I got me twenty husbands all over the Seven Seas."

No scientific historian ever figured out if it was women, booze or gambling that was the most popular. All three were available and there was majestic and fearful guzzling at all times. R.J., the wine merchant, in a letter (a copy of which is in his daybook) writes to an English spirit merchant: "There is a growth in the last decade since the gold discovery in the use of good wines, fine brandies. Mr. Huntington offers the best. Mr. Crocker is a bit of a blue-nose, even about social drinking."

Near the end of the nineteenth century there were some records which R.J. states in his daybook he looked into. "Checked and noted that 3,115 city licenses granted this year to offer beer, wines, whisky and other alcoholic beverages. I figure one mahogany bar available for every 95 citizens' elbows. Must also reckon there are at least 3,000 blind tigers, or blind pugs as the waterfront calls the dismal dives that ignore need for a license. Figured it out the other night, 10 million dollars worth of spirits consumed in the legally endowed places. Bourbon and rye whisky the favorite tipple. Rum the sailors' delight. Beer is pleasing to all classes. Women drink it even on Nob and Russian Hill. . . . Comes in huge heavy glass schooners for a jit (nickel). Potent enough to send a person reeling after three or four. Schooner makes a fine weapon; a broken one with some of it knocked off on the table edge; just the handle and a few inches of raw gashing glass. Very murderous.

"Mexicans and upper middle class approve of wine. Average

citizen and denizen of the waterfront consider a man who drinks wine a weakling, milksop, mollycoddle. Mexicans have produced a group of drunkards they call *winos*.

"*Margarita*: invented by a Virginia City bartender in memory of his girl. She was killed by stray bullet in a brawl, died in his arms, they claim. *Manhattan*: in 1846 a bartender made a drink for a wounded duelist. Filled a glass half full of rye, syrup and bitters, vermouth added."

The upper classes, if of a sporting and lively nature (and many were, being only a few years away from a pick-ax, a store counter or even from a Sydney convicts' camp) enjoyed the pleasure of variety and music halls. Vulgar places, they admitted, but good for a bit of amusement for menfolk. These places were strictly stag. There was Bert's New Idea Melodeon, the Pacific, Adelphi, Gilberts' and the best remembered, the Bella Union at Washington and Kearny. They were not all revoltingly obscene, but gave as the ads read: FREEDOM FROM CONSTRAINED PERFORM-ANCES. The Pretty Waitress Girls were done away with here, but ornate private boxes were at the disposal of the lady entertainers after their stage work, where they insisted on the men buying the drinks. Of course they got cold tea and a percentage of the bill, and could add to their incomes on the sofas. Professional prostitutes were not admitted. Many really fine talents (show business) were developed at the Bella Union, from where they went on to Broadway to vaudeville and theater stardom. Eddie Foy, Lotta Crabtree, Ned Harrigan and others. Harrigan, a ship's calker, was pushed onto the stage and told to be amusing. He proved a hit, and later in New York he and Tony Hart became the most famous comedy team in the nation.

The Bella Union was called tony, classy, a "peach of a place" by the top-hatted young men of the town. It burned down several times—as what building didn't in the raw wooden city—but the place existed for over half a century. It died at last as a Penny Arcade showing waxworks called the Eden Musée. (Wrote R.J.: "Its customers had been stiff in the past but never as stiff as the final dummies.")

26. *Pretty waitress girl as advertised in all the rough joints.*

Death by violence, as so often in the history of the town, seemed to be the fate of its owners. Samuel Tetlow ran the Bella Union and shot his partner, one Billy Skeantlebury, most likely over the division of income in the days before cash registers and sales slips. Sam was acquitted, the plea being "Self-defense." As a reporter wrote: "Self-defense is a valid plea in any killing unless you're seen running over a man with a steam roller."

For a close-up of what high living was like at the Bella Union in its glory we quote from the San Francisco *Call*, in 1869, carried away by the Bella Union's fame.

"Who has not heard of the Bella Union? . . . We enter and passing through a large bar room find ourselves seated in a very pretty little theater, surrounded by a circle of curtained boxes, that resemble so many pigeon holes. After giving the audience time to admire a drop curtain execrably painted, it is drawn up and exposed to view is a semi-circle of male and female performers seated on the stage; the latter generally quite pretty and in no way diffident in displaying their charms to the audience. Songs and dances of licentious and profane character while away the hours of the evening, and all that can pander to that morbid desire of the rabble for obscenity is served in superior style. If you have remained long enough below we will intrust ourselves to a pigeon hole above. No sooner are you seated than the curtain drops on some broad farce and the orchestra prepares for the interlude. But what is this? Don't be alarmed, my friend; this is simply the pretty little *danseuse* who performed the evolutions in the hornpipe in the last act come to solicit the wherewithal to purchase a bottle of champagne. The request is a modest one, partaking of the character of the fair petitioner. 'Only $5, now don't be stingy.' But you are stingy, and the request drops to a bottle of claret. 'No?' Under the depressing influence of your meanness it continues to drop until it at last reaches the humble solicitation of 'at least a whisky straight.' In the next box are seated three or four young men of respectable family connections, said respectable connections dozing away in their residences on Rincon Hill and elsewhere, under the hallucination that their worthy scions are attending a levee of the Young Men's Christian Association. How shocked they would be could they but see them as they sit there now, 'playing particular smash' as they are pleased to term it, with the feminine attaches of the Bella Union. Well, night gives license to many strange things."

Sam Tetlow, master of publicity, was as handy with a poster or broadside as with a gun. Boys tossed and passed out his Bella Union offerings in the streets.

Unique for GRACE and BEAUTY
Wonderful ECCENTRICITY
And Perfect in Its Object of Affording
LAUGHTER FOR MILLIONS!
DRAMATIC, TERPSICHOREAN AND MUSICAL
TALENT WILL APPEAR
Emphatically the
MELODEON OF THE PEOPLE
Unapproachable and Beyond Competition.

The attraction, however, was mostly in girls, not drama. . . . Madison Avenue copywriters steeped in Proust and Freud did not yet exist to tie up the appeal of a pair of legs or a lofting set of breasts as a social asset, a goal to make a man a success and well adjusted. Sam Tetlow's prose came to the point directly.

PLAIN TALK AND BEAUTIFUL GIRLS!
REALLY GIRLY GIRLS!
No Back Numbers, but as Sweet and Charming
Creatures as Ever Escaped a Female
Seminary.
Lovely tresses! Lovely Lips! Buxom Forms!
at the
BELLA UNION
And Such Fun!
If you Won't Want to Risk Both Optics,
SHUT ONE EYE

As For the Program, it is Enough to Make
A Blind Man See—It Is An
EYE-OPENER!

We could Tell You More About it, but It
Wouldn't Do Here. Seeing is Be-
Lieving, and if You Want
Fiery Fun, and a
Tumultuous
Time,
Come to The
BELLA UNION THEATER.

The impression has been given by hasty historians that the
Barbary Coast was the only vice and pleasure district of San
Francisco. Actually the most popular of the attractions was out of
the district, at Third and Fourth streets, called first the Cremorne
and then the Midway Plaisance (somehow everything in town at
some time had a mythical French flavor warped in passage). The
Plaisance besides playing some of the earliest New Orleans jass
(later spelled jazz) with its usual ragtime, became the headquarters of the hoochy-koochy, a dance of shakers and twitchers.
That dance is still a wild thing of hip-waving, navel-gyrating and
torso-flexing, of much more interest as to what the human female
body can do than the epileptic shakedowns of today.

The Plaisance in its reinterpretations exposed the best of the
coochers. Little Egypt showed her smooth round belly there and
her headdress of gold coins, after her sensational appearance in
the Chicago World's Fair. "The Girl in Blue," a dance nihilist,
was also featured; the music and lyrics were rather blue all the
time. The Plaisance did a big business of discrete stalls heavily
curtained in Louis Quinze velvet on its mezzanine. Selling of drinks
and bodies attracted the trade of some of the socially prominent.
Rather astonishing when one discovers that the price of admission
at the door was a dime to see "Living Art" as a change from the
oils of Meissonier, Winterhalter, Boulanger.

It happened once that a customer resented it when the manager
lifted an actress off the patron's lap so that she could perform.
The irate customer had to fire a slug into the ceiling and yell, "You
put her back!" Which was done with apologetic humility as she
was replaced on the lap.

The girls carried their money in a small purse attached to a garter, or they folded the bills in under the top of the stocking. Gentlemen would ask for the privilege of slipping a few banknotes under the high top and pat them into place. Some of the girls who were paid in silver in the low class deadfalls and hook shops, having no clothes on and no place to hide their earnings, kept the coins in their mouths, thus starting a legend that many of them were deaf and dumb.

A sight of the Coast to those escaping from ennui was Big Bertha, a three hundred pound soprano, who on hitting town let escape the coy information she was a *rich* Jewish widow, too dumb to invest her wealth without a good man to help her. The gentry who appeared for wooing, with financial advice, were made to put up certain sums of money to show they had the "wherewithal" to match her investments in some project never too fully defined. She was arrested for this con game but she never was tried. After this she received billing as an attraction (in a rented store at ten cents a head) as BIG BERTHA, QUEEN OF CONFIDENCE WOMEN. Before breaking out into song, gaudy Bertha, with no aloof evasiveness, would recite her life in crime, almost all of it imaginary. This was not of much interest and her singing hardly a thing of joy, her best numbers being: "The Cabin Where the Old Folks Died," a grim lyric not followed by anything more cheering than "A Flower for My Angel Mother's Grave." The last song, it was suspected, was translated from the Yiddish. Big Bertha, years before it was a popular avant-garde term, became a great success as a "camp" character. People came from all over Southern California to see her, shrilly screaming as a singer, fail as an actress and stumble as a dancer with an insouciant hiccough.

R.J. in his daybook notes: "Last night took some German export wine men to see Big Bertha and Oofty Goofty play *Romeo and Juliet*. She, too big for the balcony, played it from the floor, Oofty Goofty safe in the balcony. Droll, but Germans not very amused, till backstage I gave Oofty a half dollar to let them hit him on the head with a baseball bat. They went to it with great relish, amazed it were not *streng verboten*."

It should be explained that Oofty went around town carrying a baseball bat, offering his services as a victim. "Come on, gents, hit Oofty Goofty with a bat for only four bits. Gents, take the bat and hit me for four bits." Oofty was actually immune to pain and had a standing standard price for sidewalk or barroom sadists. A kick in the rump, hard as you liked, a dime; beating him with a cane, two bits. The full no limit cost, fifty cents, *and* you could bring your own baseball bat. It's hard to believe that San Francisco thought this dismal rite amusing. Poor Oofty was retired from the masochist business by the prizefight champion John L. Sullivan, the gregarious Boston Strong Boy, who used a billiard cue on Oofty's back, ending the brutal eccentricity.

Big Bertha continued to make theater history of sorts. A popular play of the period that San Francisco enjoyed was *Mazeppa*, in which Adah Isaacs Menken, a flamboyant actress of no great skill but possessed of a marvelous body, made a hit by being attired in little but close close-fitting flesh-colored tights. She rode a real horse on stage, which was whipped up and run out of breath on a treadmill in sight of the customers. Adah played it thousands of times and wore out hundreds of livery stable horses. Adah was the "intimate" friend (Encyclopedia Britannica) of Swinburne, Dickens, Gautier, Dumas. Big Bertha played Mazeppa strapped to the back of a donkey. It was a sight of the town to see three hundred pounds of busty, hippy woman tied to the back of a small donkey. One night the animal staggered under its burden and carried itself and its partner past the footlights into the band pit in a welter of flesh, animal hide and splintered fiddles and bent brass. Bertha rose to the event with some of the strongest cursing ever heard from any actress, playing Mazeppa or not. She refused to write the new act into the script and gave up the part. In some way Bertha got control of the already declining Bella Union, but she failed after a few months as manager and was heard of no more.

These early vice-ridden places of entertainment existed nearly half a century. And while the personnel murdered each other, sold their bodies, gambled away birthrights and consumed the product of thousands of stills, the districts remained the pride of the town.

One spoke of them in a whisper in the presence of "good" women. But by the end of the century women were joining their husbands in slumming in the gay places. San Francisco was always a democratic town, and the sports, the well-to-do, the rounder (as the playboy of the day was called), the rich investor, the gentry that raised blooded horses and gave diamond bracelets to chorus girls, all mixed and mingled with the riffraff at times. Or rather often looked down at them from the private boxes, but stood elbow to elbow while a barman mixed a Blue Blazer or slid the schooners of steam beer along the solid bar surface. Poor man, rich man, beggar man, and certainly thief; all were proud to be natives on the Golden Gate and to take their pleasures raw and lusty; between ecstasy and melancholia (for the sea fogs in season in their tenacity isolated them from the outer world). The ingenuity and indefinable charm of San Francisco was never denied. To them the full life was not an inner contraction but an expansive show.

With all this low living there was also a lot of high living on the hills at the other end of the city. R.J. in his daybook records a dinner Collis P. Huntington gave for some Wall Street bankers visiting from the East on some matter of railroad skullduggery to be done with a bribed Congress.

"Twenty to table. Consommé Royal, Pheasants stuffed with prunes and chestnuts, Oysters Casino, Filet of Beef Wellington with a La Tache wine (bit corked; C.P.H. never took much interest in the wines). Fairly good salad, Camembert, brie, port l'Eveque. An extra dry champagne and Tokaji Aszu. Had chef give me recipe for the brandied Liver Paté we had started with.

> 4 tablespoons brandy
> 1 pint chopped mushrooms
> ½ pound chicken livers
> 1 pint beef bouillon
> 1 teaspoon Worcestershire sauce
> ½ cup pitted olives
> ¼ cup parsley
> ¼ teaspoon nutmeg.

"Cognac after dinner. Lunch next day: Roast Woodcock, Petite Marmite Henri IV to start—Blue Blazers & Bourbon before lunch. Cigars and brandy after dinner.

"Blue Blazer (the true mixture)

> Each drink:
> 1 tablespoon honey in silver mug
> Stir in hot water to half the mug.
> In another mug equal amount of Scotch
> Ignite whisky and while burning, pour
>   back and forth from one mug to other
>   until the flames die down.

"Dinner again tonight: duck à la Rouennaise, blazing with Calvados, sauce of duck liver, red wine, shallots, thyme, beef

27. *A good host served one of his wild boars.*

marrow. Began with fruits de mer of lobster (on ice, alive, across the nation from Maine) with shrimp, scallops. Consommé garni to start. Usual brandies, table wines. Best of all a fine Liebfraumilch. Several diners shaky on their feet with shuffling gait. Myself must go on two day fast. Stomach taut and full of wonder. After dinner talk of sex *a la paresseuse,* and *au bord du lit.* Begged out from going up the line. At home had a dose of lemon juice and syrup of radishes."

In the sporting houses and the better gambling places the food was often good but of a different nature. Nell Kimball, who ran a high class bordello for some years in San Francisco, writes in her unpublished memoirs:

"The tonier johns liked a mulled wine or a whisky toddy when the wind from the Golden Gate was chilly. The ones that were once miners favored a hot buttered-rum-and cider. If they stayed over the night I always had Lacy Belle, who came up with me from New Orleans, where her kitchen was the damn best ever in the sporting houses, I'd have her whomp up some beer-batter fritters, and slice some cold pheasant and thin ham and have lots of good strong black coffee, which she ground up from the bean herself right smack before brewing it. Some of the eastern sports from Philadelphia and Boston liked a chuck steak with mushrooms for breakfast, and it seemed crazy to me, but I let them have it. A good hot leek and potato soup seemed to help, I've found, more than black coffee when a guest had taken on too much drink the night before. I always had a cut glass decanter of Kentucky bourbon right at hand for those that needed the hair of the dog. Mr. C would often send me a haunch of venison when he expected to stay the night and Lacy Belle would make it into Deer Tarragon with Wine. I never cared for it myself—too gamey; but the girls Mr. C invited to have supper with him gave me a hell of a lot of trouble after one of his feasts and a night upstairs; the girls feeling they were something special as his partners at table, and in bed. I always kept a dozen bottles of Mericer's Cuvée de l'Empire, but I noticed the bourbon was what the johns really took to, with a little branch water.

"Nothing will make a whore sassy and feisty like skin full of bubbly wine, and it was a problem to keep order when Mr. C. brought some senators from Washington and judges out to the house to make a night of it. He always called it "Painting the town red," having been a store keeper before he began to deal in railroad supplies. I held on to some railroad stock he gave me, held it for a long time, but it never amounted to much the way he and his friends shivareed the company. Like owning the sailing ships buried under the city . . ."

The sailing ships the Gold Rush left to rot on the Bay still make news, at least those that were covered over to make new land for the city. At this late date they still are news in California newspapers.

Battle Under Way Over 49er Ships in New Subway's Path

Another battle on behalf of antiquity is unfolding here over the hulks of ships left buried 115 years ago when the city was built atop them.

The Bay Area Rapid Transit District is preparing to let a contract for tunneling a subway under Market St., San Francisco's main thoroughfare.

And it is possible that the tunnel drillers may crunch into the remnants of one or more of these ships, which were abandoned when their crews headed for the goldfields. They were later covered over by fill.

In any case, the excavation work, scheduled to start next fall, is expected to unearth a treasure trove of other relics from San Francisco waterfront life of gold rush days.

Charges and a Denial

The controversy revolves around who should participate in any archeological exploration under Market, with charges by one side that "the feds," in the form of the National Park Service, "are muscling in" for the "publicity" and a denial of a "takeover" from the other. Another voice says the argument is academic because the tunneling auger will undershoot the ship bottoms and the equipment employed will make it impossible to probe for remnants.

Transit district officials take the position that it will be just fine to rescue artifacts from the 1850s in the process of building a transportation system of the future—as long as the retrieving does not interfere with construction schedules.

Gold Increases Dockings

These ships sailed toward their curious destiny in the boisterous days after John Marshall discovered gold at Sutter's Mill in January, 1848, and San Francisco was transformed from a sleepy garrison of 800 people into a teeming port bustling with gold fever.

The dock area in those days was Yerba Buena Cove, a crescent-shaped indentation at the end of the San Francisco peninsula.

Records show that only nine ships sailed into the cove in 1848. But as word of the gold strike spread, dockings increased dramatically. About 775 vessels carrying starry-eyed prospectors and their supplies sailed from Atlantic ports in 1849 on the long voyage around Cape Horn for San Francisco.

Here the ships were hastily unloaded and the passengers and many crewmen dashed off to the goldfields.

Deserted, the ships lay at anchor in the jampacked cove. Meanwhile,

in booming San Francisco flatland for construction was scarce. The town turned to the shallow waters of the cove to supply its ravenous demand for more room.

At one point in the cove's crescent the shoreline was at Montgomery St. in what is now the edge of Chinatown and the financial district. Fill scooped from the sandy bluffs nearby was dumped into the shallows, gradually extending the shore as much as six blocks and eventually straightening out the crescent.

In the process, the deserted ships became landlocked. Many were converted for commercial use. Several were warehouses, one was a church and another, the Euphemia, was used temporarily to house the insane.

Hit by Fire

A fire which razed the city in May, 1851, destroyed the superstructures of some ships, but many, among them the Arkansas, which for years was a rollicking ale house, survived.

Eventually, however, all the ships were covered over by fill, their hulks compacted under 20 or 30 feet of earth.

The graves of only six could be pinpointed until construction of the Golden Gateway urban renewal project of high-rise apartments began four years ago on what had once been Yerba Buena Cove.

The museum staff also prepared a map showing the location of the 42 ships in relation to present streets.

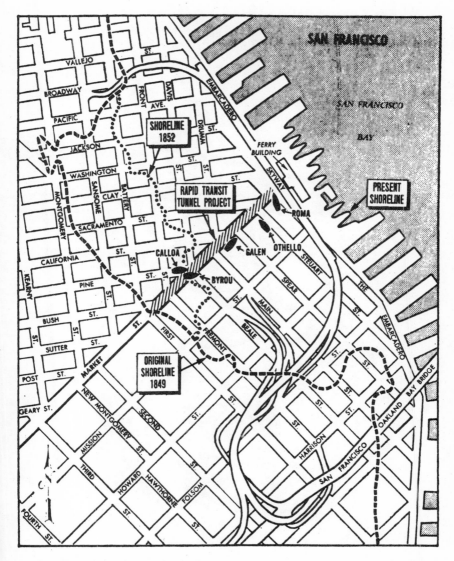

MOORED UNDER MARKET ST.?—Map showing where five old ships may be buried and which could be unearthed by rapid transit tunnel

28. *Working on the railroad and working very hard for very little.*

13

JOHN CHINAMAN AS A PIONEER

For the ways that are dark
And for tricks that are vain,
The heathen Chinee is peculiar . . .
Bret Harte

We think of the Western pioneer as tall in the saddle on the Chisholm Trail, as frankly Anglo-Saxon with a cold calm stare in his blue eyes to turn evil doers weak. As riding a palomino or paint pony, and a sure shot with a pair of pearl-handled Colt .45s at his Gary Cooper hips. Actually hundreds of thousands of Chinese were truer settlers and makers of the West than John Wayne or Gene Autry. The Chinese came from Foochow, Swatow, Canton, from Shanghai, Amoy, Harbin, from the dried-out fields of central China. They were to dig the right-of-ways, clear sagebrush, blow up mountains, lay the ties through the California passes, set out the iron rails, become gandy dancers (a gandy was an iron bar used to tamp ballast under ties). They usually made the best mining camp and city citizens.

In time they formed settlements in every large Western city, particularly San Francisco. They set up laundries and eating places serving Bo Lo Kai Chicken, worked hard and kept their private rites to themselves. They were not the simple, humble, polite people they seemed to be. They were fantastic gamblers, losing fortunes at fan-tan and other games. They smoked opium, brought over thousands of slave girls and entertainers who were prostituted in the dives and cribs of San Francisco. The Chinese made a vital, exciting, clever and solid group of citizens. They formed in *hongs* for trading, and *tongs* with hatchet men for continual warfare among themselves to control business enterprises, opium, gambling and the Chinese slave prostitutes.

The Chinese came to California early; two months after gold was found in 1848 the ship *Eagle* landed at Yerba Buena Cove three Chinese, a girl and two men. No record has been left as to why they came and where they went. Most likely they went digging for gold. In the early fifties when records were kept, in one year ten thousand Orientals came in. By 1852 the state had a population of twenty-two thousand; twenty years later there were nearly eighty thousand Orientals, nearly half of whom settled into San Francisco alleys, cellars and shacks. Exclusion Acts stopped entry of Chinese in 1882 and again in 1888. Color saturation worried the Yankees who had seized power from the Spanish-Mexicans, a coffee-colored people.

The Chinese got rough treatment in the gold fields. They were often run out, and came back to the city. One Wah Lee set up the first Chinese hand laundry in a cellar with a sign announcing:

WASH'NG & IRON'G (the sign painter, perhaps Chinese, was having trouble with certain letters).

Wah charged two dollars silver for a dozen bits of laundry. Business was so good he soon had three dozen women working the clock around at their tubs and flatirons. The rest is history; the spread of Chinese laundries like a clean snow over the West. Men dared boast they owned more than one suit of Long John red flannel underwear—one clean.

The Chinese kept to certain patterns of dress, ate special food and were as isolated as the Jews in the Russian ghettos. A newspaper seeking local color on these exotic strangers says of them . . . "One meets natives of the Celestial empire, and subject of the uncle to the moon, with their long plaited queues or tails, very wide pantaloons bagging behind, and curiously formed head coverings—some resembling inverted soup plates, and others fitting as close to the scalp as the scalp does to the Celestial cranium it covers. We have no means of ascertaining the exact number of Chinese in San Francisco, but we should suppose that they number at least three thousand. They are not confined to any particular street or locality, but are scattered over the city and suburbs."

And the Chinese would just say, "No savy" or "*Dweibuchi*" (pardon).

They lived in no *cloisonné* world, but huddled together in the smell of joss sticks, soy sauce, opium, sandlewood. They formed a colony of sobriety and gravity from the Flowery Kingdom, as China was sometimes superficially called. They held on to the upper section of Sacramento Street, all of Dupont (Grant Avenue today), and the natives (U.S.A.) called the section "Little China." It was about seven blocks long and three wide, and it swallowed thousands of Chinese a year without a burp, nor did it overflow much into white sections of town. A nineteenth century survey shows thirty thousand living in a dozen square blocks in nearly sixteen thousand sleeping bunks (two to a mattress was the rule). One-third were women, and a good majority of these were actually slaves; for the Chinese were a sensual people, and connoisseurs of female flesh.

The men were mostly cooks and houseboys. About five thousand twisted cigars for a living, the same number were workers in men and women's clothing manufacturing. The rest were behind hot irons in a laundry. They existed in calculated formal patterns, the whites insisted. But these were semi-official numberings and recordings. Actually there were smugglers, criminals, for a great deal of vice was being managed by Chinese in their elusive depots inside Chinatown. The hard cases, known as "China Boys," yellow gangsters, were very active.

In time there was created the Six Companies, a loose organization of merchants and important Chinese community members. They divided into the Sam Yup, Yung Wo, Kong Chow, Wing Yung, Hop Wo and Yan Wo companies, and had representatives all over the nation. With their special funds they also recruited coolies in China to come to the United States. The imported coolie worked off his debt to the Six Companies, and also gave up to the Six, it was hinted, a percentage of his income for life. There were rhythmic arabesques to Chinese thinking and doing.

The first Chinese buildings in San Francisco came from China in sections and were erected on muddy land, lanes and alleys. Fires soon took their toll and the buildings that followed were shacks, huts, storefronts, rooming houses. And often cellars where people lived, mated, cooked and ate in their own gamy odors.

The original Chinatown was a crazy quilt of cheap buildings, crowded living among piled-up bundles and boxes. The fire of 1906 was a blessing, for it caused the erection of the modern Chinese section of the city, for all its false dragon fronts and fake Peking reds. Huge cellars in the early Chinatown were filled with men and women and children, all living together. It is hard to believe five hundred at a time filled a cellar just beyond Kearny Street and a place named Devil's Kitchen. The Dog Kennel on Bartlett Alley was also a home for hundreds of Chinese; every place tight-packed, all without plumbing or any modern form of sanitation. The bribing of city inspectors kept everything as it was: "*Ching dzai lai*" (please come again). Early in this century only the scare of a bubonic plague sent the health department into Chinatown with a few hundred pounds of sulphur to get rid of some of the ancient stinks.

Life was not easy for the average poor California Chinese. Their long braids were cut off by saloon bullies when the jolly rumor was passed around "Each Chinese fella expects to be yanked to heaven by his braided pigtail! Without it he's doomed to hell, sure as shootin'!" He was robbed in the streets in daylight. Mark Twain wrote of dogs being set on him, his baskets of laundry tossed into the mud. Chinese were casually murdered. No one took any action. Like the Greasers and the Irish, they were suspected of being sub-human. ("No Irish" many a sign read.)

In 1852, Governor Bigler, a front for the white miners lobby, sent the Legislature a message calling attention to "the coolies" and asked laws to keep them from landing. With no real Indian wars—somebody had to be "the hostiles." There were bloody riots in Shasta. Chinese were lynched. The mining towns drove out or murdered all but their own Chinese cooks and laundrymen. It was a beautiful basic time of bigotry and white power at work.

The Yanquis, themselves intruders in the land, were mostly simple folk, not well educated, and the Know Nothing Party fed them the race nonsense that was to cause so much horror in our own century.

The *Annals* explains why the Chinese were frowned upon and always in danger of violence.

"Of different language, blood, religion, and character, inferior in most mental and bodily qualities, the Chinaman is looked upon by some as only a little superior to the negro, and by others as somewhat inferior. . . . In short, there is a strong feeling—prejudice it may be—existing in California against all Chinamen, and they are nicknamed, cuffed about, and treated very unceremoniously by every other class. . . . It was only in 1851 and 1852 that their rapidly increasing numbers began to attract much attention. Considerable apprehension then began to be entertained of the supposed bad effect which their presence would have on the white population. Large bands of Chinese were working at the mines upon conditions which were supposed to be closely allied to a state of slavery. Much misunderstanding arose on the subject. It was believed that the gangs were receiving only subsistence and nominal wages—some four or five dollars a month for each man—and that speculators, both yellow and white, were setting them to work on various undertakings which free white laborers conceived should be executed only by themselves. If these vast inroads of Chinese were to continue, the white miner considered that he might as well leave the country at once, since he could not pretend to compete with the poverty-stricken, meek and cheap 'coolie,' as so John Chinaman was now called by many. It was true that the latter never sought to interfere with the rich claims which the American miner wrought, while he submitted very patiently to be violently driven away from whatever neglected spot he might have occupied, but which the white man suddenly chose to fancy. It was true also that the Chinaman regularly paid, as a foreigner—and was almost the only foreigner that did so—his mining license to the state; and was a peaceable and hard-working subject. These things did not matter. . . . Angry words, much strife, and perhaps some bloodshed, were generated in the mining regions, and the hapless Chinese . . . their lives made miserable."

The founder of holy Stanford University, which bears his son's name, when governor, speaking to officials, said the Chinese, as a "degraded and distinct people would exercise a deleterious effect upon the superior race." Can anyone wonder, a recent report states, that the Birch Society is strongly entrenched in California today and controls many police departments and dominates a political party in a state where intolerance and superior race non-sense started so early. Up to Governor Stanford's utterance there had been only the statute of 1850 making official the natural frontier discrimination against "Negroes, mulattos and Indians." Now a law appeared taking away from the Chinese "the rights of testifying in any legal action in which a white person is involved." Later laws did not permit Chinese to work for corporations, and took away any voting rights they may have had. They were also ghettoized by restrictions as to where they could live. Instead of howling *Yellow Power!* in that shotgun-and-Colt-.45 age, the Chinese began to educate themselves.

By the seventies there were Native Sons' meetings to deport all Chinese in the cities and the state. Resolutions were sent to Congress and some of the text is modern enough to read like *Mein Kampf*, or the China reporting of today:

"That not one virtuous Chinawoman had been brought to America, and that here the Chinese had no wives or children.

"That the Chinese had purchased no real estate.

"That the Chinese ate rice, fish and vegetables, and that otherwise their diet differed from that of white men.

"That the Chinese were of no benefit to the country.

"That the. Six Companies had secretly established judicial tribunals, jails, and prisons, and secretly exercised judicial authority over the Chinese.

"That all Chinese laboring men were slaves."

All this certainly has a breadth and spaciousness not to be heard up to today's reports on whatever side we were trying to dominate or destroy in LBJ's Asian crusades. At least the early Chinese escaped the cry of "being Godless, atheistic Marxists."

There was a sexual tinge to the California bigots' hatred of the Chinese, a desire and yet a revulsion that head shrinkers have seen in the attitudes of the Southern whites to the Negro; the dramas of Faulkner and others of mixed skin hedonism. The Chinese "problem" was touched upon in the answer sent in reply to the resolution by one Lee Tong Hary, president of the Chinese Young Men's Christian Association (a segregated group).

On the matter of Chinese families he boldly stated: "They are *all* chaste, pure, keepers-at-home, not known on the public street. There are also among us a few hundred, perhaps a thousand, Chinese children born in America. . . . Chinese prostitutes have been brought to this country by unprincipled Chinamen . . . at the instigation and for the gratification of white men . . . the proceeds of this villainous traffic goes to enrich a certain class of men belonging to this honourable nation—a class of men, too, who are under solemn obligations to suppress the whole vile business, and who certainly have it in their power to suppress it if they so desired. A few years ago, our Chinese merchants tried to send these prostitutes back to China, and succeeded in getting a large number on board the outgoing steamer, but a certain lawyer of your honourable nation (said to be the author and bearer of these resolutions against our people), in the employ of unprincipled Chinamen, procured a writ of habeas corpus, and the courts decided that they had a right to stay in this country if they so desired. Those women are still here, and the only remedy for this evil, and also for the evil of Chinese gambling, lies, so far as we can see, in an honest and impartial administration of municipal government, in all its details, even including the Police Department. If officers would refuse bribes, then unprincipled Chinamen could no longer purchase immunity from the punishment of their crimes."

Chinese girls as young as twelve years of age were imported to work in Chinese brothels early in 1850. The *Chronicle* reported this item of trade as if it were imports of fish, lumber or window glass. "There are new faces among the Chinese street girls."

At the height of this import of teen-age odalisques there were two thousand Chinese whores in San Francisco, most being slaves imported and owned by Chinese landlords and merchants. Ships were often raided by the police at the request of the Six Companies and one load seized consisted of 44 girls from eight to thirteen years of age. They were transported to the Magdalen Home, to be trained as house servants, but many somehow ended up in the hands of brothel keepers. Restriction and cessation of Chinese immigration only increased the value of the girl as an erotic asset.

Nell Kimball, whose memoirs of her life as a sporting house madam give a valuable picture of brothel life wrote: "When I got to S.F. in 1898, I had as a laundry woman an old harridan named Lai Chow, who was once a slave girl, brought in for the sports in Little China [the early Chinatown]. She told me she came in with twelve year old girls, two dozen of them in padded crates billed as dishware. The customs men were handed cash bribes to pass the bales in unopened. When she ran her own house, Lai said she got the young girls through ports in Canada and they were sent down by coach. She never had much trouble with John Law, for when they raided her place during some reform time, she always had Chinese waiters on tap who would claim her whores as wives. Lai knew the famous Ah Toy. From 1850 on in San Francisco Toy was a Chinese hooker and hustler, maybe the first one to make a reputation as a pleaser. She was a slave but after a few white johns with a lot of money became her patrons, she bought herself free and began to import Chinese girls on her own, being smart and businesslike. Lai was one of them and worked for Madam Ah Toy for many years in various cribs and knocking shops. Madam Toy did a big trade in selling girls all over the United States. As Lai put it to me: 'You hear hey, all Chinese girls they have parts go east west, not north south like white girls hey, you hear?'

"I said, sure I had heard that the vagina of Chinese girls was peculiar that way but that I didn't believe it myself being from Missouri—St. Louis at that.

29. *Chinese slave girl—seller of "looksee" and other delights.*

"Lai agreed with me 'All big sailor lie. But white fella they want to be sure for himself. So Madam Ah Toy she do big business selling Chinese girls. She have places all over Frisco, Sacramento, other places.' Places I never ran a house.

"I myself [goes on Nell Kimball] knew Selina, a Chinese tart, the best looker I ever saw among them, what was called a stunner. She had a marvelous body, thin and yet just right in hips and breasts, not skimped as with most Chinese. She could chatter the artistic come-on to a john—about scrolls, screens, and give off a sense of culture, which a man likes sometimes when he's buying a woman's time and he's budgeting his vitality. She had a place, a three room kip in Bartlett Alley and it was: *For Whites Only*. She never had anything to do with a John Chinaman during business hours. She used her head as well as what she sat on. Customers had to book her three days ahead, she was that much in demand she claimed—and she got a whole buck, not the usual seventy-five cent price. She was a *looksee* seller, taking off her clothes for fifty cents so the trick [customer] could check for himself—as Lai had told me—that in her sex parts she ran north to south like the white girls, and not east to west. *Looksee* [*Touchee, Doee* was extra] was a big money maker for all owners of Chinese whores who went down to a dime in price in the cribs for the *Looksee* trade."

In erotic circles the north-south, east-west question was as much debated as the Northwest Passage among explorers. For a scientific answer the writer Buel, in his book *Metropolitan Life Unveiled* (1882) smugly tells us: "Being bent upon investigation, we enter . . . paying . . . for the privilege of witnessing the physical configuration of these poor, degraded creatures. . . . In order to set at rest a question which has been fiercely debated by students of nature, our investigation justifies the assertion that there are no physical differences between the Chinese and American women, their conformation being identical." Victorian prose perhaps, but settling an international controversy better than the United Nations does today.

It will be noticed men are hardly ever condemned as the source of all this demand for whores. This image of women as depraved creatures was not new to San Francisco. The most corrupt branch of the church, the Holy Inquisitors, who had come to California once—had the worst to say about the sexual monster, woman. "A woman is beautiful to look upon, contaminating to the touch, and deadly to keep, a foe to friendship, a necessary evil, a natural temptation, a domestic danger, an evil of nature, painted with fair colors, a liar by nature. She seethes with anger and impatience in her whole soul. There is no wrath above the wrath of a woman. . . . Since women are feebler both in mind and body, it is not surprising that they should come under the spell of witchcraft more than men. A woman is more carnal than a man. All witchcraft comes from carnal lust, which is in women insatiable."

This attack on woman as a carnal animal filtered down through puritanism. The American strain was always active in matters of morals and the sins of pleasure. The Inquisitors saw woman as the tool of witchcraft and her own filthy desires. "These women satisfy their filthy lusts not only in themselves, but even in the mighty ones of the age, of whatever sort and condition, causing by all sorts of witchcraft the death of their souls through the excessive infatuation of carnal love."

Poor little Chinese slave girl. She had no answer to any of this but the doorway cry of "China girl velly nice. You come inside please?"

30. *Inside Chinatown.*

14

THE GIRL SLAVES OF CHINATOWN

She took all his jewels, she took all his gold,
She took all his costly a-ware-O.

Chinese slave girls in San Francisco offered themselves in either parlor houses or cribs. A parlor house with Chinese girls would be on Grant Avenue, Waverly Place, Ross Alley. There were not too many of them, but they were a white man's idea of China, choking in musk, sandlewood, bad teak, sleazy silk hangings, grotesque ceramic gods, scrolls and wall paintings; all helped add to the idea that the Chinese, wise in all things, certainly knew how to run a bagnio. A parlor house kept from six to twenty-four girls on hand in thin Oriental costume, hair piled up and shiny, girls all very much ready to be treated by the white master as a willing slave or toy, a reed to his needs or perverse impulses.

Cribs had no stage settings, little perfume; everything was for speed and the business at hand, or at bed. Cribs lined Jackson and Washington streets and the alleys called Bartlett, China, Church (and other names not for print). Some alleys had only a fifteen foot passage. A crib drew no color line; men of all colors were welcome. *"Ni syihwan cha ma?"* (You care for tea?)

Japanese girls came later, inmates of the Yoshiwara, the traditional vice district of Tokyo. They retained some of their exotic ritual training, insisting the customer take off his shoes at the door, and they were shined for him after he attended to romance. Often he received a terrible Japanese gift cigar on departure from the bowing Madame Butterfly of Broken Blossom Alley.

It wasn't that all the girls used in Chinatown were Chinese. "Rich Chinamen liked to cross the color line." So wrote Nell Kimball. "But I never let the Oriental into any place I ever ran. The truth was they always tried to get the white kid tied on the smoke (opium); then they'd take her away and set her up as a concubine in some cellar dive. John Chinaman has a yen for having ten or twelve women at hand if he can afford it. One or two white ones give him a feeling he's done well. The only time I was in a white sporting house for the Chinese with Lai. I didn't think much of it. The women all had small rooms with bars on the windows. They looked glum and washed out to me, but maybe they were getting over a session of smoke. The novelty of having a white girl soon wears off and the rich Chinaman would rather import girls from home and sell them off when he gets bored with them. White girls, unless sunk real deep in smoke, act up and get mean. Chinamen like a girl who is placid—as if in a pantomime—she doesn't hardly look up at his face, and doesn't mind being given a knock, a cuff. Lai explained a Chinese girl respects a man for being a superior being and a master. She says it's Confucian teaching. Well, —— to that. Once a white whore has worked in a Chinese dive she's never any good in a decent house. I've seen that a dozen times. The spunk and spirit have seeped out of her and there's always the danger she'd bring her pipe and *gow* pills with her and give the habit to the other girls."

There is no doubt that the lure of young and immature Chinese girls was what brought the town's gentry to the parlor houses and the sailors and workingmen to the cribs. Just as with plenty of fine crab and fish dinners on the wharfs, there was always a supply of Chinese girls in San Francisco, no matter how many visitors there were "going down the line."

In 1869 the San Francisco *Chronicle* reported a cargo of Chinese girls as if it were a stock market commodity. "The particularly fine portions of the cargo, the fresh and pretty females who come from the interior, are used to fill special orders from wealthy merchants and prosperous tradesmen. A very considerable portion are sent into the interior under charge of special agents, in answer to demands from well-to-do miners and successful vegetable producers. Another lot of the general importation offered to the Chinese public are examined critically by those desiring to purchase, and are sold to the 'trade' or to individuals at rates ranging from $500 down to $200 per head, according to their youth, beauty and attractiveness. The refuse, consisting of 'boat-girls' and those who come from the seaboard towns, where contact with the white sailor reduces even the low standard of Chinese morals, is sold to the proprietor of the select brothels."

The last sentence suggests a secondhand car lot in worn models: Sam's Surplus Seraglio, Reconditioned Concubines. It was an abominable and dreadful condition of human slavery years after Lincoln's Emancipation Proclamation. And it was all as modern as today's Mafia dealing in bodies and narcotics—and as little was done about it, or its protectors.

There is no doubt that opium formed a fine combination offer with the Chinese girl trade, and that the importers of flesh also brought in the sticky black tar that the pills were rolled from— often aided by bribed officials, and that the opium rooms (always called "dens" by white journalists) were under the same management (and police and political protection) as the parlor houses and cribs.

Protection knows no color lines. The Chinese dealers in crime and vice paid the same police and City Hall politicians, white lawyers, as the Barbary Coast and Tenderloin owners.

Depravity, yellow or white, was available not only in dance halls or concert saloons, but also in gambling houses with annexes of brothels and opium rooms. There was also a popular Chinese lottery, which was said to run into millions of dollars in gain for its owners, *not* the buyers of its tickets. In one year over two dozen places for off-the-street opium smoking were known to a special commission, catering to nearly two hundred and fifty bunks and as wide open as a motel serving anybody. Rich men, white gentlemen and ladies often had their own private smoking room, just for themselves and their friends, the way "pot" and LSD are used today. Exclusive clubs for opium smoking were run for white and yellow opium lovers. Service there was discrete, comfortable and costly; the gum of good quality, the pills cooked just right, the sofas soft. The so-called "opium dens" that the tourists were led to were a racket of the tight union of guides and cellar owners. The Chinatown Guides Association was a licensed group and their dismal creepy joints, with Fu Manchu types, bleary-eyed, slipping knives and hatchets out of their sleeves, were only actors on stage in subterranean passages where it was said—but never shown—white slavery, demon worship and ghastly rites were carried on. Such a tour was actually hardly as dangerous as eating a Chinese meal. The gooseflesh lasted as long as one's appetite after some Egg Foo Yong and Lobster Cantonese.

R.J.'s daybook is more interested in the gambling scene. "Chinese gamble on anything. Took party of Newport folk from the East to the heel of Sacramento Street. All a row of gambling establishments. Went to Lee's. Much kow-towing, bland smiles. Smoke thick, voices shrill. Chinese not at all silent and solemn. Lust for gambling on many faces. Fan Tan and poker most popular. Chinese drinks interesting. But drunk warm."

The frugal Chinese of legend was a madman when at a gambling table. Savings, fortunes changed hands over plain tables to the click of fan-tan gear, a form of lotto, and other games. The *Annals* takes us into some of the gambling rooms which offered music. ". . . There is an orchestra of five or six native musicians, who produce such extraordinary sounds from their curiously shaped instruments as severely torture the white man to listen to. Occasionally a songster adds his howl or shriek to the excruciating harmony. . . . Heaven has ordered it, no doubt, for wise purposes, that the windy chaos is pleasant to the auricular nerves of the natives. Occasionally a few white men will venture into these places, and gaze with mingled contempt and wonder upon the grave, melancholy, strange faces of the gamblers, and their curious mode of playing. . . . There seems to be only one game in vogue. A heap of brass counters is displayed on the plain, mat-covered table, and the banker, with a long slender stick, picks and counts them out one by one, while the stakers gaze with intense interest on the process."

The life of the Chinese girl slaves—many were mere children—
is hard to believe today. The crib workers were exposed like chickens
in actual slatted cages, and that is what they were, crates, size
twelve or fourteen feet deep and wide. They contained a front
room and a back room, made by a dividing drape. Any number of
girls up to half a dozen worked in each crib. The girls' style of
undress was bottomless instead of topless; they wore only a short silk
blouse, usually black in color, with some added decor of flowers. In
cold rainy weather they might add black silk pants. Furniture was
simple. Out back was a pallet or two resting on a wooden door
form, the usual washbasin, a chair or two. Out front there was
a rug of sorts, a set of drawers and a mirror. The door, even if it
contained glass, was barred, and the girls stood at the bars like
prisoners, talking up trade. Ancestor worship was still strong, and
the girls shouted, your father has already been here, just left. It
was an honor to have a woman your father had just departed from.
"*Ching dai wo wenhou ni jyali*" (Please remember me to your
family).

The usual sales pitch was "Oh Chinee girl much much nice."
Followed by a plea to come in and inspect the merchandise. A
catalogue of tricks, games and rates was also cried out for all to hear.
Several writers have reported their sales pitch, so we can accept as
true their cries of "*Lookee* two bits, *feelee* floor bits, *doee* six bits."

Parlor houses had an age limit for males. Boys of fourteen and
up to sixteen were usually refused service. Crib girls however, took
what came, and white boys of ten and twelve were often arrested
inside a crib. Some confessed that if they could afford it they would
visit their favorite crib two, three times a week. Rates were low. Boys
under sixteen, fifteen cents; adult males twenty-five or fifty cents.
Reformers and some medical reports list at least ninety percent of
the Chinese whores as sick or diseased. While in time Lincoln freed
the Negroes, Chinese brothel girls were almost all slaves after the
Civil War. They were often sold at the age of five by their parents
in China. A syndicate of four Chinese was once said to own eight
hundred girls, ages two to sixteen. Of course some of the stock was
just growing up for future markets. The going price in Canton or
Shanghai for a prime girl slave was seventy to eighty dollars. In San

Francisco she was marketable at five hundred to a thousand dollars in the inevitable sequence of events.

Suey Hin, a woman wholesaler in girl slaves, always had a stock of fifty to sixty girls on hand. The Salvation Army converted Suey to the true Christian faith and as a pious convert she sold off for a good price her girls, but for half a dozen, which she held back in case she found the white man's God not to her taste. In time the Salvation Army got her to toss the last half dozen slaves onto the drum and they were free. One was three years old; Suey had bought her at the age of ten days as a long range investment.

The practical Chinese in the slave trade of San Francisco were efficient and skilled. Waste was an impiety. The order for slave girls was placed from San Francisco with procurers in China for delivery in groups; from a half dozen to a hundred at a time. Brothel keepers, jobbers in girls who resold to smaller buyers—say to a man looking for a special sort of housemaid—were alerted that a new batch of good ones was on its way. A selling room was set up with closely guarded doors. The girls were marched singly onto a platform, stripped naked and examined like blooded mares or some special form of prize cattle. Chinese doctors, some still in the medical Stone Age, chanted the health and primeness of the stock. "Ha yung chi!" (Good luck).

The bidding was done by crying out a price, and if accepted it ended by the buyer putting coins of bills into the girl's hand. She turned this money over to the seller. A bill of sale appeared and the girl was told to make her mark. For example:

> For the consideration of 800 dollars agreed upon, paid into my hands this day, I, Pia, promise to prostitute my body for the term of 8 years. If, in that time, I am sick one day, two weeks shall be added to my time; and if more than one day, my term of prostitution shall continue an additional month. If I run away, or escape from the custody of my keeper, then I am to be held as a slave for life.

XX

31. *Chinatown did a brisk business of selling and buying girl slaves.*

In translation this lacks the Confucian grace of proper Ch prose. If there was a clause about repayment of passage and the document could, amazingly enough, be held as legal in American court of law! There was no interest in most courts a body sold into bondage *if* it were Chinese.

After the immigration laws made it difficult to import girl prices rose, comparable only to the modern market for works of art, which have jumped beyond reason. A one-year-old girl child to be raised and trained like a prize doggy came at one hundred dollars. But a nubile fourteen-year-old was like a Rolls Royce or Jag, and cost twelve hundred dollars, FOB San Francisco. No price was set on melancholy, lassitude, shame or despair. Near the end of the nineteenth century prices rose as high as twenty-five hundred dollars a girl. The all time high price known was paid in gold: twenty-eight hundred dollars for a fourteen-year-old.

A bill of sale of some transactions involving other goods has survived.

Loo Wong to Loo Chee

Rice, six mats, at $2	$ 12
Shrimps, 50 lbs., at 10¢ . . .	5
Girl	250
Salt fish, 60 lbs., at 10¢ . . .	6
	$273

RECEIVED PAYMENT.

The girl slave's life was cruel to the extreme. Of course they got neither the payment for their sale or debauching, nor any of the income from their prostitution. They went out a few times a month under heavy guard to "take the air." The rules were like those of a medieval prelate's prison. Beatings were common, and burning with a hot iron was done, but since that would mark the merchandise it was only for extreme cases. Failure to please a customer of any kind and in any condition brought starvation, flogging and subtle punishment from traditional torture manuals; the Chinese are as a race greatly addicted to classical old forms. They disregard modern talk of neurotic obstinacy, psychological obstacles.

Some people who have studied the condition have stated that a crib girl lasted from six to eight years at her degrading task. The frugal owner, when a girl became diseased, broken-minded, senile before her time, often made her "escape" to the Salvation Army, thus avoiding the problem of disposing of a worn-out item. If the owners of slave girls had to end the career of a crib inmate themselves, they provided what were called "hospitals."

A newspaper reporter found conditions grim. "When any of the unfortunate harlots is no longer useful and a Chinese physician passes his opinion that her disease is incurable, she is notified that she must die. . . . Led by night to this hole of a 'hospital,' she is forced within the door and made to lie down upon the shelf. A cup of water, another of boiled rice, and a little metal oil lamp are placed by her side. . . . Those who have immediate charge of the establishment know how long the oil should last, and when the limit is reached they return to the 'hospital,' unbar the door and enter. . . . Generally the woman is dead, either by starvation or from her own hand. . . ."

Order among the crib and parlor house owners and the illegal businessmen was a Chinese affair, dominated by *tongs* (mutual benefit associations). The first tong war was, novelists will be delighted to hear, over a woman. The tongs, as they developed, blackmailed or protected the rich, policed the slaves and also did any executions ordered by the syndicate. These tongs, the Chinese Mafia, had a romantic side. A Hop Sing hood had his girl stolen by a Suey Sing hatchet man. A half dozen killings followed, mostly by means of a razor-sharp hatchet that fitted up a loose Chinese sleeve. The girl came back to her rightful master. The first California tongs we know of, the two mentioned above, came into being in 1860 to protect the Chinese miners from lynching or being run out of their diggings.

When the railroad gangs of coolies were building the lines east, the tongs went along to protect and press out a little blackmail. Like the Cosa Nostra of today, the tongs spread all across the

United States. They knew how hard to push. At their height nearly two dozen rich and powerful tongs ruled San Francisco's Chinatown. While they would turn an honest dollar if they could, opium, slave protection, the gambling games were their special interests.

The *boo how doy* or gangsters of the tongs, had specialists for killing, or merely breaking bones, or offering a few scientific punishing chops with the flat or side of the hand. Sometimes a Chinese bringing a wife from China had to pay the tong a head tax on her just as if she were a slave whore. The hatchet remained the favored weapon, but knives and the blackjack or sap were also used. The dress uniform of a mobster tong member was as ritual as Al Capone's green silk shirts or George Raft's snap-brim hat and spinning coin. The tong gunsel or hood favored winding his long queue around his head and on top wore a black broad-brimmed flat hat, like the Pennsylvania Amish, pulled down to shade the eyes.

To give warning to others the weapon that killed was left by the side of the dead victim. For all their opium, gambling and skill in murder the *boo how doy* boys always seemed to have romantic girl trouble. They found in sex a quivering personal uniqueness, perhaps a calming hope for some different experience.

R.J.'s daybook of 1875 gives us some details of a passionate tong romance, its violence and its aftermath.

"Town gossip full of the Low Sing affair. He member of the Suey Sing tong, biggest and strongest of the town tongs. Was in love with Golden Peach (Kum ho) a slave girl. Saved his income to buy her, but girl was also desired by the Kwong Dock tongman, Ming Long, who was the master hatchet man often sent to tour mine and railroad points at end-of-track to keep order. Ming already had a harem, but warned Low Sing the crib girl was to be his. Low Sing's skull was split by Ming's hatchet, as Low held hands with Golden Peach. The Suey Sing tong issued a *chun hung,* an offer of battle, done up fine on scarlet paper, posted for all to see on Grant Avenue. (Hip Lee of the Six Companies translated it for me.)

Kwong Dock tong is sincerely, earnestly asked to send the best fighting men to Waverly Place midnight tomorrow to meet our *boo how doy*. If challenge is ignored, Kwong Dock tong must admit defeat, make compensation, apologize for assault upon Low Sing. We sincerely hope Kwong Dock tong will accept challenge, and put by side of this its *chun hung*.

Sealed by Suey Sing Tong.

"The Kwong Docks sent out their own red paper. That night the two mobs met to face each other, two dozen on each side. Gambling house bets were made on the number of dead and mutilated expected. The tongs attacked each other screaming and were at it hatchets and voices when the police stepped in swinging clubs. The tong members fled leaving ten well chopped up *boo how doy*. Six were Kwong Docks. Kwong Docks then sent a document of regret, offered to pay indemnities to be settled at a great feast. Poor Ming Long was now prey for both tongs, such being the ground rules for a tong peace-pipe gathering and frolic. Ming got away, some say to China." As for Golden Peach, no records survive.

Meanwhile the mansions of the railroad kings were rising to dominate Nob Hill, and the sailboats skidded and clewed in the bay. At Berkeley the intellectuals talked of Zola and women's rights, and recited with a giggle the verse of Omar about thee, a tree, wine and a loaf of bread.

The early days of the great bonanzas were gone, but the rich mines were pouring out ore to the great combines. The best people learned the waltz.

Not far from the cribs of the slave girls Ned Greening, the society king of the era, held his cotillions as the pinnacle of coastal elegance. The Bohemian life existed already at North Beach where the readers of *Trilby* and Oscar Wilde paraded in bow ties very large and loose, smoked Sherlock Holmes' pipes, and talked of *Art Nouveau* and impressionism over their steam beer and breaded fried crabs.

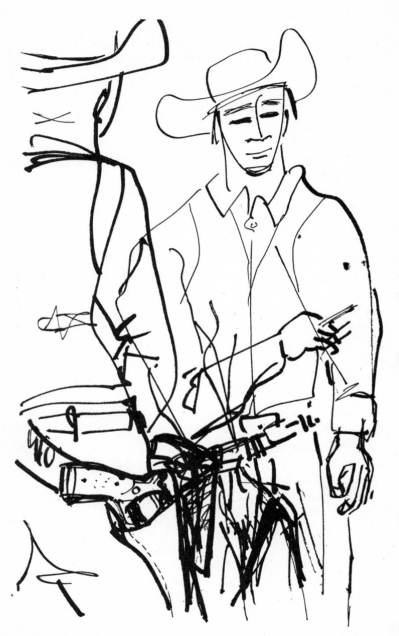

32. *Hard men became the folk heroes of early writers like Bret Harte.*

Behind thousands of bay windows people thrilled to the poetry of "The Man with the Hoe," and polished their shoes to go see and hear Patti and John Drew, Mojeska and Tetrazzini on stage. For low tastes there was Eddie Foy, and the Irish tenors, the acrobats and the trained seals. For swank theatergoers the town was host to Irving (like a later Garbo—one name would do) and Ellen Terry under pseudo-Gothic spires, mansard roofs and cupolas that took on a patina from the salt breeze of the Golden Gate.

It seems impossible that people made little or no protest against the vice and horror of the slave girls of Chinatown, so near the good cuisine at Marchands and the Poodle Dog. The early "scorchers" rushed by on the first bicycles in Golden Gate Park, the Gibson girls went boating on the ferryboat *El Capitán* singing "Bill Bailey, Won't You Please Come Home." And the town remained docile, passive, and yet somehow uneasy over the inhumanity of actual slavery in a major American city.

Book Four

MONEY IS FOR SPENDING

15

ALWAYS A WRITER'S TOWN

> Get six jolly boys to carry my coffin;
> Get six pretty gals to carry my pall;
> Put bunches of roses all over my coffin,
> Roses to deaden the clods as they fall.
>
> It don't take such a lot of laws
> To keep the rangeland straight,
> Nor books to write 'em in, because
> There's only six or eight.

San Francisco owes a great deal of its historic fame and notoriety to its literary figures. Writers found on its streets and in its houses the material and the characters that gave it a flavoring it has never lost—a taut grin suffused with life and sadness. The first was Francis Brett Hart (he took a *t* out of Brett and his father added an *e* to Hart). He was related to the Jewish family that became Hart, Shaffner and Marx, the clothing makers. Bret got to San Francisco in 1854, he and his sister sailing to join his mother who was already there. (Causing Mark Twain to say, "He threw his mother into the battle of life for him.") Harte worked some diggings without luck on the Stanislaus River, and his claims to having served for a short time as a shotgun guard for Wells Fargo may be true. *That* job had no illusory feeling of permanence, everyone admitted.

Harte was a dandy in good tailoring with glowing side whiskers. He invented the Western story, the movie and TV versions of the prostitute with heart of gold, the noble self-sacrificing gambler, the comic miners, the robbers, town bullies, sporting house set. They have all entered American legends and become our epics, our sagas of the West. Harte knew early San Francisco as he knew the gold camp miners, and in his two best stories, *The Luck of Roaring Camp* and *Outcasts of Poker Flats*, he began what was to become the traditional way of writing about the West Coast. His famous poem, often called the "Heathen Chinee," but actually titled "Plain Language from Truthful James," was the first appearance of a Chinese in popular writing, even if the Chinaman in the verse is hardly anything but wily. Harte was the master of allusion and evocation. His West smells right.

The later story of Bret Harte became just the decline of a popular writer who went East and then to England where he continued writing too much, long after his popularity had left him. But in San Francisco Harte was the teacher of Mark Twain when Twain appeared there in 1864, with no reputation as yet save as a drinking, fun-loving tramp newspaperman, an unemployed riverboat pilot, failed miner, and a few other things, some unsavory. There is a story that he was arrested for wrecking a brothel while he was full of bourbon, and spent the night in the city jail. He wrote later: "It was a driving, restless population in those days. There were none of your simpering, dainty, kid-glove weaklings, but stalwart, muscular, dauntless young braves, brimful of push and energy. . . . For all the slow, sleepy, sluggish-brained sloths stayed at home—you never find that sort of people among pioneers." Well, maybe.

Mark Twain wrote his famous story *The Celebrated Jumping Frog of Calaveras County* in San Francisco, and after a trip to Hawaii, he returned to the city, where he gave his first public lecture, and San Francisco greeted him as a new rising star. He went East to fame with his jumping frog. Mark Twain had various opinions about San Francisco. *Roughing It* is a magnificent picture of the times, and later Twain looked back on the Golden Gate with nostalgia as a place where he had tarried in his youth. (It was Ernest Hemingway who said: "We all had a girl and her name is Nostalgia.")

The man who really put San Francisco on the literary map was Benjamin Franklin Norris, who cut it short to Frank Norris later in life. Born in Chicago Norris spent much of his boyhood in San Francisco, and at seventeen he went to Paris to study painting, but was overwhelmed by the realism, or naturalism, of Emile Zola's novels—their idea that our only act of faith is avoiding (if we can) what we are. Norris decided to see if he could re-create the actual life of San Francisco in a new literary form, the utter commonplace reality of things, the instability of time, the constant quality of stress. He began *McTeague*, the story of a simple lout of a San Francisco dentist, living the life of the town, falling in love, getting into trouble, and when forced at last into murder, fleeing the city. It was one of the first realistic novels of an American city. From it we learn the town, its habits, its everyday routines among a collection of characters that, taken directly from life, appear to communicate with the city as part of it. Norris' next novel (not published till after his death; it survived the 1906 fire, but was once thought lost) was *Vandover and the Brute*, a study of the breakup of the mind of a playboy San Franciscan, done in detail with a kind of fascinating horror—a man destroyed without reason. Social patterns of the town's upper middle class are pictured; almost Proustian details are presented of bars, clubs, dances, parties, the daily habits and some of the vices. It is a novel that should be better known. Norris also did a small charming novel of San Francisco life called *Blix*, which had the sound of the streets, the color of Chinatown, the horse traffic and the Golden Gate as seen by two lovers. Norris died young, in 1902, the result of an operation for appendicitis.

The life of John Griffith London, better known as Jack London, reads like a bad melodrama of some ultimate jest on the Frisco waterfront. He is supposed to be the son of a showman, astrologer and spiritualist, W. H. Cheney (whom Jack never met), and Flora Wellman, an addled, perhaps mad personality. She married a widower with eleven children after Jack's birth, a John London, who gave the boy his name. Jack grew up on the Barbary Coast, along the waterfront. He knew the dives and the brothels early. He stole little boats, was a kind of bay pirate, worked for the fish and game patrol after having peddled newspapers in the Tenderloin and on the Coast, drifting in and out of the saloons, learning to drink, and drink hard. London was a longshoreman, a cannery worker. He saw San Francisco from its seamy and sinful side with a devastating lucidity. Much of this city appears in scenes in his various novels as solid, brutal incidents, tinged with his ideas of an early socialism; when the future would be better for the poor and the outcasts, and their wretched forbearance and inadequate life would change.

After a whirl as a sailor to the Japanese Sea, Jack London went to the Klondike for gold, and came back broke, to write of men and wilderness with great success. But success—to be banal on the subject—success destroyed him, his hopes, his ideals. London wrote too much in haste, spent money recklessly, overburdened himself with debts, drank till he was an alcoholic, and by the time he was forty was ready to commit suicide. He did. His life resembled that of a miner who hit the mother lode and went on a spree in town.

London set the pattern for the life of George Sterling, poet, critic, bohemian and lush, one of the sights of Carmel and San Francisco; he was always full of the grape. He was a member of the Bohemian Club, and it was in one of its rooms that he took his own life "by his own hand" as one report had it. Sterling's wild San Francisco verse, his imagery were well known in their day but are now forgotten as too naive and romantic.

Much more vivid was the San Francisco poet (and sensual leering figure), Joaquin Miller, who was born Cincinnatus Hiner Miller in 1837, but took to naming himself after the bandit Joaquin Murieta. Miller invented many juicy legends about himself. He claimed to have been born in a covered wagon, but wasn't. He came West in 1852 along the Oregon Trail to settle with his family in Oregon. At seventeen Miller ran away to dig for gold in California. He claimed to have married a Digger Indian squaw, and also, like so many, failed to find gold. Miller was part Grand Guignol and part Rousseau's not-so-simple savage.

After some books of Miller's poetry were published, San Francisco seemed unfriendly, so with shoulder-long hair and flowing chin-touching moustache, under a huge sombrero and wearing fringed buckskin shirts, he went to England. He was accepted as the real stuff, a genuine simple Western genius from the popple and red oak trees. The Londoners loved him as a stud 'possum, when he smoked three cigars at once, and snapped at the ankles of girls with his teeth in the best drawing rooms. This to the English, was a hero out of *McGuffey's Reader,* their idea of how a man from San Francisco and the West should act. Miller became engaged, but not married, to the daughter of a baronet, and soon other wild primitives replaced him in the society of the day.

In 1886 Miller got hold of some land in Oakland across the Bay from San Francisco. He erected a strange house in his own eccentric style. Full of promiscuous naiveté, he was one of the sights of San Francisco, visiting celebrities coming to see the old reciting fraud with his long beard and strange habits of life; including a sort of harem of admiring women. For all his ubiquitous vulgarity Miller was a true voice of the wild and uproarious West, a man of root, hoot and holler, made for the gala that was so much of San Francisco in its youth. It is to be regretted that his best remembered poem is not about the town but that battered bit of national idolatry, the school favorite, "Columbus," with its refrain "On, sail on!"

The wittiest writer, the most cynical ever to take over San Francisco and have it bow to him, was Ambrose Gwinett Bierce, born in Ohio in 1842. Bitter Bierce they called him. After he fought in the Civil War, he was offered a pension, and he replied, "When I hired out as an assassin for my country, that wasn't part of the contract." The most reasonable remark ever made about the philosophy of war by those who actually have to fight them.

Bierce came out to San Francisco as a watchman at the U. S. Mint. From the dreary job of watching money he took on journalism and became in time the literary dictator of San Francisco. Being feared he was admired and wondered at for the sharpness of his tongue and the skill with which he handled the language.

He was the friend of Bret Harte, Mark Twain and Joaquin Miller. He was also a gourmet, a wine expert, part-time hedonist married to a shrew, a hater of facades and the ways of man too facile in the destruction of his own earth. His column in the *Argonaut*, "The Prattler," made his reputation and raised the hackles of the smug; it ended up on the pages of the San Francisco *Examiner*, harpooning people under the gleeful pleasure of its owner, William Randolph Hearst, the over-obsessive son of that Senator Hearst who had hit it big in silver mines.

Bierce, like most writers, had what is politely called woman trouble, and he wrote, "Woman would be more charming if one could fall into her arms without falling into her hands." (R.J. reports he once said, "Sex being metaphysically sinful, is best when physically a bit revolting.")

San Francisco got excited when Lillian Russell refused to wear tights on stage. Bierce wrote on tights and the event: "TIGHTS, an habilment of the stage designed to reinforce the general acclamation of the press agent with a particular publicity. Public attention was somewhat diverted from this garment to Miss Lillian Russell's refusal to wear it, and many were the conjectures as to her motive, the guess . . . that nature had not endowed Miss Russell with beautiful legs. This theory was impossible of acceptance by the male. It is strange that in all the controversy regarding Miss Russell's aversion to tights no one seems to have thought to ascribe it to what was known among the ancients as 'modesty.'"

Of rich thieves, like a Huntington, endowing things, he wrote: "PHILANTHROPIST. A rich old gentleman who has trained himself to grin while his conscience is picking his pocket."

Of the fashion of lynching going out of style: "GALLOWS. A stage for the performance of miracle plays, in which the leading actor is translated to heaven. In this country the gallows is chiefly remarkable for the number of persons who escape it."

Rich San Franciscans began to collect art, not writers, as social status (as is the fashion today); they were a natural prey of dishonest dealers. Bierce wrote of this art nonsense: "PAINTING.

The art of protecting flat surfaces from the weather and exposing them to the critic. Formerly, painting and sculpture were combined in the same work; the ancients painted their statues. The only present alliance between the two arts is that the modern painter chisels his patrons."

And a final impromptu word, before Ambrose Bierce, weary of life and men (also women) traveled south to disappear into Mexico, to be killed, it was rumored, by either Pancho Villa or Carranza. "ALLIANCE. In international politics, the union of two thieves who have their hands so deeply inserted in each other's pocket that they cannot separately plunder a third."

No writer since Bierce has added to San Francisco so much acid irascibility and spice. He was to the literary set of the town, as miners used to claim, "half catamont, half man-eating alligator."

"Standing at a bar"—as reported by R.J. of the daybook—"a silver gaboon at their feet and glasses of bourbon in their fists, to men the words of Bierce bring back an era as clearly as the sight of a tall plug hat, a ruby tiepin or a carpetbag portmanteau."

Some of the folk ballads sung in the dives of San Francisco had no known authors but contained the full flavor of the memory of early hard times.

Oh, don't you remember sweet Betsy from Pike,
Who crossed the big mountains with her lover Ike,
With two yoke of oxen, a large yellow dog,
A tall shanghai rooster and one spotted hog?

One evening quite early they camped on the Platte,
Close by the roadside on a green shady flat,
Where Betsy sore-footed lay down to repose.
With wonder he gazed on his Pike County rose.

The shanghai ran off and the cattle all died;
The last piece of bacon that morning was fried.
Poor Ike was discouraged, and Betsy was mad;
The dog wagged his tail and looked wonderfully sad.

There were dozens of verses—many of them bawdy.

> They went by Salt Lake to enquire the way,
> When Brigham declared sweet Betsy should stay.
> Betsy got frightened and ran like a deer,
> And Brigham stood pawing the ground like a steer.
> At length they arrived on a very high hill,
> With wonder looked down upon old Placerville.
> Ike sighed, and he said, when he cast his eyes down,
> "Betsy, my darling, we've got to Hangtown."

That was what the whisky-seared palate of the town liked. It had little room for the eloquence of literature among the incessant hawking of tobacco chewers.

A lean skeleton of a man with a stringy Chinese moustache, he coughing and smiling, at twenty-nine had met an older Oakland woman in France and had fallen in love with her. He was not yet an established writer, this Robert Louis Stevenson. Fanny Van de Grift Osbourne, with her two nearly grown children, didn't know what to make of this Scots admirer with his not too clean fingernails. Fanny's son remembered how Stevenson appeared: "He looked ill even to my childish gaze; the brilliancy of his eyes emphasized the thinness and pallor of his face. His clothes, no longer picturesque but merely shabby, hung loosely on his shrunken body." Yet he wrote so much he wondered if he "might have affected the price of paper on the Pacific Coast." Despite sickness and the difficulties of Fanny's divorce, he found some part of California "a lovely place, which I am growing to love." People helped; a doctor who treated him, a French restaurateur who fed him, a Jewish merchant who found him the abandoned mining cabin on the Silverado which became the setting for not only a honeymoon but also the subject of his only book with an American setting.

He himself did not question his passion for the older woman even if earlier he had written: "Falling in love is the one illogical adventure . . . the effect is out of all proportion with the cause." In 1879 Stevenson followed Fanny to California, settling in a

33. *Robert Louis Stevenson in San Francisco, where he came to steal a man's wife.*

Bush Street San Francisco boarding house of Mrs. Carson to moon at Mrs. Osbourne over the Bay at Oakland. He was so poor he was always hungry and ate ten cent meals when he had a dime. He was also often sick, his lungs already giving out; an unknown stranger from the East, trying to write. The love affair had a happy ending. Fanny Osbourne got an early California divorce and the strange couple were married; plump Fanny to her younger bridegroom, the lean stick of a man, married in a Post Street church. Some time later they were bound for Honolulu, Tahiti, the Marquesas. He finally to die in Samoa.

While living at Mrs. Carson's boarding house, in hunger and in despair he had written:

> It's there that I was sick and sad.
> Alone and poor and cold.
> In yon distressful city
> Besides the gates of gold.

The city saw many young writers, full of incorrigible curiosity, all of whom also left her after hungry days. Kipling came passing through as a young man on the run, and called San Francisco one of only two American cities worth writing about. (New Orleans was the other.) It was a town for receptive grasping minds rather than creative ones. It was too lusty and busy to be a poseur addicted to attitudes. Its most civilized writer, Ambrose Bierce, felt what the city had was valor, which he defined as a "soldierly compound of vanity, duty and the gambler's hope."

Another voice said:

> In sparkling wine our glasses jine,
> They make the nectared drink divine
> Since mirth and laughter rule the hour.
>
> While roses plucked from friendship's bower
> Around our moistened temples twine
> And add fresh fragrance to the wine . . .

So wrote the early California judge and poet, Ned McGowan, of high life in San Francisco (most likely after a session of "moistened temples"). In the upper world of the newly rich, the powerful forces that bribed the law and intimidated the courts, there was a desire to outshine the society of the East, the Astor-Vanderbilt snobs of Fifth Avenue, the Goulds of Newport, the sybarites of Saratoga's inner circle, and what was soon to be the smug protected porch rockers of Widener's and Frick's Palm Beach, awaiting the serving of clams casino, paté maison, crab legs poulette. No camp beans tonight.

They were turning away from their own early beginnings, leaving behind the great mass of seacoast faces, of the miners who failed, now employed at so much a day. Some saw in old comrades enemies who might attack wealth and position. Henry James visiting his native land, after the years of exile (since he ran away from the Civil War as a young man ripe for service in the Army) already wound up in his long-winded sentences like so many scarves against the common air—James saw the true conditions. "I have the imagination of disaster—and see life as ferocious and sinister." With that he scurried back to London and to the teacups. The new voices were more like William Vanderbilt, who when accused of forming trusts against the general interest said: "The public? The public be damned."

The silver and gold millionaires, the bankers, railroad builders of San Francisco saw their chance to be welcomed by the Eastern interests against a common enemy. There was Jack London with his talk of "Yours for Revolution," and Henry George moving East preaching his Progress and Poverty, his Single Tax; the very word *tax* was an obscene one to the robber barons. How much better the coal man, George F. Baer, who saw the divine position of the poor: "The rights and interests of the laboring man will be protected and cared for by the Christian men to whom God has given control of the property rights of the country."

The historian Charles Francis Adams looked in horror on these new rich. "I approach the end . . . I am more than a little puzzled to account for the instances I have seen of business success—money-getting. It comes from rather a low instinct. Certainly so far as my observation goes, it is scarcely met with in combination with the finer or more interesting traits of character. I have known and known tolerably well, a great many 'successful' men—'big' financially—and a less interesting crowd I do not care to encounter. Not one that I have ever known would I care to meet again either in this world or the next; nor is one associated in my mind with the idea of humor, thought or refinement."

Darius Ogden Mills of San Francisco, one-time storekeeper, mine developer, now banker, invaded the East to build himself a bit of a home on land bought away from home. A contemporary business historian, Henry Clews, notes concerning the house: "After purchasing Mr. Mills gave carte blanche orders to a noted decorator of New York, and during a trip to California the work of decoration was done. On his return he at once took possession of a mansion of which a Shah of Persia might have been proud. He was delighted with all that had been wrought . . . the richly carved woodwork, the gorgeously picturesque ceilings, the inlaid walls and floors and the ensemble of Oriental magnificence. His contentment was complete. But the decorator's bill, $450,000, it is said, slightly disturbed his serenity. It caused him to look with a critical eye on the splendid decorations which constituted a study of the fine arts at such high rates of tuition."

Collis P. Huntington, not to be outdone, built a two million dollar gray-stone on 57th and Fifth Avenue. It was noted "after it was completed he could never be persuaded to live in it. His reason was a belief in the superstition that men build houses only to die in them."

The Californians who sought the sanctifying life of the East were trying to get away, a long way from the days when the cry was:

> Bacon in the pan,
> Coffee in the pot!
> Come up an' get it—
> Get it while it's hot!

They were regal spenders and yet they were only accepted in part. As one perceptive hostess wrote: "The West was yielding tremendous riches . . . Steel barons, coal lords, dukes of wheat and beef, of mines and railways, had sprung up from obscurity. Absolute in their territory, they looked for new worlds to conquer. The newspaper accounts of New York society thrilled the newly rich. In a great glittering caravan the multimillionaires of the midlands moved up against the city and by sheer weight of numbers broke through the archaic barriers."

Well, hardly broke through in enough numbers to dilute too much the Eastern snobbery of "the four hundred." ("There are only four hundred people worth knowing in society.") When they did, an eyewitness could set down notice of "its restless activity, feverish enterprise and opportunities . . . but more particularly by its imperial wealth, its Parisian, indeed almost Sybaritic luxury and social splendor . . . the roll of splendid equipages . . . the constant round of brilliant banquets, afternoon teas and receptions . . . beautiful women and brave men threading the mazes of the dance; scenes of revelry by night in an atmosphere loaded with the perfumes of rare exotics, in the swell of sensuous music. . . . Soon nothing remains for the wives of the Western millionaires but to purchase a brownstone mansion, and swing into the tide of fashion with receptions, balls and kettledrums, elegant equipages with coachmen in bright-buttoned livery, footmen in top-boots, maid-servants and man-servants, including a butler. . . ."

Butlers were the true sign that an ex-miner or peddler, storekeeper, cow puncher, had made it socially. *Ruggles of Red Gap*, a novel of an English valet taming a Western town, was a best seller.

Sometimes the memory of a hard past took on a romantic glow, now that all hardships were over with. Often it would be a ritual to reenact what came to be called a "Poverty Social." One such was held at the home of a Western millionaire; "guests came in rags." Cost? Fourteen thousand dollars. "The scraps of food were served on wooden plates. The diners sat about on broken soap boxes, buckets and coalhods. Newspapers, dust cloths and old skirts were used as napkins, and beer served in a rusty tin can. . . ." *Très* fun indeed in memory of fervid scurrilous days in the rough West hunting for the wealth to take them away from it all, to what Ward

34. *Beans and coffee days of the miner soon ended—he found wealth or drifted away.*

McAllister, social leader, describes as a fancy dinner—not of scraps *or* beer. "Soft strains of music were introduced between the courses, and in some houses gold replaced silver plate and everything that skill and art could suggest was added to make the dinners not a vulgar display but a great gastronomic effort, evidencing the possession by the host of both money and taste."

And no sleeping in red flannel underwear on a scuffed blanket. Sir Joseph Duveen, formerly a dealer in secondhand furniture and trash, used to send cargoes of Louis XV, Renaissance debris, oriental rugs, European tapestry, bad Corots, strange English portraits, massive silver services westward. Paintings were popular: Millet, Meissonier, Rosa Bonheur, Bouguereau, Breton, Daubigny, Fromentin and others of the Salon school of Napoleon; also overpolished nudes, prancing horses, still lifes of murdered animals, or romantic sunsets. Some were bought for two hundred thousand dollars in old-fashioned currency, representing a value of over a million dollars in today's money.

Soon the protean opulence of the wealth that sprang up in San Francisco and the West in so short a time moved far from its early days of crude fun and frolic with such frontier stuff as:

Oh, Tom King's wife of the Federal city,
 Tom King's wife of Federal city,
I wat you how she cheated him,
 When he went off to the Western country.

She vowed so fair, so dear did seem,
 He little thought that she was tricky,
But oh, the cruel, faithless queen,
 She left her King and *spread* her dicky.

Dicky-spreading was still in vogue but on a grander scale. The granddaughter of a Sydney Duck on the Hangtown diggings went after an English duke or a French count. Mark Hopkins' adopted daughter married a title, she carrying a dowry of over twenty-three million dollars across the sea—whereas her grandmother most likely was shivareed by the banging of crude miners on tin pans while honeymooning in a tent.

R.J. reports the rich grandsons of forty-niners riding to a fox hunt after a bag of cotton rags soaked in fox urine—it being a season bare of wild foxes (recalling an unpublished line in a lecture Oscar Wilde once gave in the West: "To have taste, avoid having acres of it").

16

DANGER ASHORE

Then three times round went our gallant ship,
And three times round went she.
For the want of a life-boat they all went down,
And she sank to the bottom of the sea, the sea, the sea,
And she sank to the bottom of the sea.

When the age of the gold-panning miner, the dry gulch hunt for gold passed, large combines and modern scientific methods to get gold out appeared. The role of the miners as the pleasure seekers in San Francisco was taken more and more by the sailor. San Francisco had become a great port; its vice district, the Barbary Coast, as notorious some proudly claimed as any sailor's harbor in the most dissolute city in the world. The sailor was a potent victim for the city. Months at sea had driven his desires into fantastic dreams, and on reaching port he leaped forward, earnest, eager, usually witless and shouting, aching to stage his long pent up dramas of palpable images. He had money too, for no matter how poor the pay, at sea he had no opportunity to spend. So there was Jack Tar, the topsail men, the able seaman, the galley cook and the cabin boy with fuzz on his cheeks, talking a hundred languages, all in search of women, alcohol, gambling, wild laughter and companionship of a kind. To be met with a sea of platitudes, bottles and cheerful obscenities.

This welcoming they got near the waterfront was as close as it could crowd to spare the sailor the task of climbing too far up

San Francisco's hills. The sailors passed their shore time mostly on Davis, Drumm, Grant and Battery streets, east on Washington, Jackson and Pacific Avenue; all along here the boarding houses, whorehouses, the saloons stood elbow to elbow with welcome signs out and the pervasive smell of spirits, available flesh in every doorway. Crimps—men who sold sailors' bodies—(usually drugged) for shanghaied voyages, too long, unpleasant trips under bad captains— were on hand; for the waterfront made it a business to entertain, strip, drug and ship the remains of a man out on a hell ship, a cattle boat, a sinking wreck about ready to claim the insurance money. Dive keepers in nankeens and frilled shirts, boarding house owners, crimp masters, made fortunes in selling sailors, happy or peevish, jolly or querulous.

The police walked in pairs along the waterfront. They carried clubs with lump lead embedded in the heads, but their main weapon, oddly enough for gun-happy Americans who disdain cold steel, was a foot-long version of the early frontier Bowie knife. With this the waterfront cop could inflict fearful damage. The terror of the Coast was a Sergeant Tom Langford, who when attacked by half a dozen men robbing a shop on Pacific Avenue, all alone and braving a rain of bullets, drew his knife and decapitated one of the men and carved up a few more.

The trip from ship to shore was dangerous for the sailor. Ships were anchored away from the wharves and the small Whitehall boats took sailors and passengers ashore like taxis, for a fee. Sailors and even passengers were knocked on the head during the passage, stripped, sometimes even murdered by such boatmen as Ol' Activity, the Latin one called Red Shirt, or Old Buzz and Solly; they all claimed to be the sailor's friend as they steered him to the dive to be plucked. Solly would stop rowing half way to shore and announce: "Double the rate to shore or all of you go over the side, and be damned to you." This worked for Solly with a cruel boathook in his hand until he took on the mate of a British ship and stopped half way from shore with his demand. The mate calmly pulled out a pistol and shot Solly as dead as he would ever be.

Runners were loafers and hangers-on who touted for the boatmen and for the boarding houses, the saloons and gambling places. A good runner got three dollars for every sailor delivered to a boarding house. They came on board the vessels entering Golden Gate from the boatmen's skiffs, and they were loud, pleading, demanding, and hardly ever let go of a sailor once they had latched onto him. A newspaper report of the early sixties states: "The crew are shoved into the runners' boats, and the vessel is often left in a perilous situation, with none to manage her, the sails unfurled, and she liable to drift afoul of the shipping at anchor. In some cases not a man has been left aboard. . . ."

It was of a sailor that followed the sea.
Let the winds blow high or blow low O.
"I shall die, I shall die," he did cry,
"If I don't get that maid on the shore O,
If I don't get that maid on the shore."

Ashore or afloat the American sailor on American ships was exploited and starved, beaten and ill used, to say nothing of being underpaid. Dana in his *Two Years Before the Mast* pictured the brutal lot of the American sailor off the California coast. Mostly the sailor was paid twenty-five dollars a month and served greasy spoiled food. Naturally only the most depraved, foolish and brutal man went to sea as a common sailor more than once.

On shore the game was to get the sailor to sign up again to ship out as soon as he could make his mark, for he got two months' pay in advance to buy some kind of outfit for himself out of some slop shop. Actually by the time the sailor was signed on he was groggy and in the hands of the waterfront harpies, so it was usually the crimp or the boarding house keeper who got the advance. The whore got little but a clout on the head from her mack.

Sea voyages often lasted two to four years between home ports and an agreement between bad captains and crimps was often to give the sailor such bad treatment that he'd desert the ship and so forfeit his salary. Other captains' and owners' tricks were to make pacts with San Francisco clothing dealers to charge all the sailor bought to the captain against the sailor's pay. Everything was triple priced, and the surplus divided between the captain and the dealer when the captain settled the account.

Comradely kind words and glorious depraved promises were the runner's stock-in-trade, but he also carried a sailor's dirk, a blackjack or sap, and protected his hands from roughness with brass knuckles. The runners treated their clients to bottles of whisky dosed with Spanish Fly to increase the sailors' sexual irritation, and often a bottle of liquid soft soap was poured into the galley soup pot to convince the sailors that the grub on board was not fit to eat.

The drugged booze was helped along by the runner's collection of obscene picture postcards depicting depraved sexual games to be had ashore, and talk of the kindly boarding house keepers of San Francisco, so willing to advance cash on future sailings; who were keepers too of the young and delightful tarts always waiting for their sailor lovers. Few common seamen escaped the runners of the Whitehall boats. The willing drinking sailor was helped down into the bobbing shore boat; the unwilling man who wanted to save his money and get away from the Coast dives was often blackjacked and beaten and tossed down into the boat to come awake in some fearsome dive with offerings of drink and women.

A sailor was anybody's game until he called out the name of the boarding house he preferred. The unwilling sailor could be grabbed by two crimps, each holding an ear of the seaman in his teeth and not setting him free till he yelled out the name of the house whose hospitality he desired. Good captains—and there were a few—fought off the runners, but the shore vultures were armed and it was *their* harbor, and the police usually were bribed to look the other way. In 1870 an English passenger, Charles Ridgway, gave a good view of the system, when several loads of runners got on deck from their boats, though they "had been told once or twice to let go and leave the ship. But they flatly refused to do so.

"Whilst the crew was busy furling the sails, the men not only climbed on deck but mounted the riggings, and were soon seen very assiduously to importune, and at the same time hand bottles from which the sailors took long draughts. At first the sailors evaded them, but as the liquor began to work its effect, they gradually gave way, and allowed themselves to be cajoled. The captain several times called them down and threatened to have them arrested if they did not leave the ship. Two of them not only refused, but actually pointed a revolver at him, and told him that he was not in a 'B—— Lime Juice' country, but in God's own free land, where one man was as good as another. The captain appeared to be cowed and did not interfere with them again. . . .

"At short intervals I noticed that the sailors climbed over the side and lowered themselves into the boats, accompanied by the villains and were being rowed ashore. . . . I arose earlier than usual the next morning. Whilst partaking of coffee I heard the second officer calling all hands on deck, but receiving no response except from Dick and the apprentices; he looked into the forecastle and found all the berths empty. After partaking of breakfast I was about to leave when I saw two men drag old Dick towards the companion ladder. I attempted to stop them, but received curses and several blows on my face. I returned the insult, and letting go of old Dick we engaged in a close contest, during which I knocked him down. Meanwhile, Dick was not idle, but fought his man in order to free himself. I was about to spring to his assistance, but on account of the hatch which was close behind him, the impetus in trying to free himself caused him to reel backwards, and before I could grasp him poor old Dick fell headlong down, striking his head against the keel of the ship. I called for assistance, and after securing the two men, we descended and found poor Dick quite dead, his head and body being frightfully mangled. The captain at once hoisted a police flag, which was quickly responded to by two water-policemen, who took the two villains in custody. The two culprits, being well represented by counsel, got off with a light sentence of six months hard labor."

Actually it could happen that a drugged sailor remained ashore less than a day. Drunk and drug-drenched he hardly had much chance to note the time or the date. A captain seeking a fresh crew would appear and the sailor told to make his mark and sign on not only for the trip but also for the crimp and boarding house owner to take over his two months' advance pay. If the sailor was too ill or drunk to sign or make his mark, the crimp would do it for him as an added service. If the sailor objected, he got a going-over with some blackjack and fist work, was treated to more drugged whisky, and before he was dumped like a dirty bag on the deck of his new ship, he was searched, his valuables taken, his best clothes removed and rags put in their place. He was now ready to represent American shipping on the high seas. All this sounds like melodrama, but it is fully documented over and over again.

The captain paid off to the crimp only when the bodies were delivered on deck, and usually added a bonus of fifty to a hundred dollars a body. When the traffic was on in the early days of the Gold Rush, a captain would often offer three to four hundred dollars to a crimp for an able-bodied seaman, who would have preferred digging for gold to taking a bully mate's rope on his rump on a deadly trip around the Horn.

Were there laws against this? All you wanted: city laws, state, even national laws. From a hundred dollar fine to come aboard any ship without the captain's permission, up to hanging for murder done in the Bay. But politics, police, shop owners, dive runners and the respectable folk who owned the shore front property used for saloons, whorehouses and kidnaping of sailors preferred to let things go on as before. ("They're a rough crowd and love a rough life.") Some of the most notorious properties, reformers claimed, were owned by the city's best churches, or at least by the most pious churchgoers.

> While the raging seas did roar,
>   And the stormy winds did blow,
> While we sailor-boys were up into the top,
>   And the land-lubbers lying down below, below, below,
>   And the land-lubbers lying down below.

While the Mafia ("the second government of the nation") invented the modern method of getting rid of an enemy by setting his feet, while still alive, in a bucket of cement, and when it had

35. *Seaman's rest—a place where he was the prey of all—and worth money to the crimps.*

hardened, tossing it and him into the nearest body of deep water, it was the San Francisco crimp who got rid of unwanted bodies in the city by shipping them off as drunken sailors who had to be carried on board ship. By the time the captain found his drunken able seaman was actually a corpse, there was nothing to do but curse the crimper and toss the remains overboard, as "died at sea," rather than face legal explanations on shore.

Women were very active in the trade of shanghaiing sailors. One of the best remembered of the rancid biddies was Miss Piggott of Davis Street. (A clout on the head with her favorite bung starter if you asked her first name. There is no record of it.) The other harpy was Mother Bronson of Steuart Street, who kept order by biting the victim with her huge teeth. Both monsters did a little of everything; saloon keeping, sailor boarding, brothel booking, selling sailors alive or dead.

Mother Bronson wore a twelve and a half shoe and was also an expert kicker. She once held the indoor distance record for drop-kicking an unoffending Chinaman from the sawdust on the floor to the top of her mahogany bar. There were bets she could knock down a bullock with one blow, but Mother never found anyone who brought a steer into her place. Miss Piggott (how like a character from Dickens she sounds), while not less ferocious, was more subtle. She had a trapdoor set in front of her bar. An unwary sailor would be treated to the "Miss Piggott Special," a potent mixture of whisky, gin, brandy and laudanum. The dazed victim was then tapped by Miss Piggott with her bung starter as she pulled a lever that dropped him down into the cellar where he remained numb and serene, unmoving until he was carried to some ship leaving the harbor. There was always a goodly crowd of regulars present— who avoided the trapdoor—who cheered as the drugged sailor fell through the opening that suddenly appeared at his feet. A crimp named Nikko, who worked for Miss Piggott, spent his spare time, when sailors were scarce or hard to lure over the trapdoor, making stuffed dummies to take on board when hurried calls for seamen came for some ship about to sail. To give them life and animation he tied a live wharf rat in each sleeve, so that sound and movement gave life to the sailor dummy. (Today any *avant-garde* New York art gallery would consider Nikko's work worthy of a gala art showing.)

Most of the crimps were rough and inhuman males. The most notorious was Shanghai Kelly, or Jimmy Laffin, who was the man to see for whaling ship crews, a specialist in harpooners and boatmen. Or George Ruben, who ran a boarding house for Teutonic sailors and served a fine hot sauerkraut. And there was Horseshoe Brown, whose call to fame appears to be the fact that in front of his establishment on Kearny Street he calmly murdered his wife and then took his own life. No reason for the deed has survived.

The most amazing tale of a crimp is that of a character known only as Calico Jim, and while some doubt has been cast on parts of the story, it's too astounding not to retell here. Calico Jim was a Chileno who actually came from Peru, from Callao. He ran a sailor's shanghai collection center and bar at Battery Point. His political protection seems to have been faulty, or he refused to bribe the right people. Policemen were sent to arrest him; six in all, one at a time. And Jim shanghaied each one and sent them on long sea trips to far-off ports. He then packed up and left the city. In time the sea-tossed police, horny-handed and scarred by hard sea mates and duties on hell ships, came back to San Francisco. They met and formed a Hate Calico Jim Club. They collected funds and appointed one of their number to go find Calico Jim in his hometown of Callao, Peru. Find him he did, and in broad daylight in the street he shot Calico Jim six times; the story being he cried out, "That's one for each shanghaied policeman!"

The San Francisco Police Department, not the most ethical or honest in history, has always denied the story. No record exists today of the six missing officers; but records *have* disappeared from files before.

Often a good man appears to stand out from the crowd. Such a man was Fred Harvey. The railroad kings were interested in making money, not in furnishing comfort to passengers. The customer usually came last, and when it was a question of feeding the passen-

ger, many a gut-aching traveler staggered off the train in San Francisco or Los Angeles with the biggest case of indigestion of his or
her life. There was the habit of stopping a transcontinental train
three times a day in the West at some sunbaked weathered depot,
then announcing there would be a half hour stopover for feeding.
The hungry passengers would descend like an Indian raid on the
station counter or lunchroom for iron-hard sandwiches, cold greasy
singed meat of sorts, boiler-muck coffee and stale rolls and bread.
The food was dropped or sloshed down by a frowsy waitress, often
the town harlot, and while the passenger gulped, the steam train
waited groaning with impatience. To aid in the food swindle—
meal payments were in advance—the station poisoner would bribe
the train crew to cut the half hour layover by fifteen or even
twenty minutes; whistle and bell would sound, passengers would
run, leaving much of the food on their fly-buzzed plates, which
food could be brushed off and sold again to the next set of pioneer
victims. The West was rough on man, beast and digestive tract.

It was the stomach ulcer of a freight agent named Fred Harvey
that changed a great deal of this. Born in London in 1853, at fifteen
he crossed the ocean to wash dishes in New York City, later opening his own eating place in St. Louis. The Civil War upset the
trade and Fred Harvey became a mail clerk on the Hannibal & St.
Joe Railroad, better known to its bone-shaken passengers as the
Horrible & Slow Jolting. Harvey's stomach pains because of the bad
depot food caused him to open the first Harvey Restaurant in the
Topeka depot.

The effect on travelers going West was amazing. Wrote one
ironic and surprised passenger: "Travelers positively declined to
go further once they had eaten with Fred Harvey. Traffic backed
up and it became necessary . . . to open similar houses at other
points along the way in order that the West might not be settled in
just one spot." So there was a rational exultation as Fred Harvey
restaurants spread into other depots—and it is hoped his ulcers
faded away.

The gamblers, madams, light ladies, ministers, land agents, fortune hunters, sportsmen out to get a grizzly, businessmen dreaming

of wealth in the West, all had, if they could afford it, good food at all station stops all the way to the Golden Gate, and down coast to the City of the Angels. They rode in cars ornate in fumed and golden oak, with great flaring oil lamps, walls inlaid with real gilt, and as they crossed the mountains, the deserts and the plains it was dusty and cindery; the heat could make one wonder how men made it with covered wagons. Yet there was luxury awaiting them at journey's end—at the Palace Hotel, with one of its four hundred and thirty-nine bathtubs for the dainty. Meanwhile Harvey, or copies of Harvey, waited in depots with reviving food, piping hot, to ease them on the way.

The average citizen in the jolting coaches—the Big Four never seemed to use perfectly round wheels on them—had to buy the offerings of "candy butchers" (the boys and men who peddled food, candy and magazines from baskets on trains). Of course the canny frugal traveler brought his own food; in a shoebox for a short journey, or in a well-packed basket from Mom's kitchen for a long one, fondly handed out as she kissed good-by, for often a member of the family disappeared forever in the West. As one man wrote who remembers those who couldn't afford Fred Harvey dining: "when you went for a trip on the cars, somebody kindly put up a fried chicken in a shoebox for you. It was accompanied by a healthy piece of cheese and a varied assortment of hard-boiled eggs and some cake. When everybody in the car got out their lunch baskets with the paper cover and the red-bordered napkins, it was an interesting sight. . . . The bouquet from those lunches hung around the car all day, and the flies wired ahead for their friends to meet them at each station."

Fred Harvey, set in his purpose, moved westward following the sun, opening Harvey eating places along the rail lines. The Santa Fe system was the first railroad to see his merit and they began to furnish the premises, the cooking equipment, tables and chairs. Fred Harvey took care of the feeding and service. At Dodge City— while frontier gunslingers still played their epic battles—he set up in two box cars, one to cook in, one to serve the results. "Each age creates its own Greeks," a historian had said, and Harvey was the creator of a female image—American-style. The Harvey Girls he hired, designed and trained became as famous as the Pretty Waitress Girls in the dives of San Francisco, but not nearly as notorious. Mostly they insisted on marriage before handing over the pneumatic bliss of the body. Harvey ran advertising in the major Eastern newspapers to get his girls.

WANTED

YOUNG WOMEN OF GOOD CHARACTER,
ATTRACTIVE, INTELLIGENT, 18 TO 30.

They were paid $17.50 a month, plus room and board and required to be in every night by a 10 P.M. curfew. To dusty sun-baked cattlemen, to miners with stuffed pokes, to travelers in a rough land the Harvey Girls were beauty, grace, desire.

Fred Harvey's food and service have become a legend. His menus were full of luxury too, in place of the burned beans and poor coffee of ranch fires, mountain camps, dead-end towns. He brought white fish from the Great Lakes on beds of ice; you could get deer and antelope fillets or Mexican quail. And he paid top prices for his supplies: $1.50 for a dozen plump prairie hens, 75 cents for the same number of quail, and he went as high as 10 cents a pound for sweet country butter. But it was worth it. All this and the clean faces and fingernails of the Harvey Girls (every girl was passed on for starch and character by the stern Mrs. Harvey) resulted in service to fit menus free of pork belly, hog jowels, skillet grease on a tin plate with a rusty fork.

Like the airplane hostesses of today, a lot of the girls married the customers, and Fred Harvey usually gave away the girls at a proper legal wedding, even if the justice of the peace wore guns. Some claimed that as a result four thousand babies were named either Fred or Harvey. For the healthy Harvey Girls, besides practicing their little coquetries, flatteries, flourishes with a tray, and cooing limited vocabularies, were usually very fertile; Mr. Harvey had an eye for things.

"He kept the West in food and wives," said Will Rogers.

There was no bolting and running when Fred Harvey fed the Western trains. No bribing to cut down on the half hour feeding.

36. *Many a Fred Harvey waitress married into society.*

You sat at ease, eight to a table with a full arrangement of clean cups, dishes and glasses, and the smoking hot roast came in ready to carve, and the steaks sizzled on a great platter; the heavy silverware came from England, the best.

William Allen White, a Western traveler and editor famous in his day, said simply: "It is the best in America . . . in the past six months . . . eaten meals on ten of the great railway systems of the country. Harvey meals are so much better than the meals of other railroads, east, west, north and south, that the comparison seems trite."

Change came by the end of the last century; trains were faster and pride in time cut down between terminals was so great that the depot dining rooms were outmoded. So dining cars were built and put on the top-flight trains and Fred Harvey ran the best. In 1892 the *California Limited* was the train where travelers were served Fred Harvey menus while in motion, enjoying the smooth service by crews of Negro waiters in starched white. Irish table linens were fine and thick and snowy and the Sheffield silver so heavy one was amazed when lifting it.

Soon there was this kind of service on the *San Francisco Limited,* the *Grand Canyon,* the *Navajo* and other trains. But railroads left out of the Harvey circle had to bring on their star food managers to compete. Wild Bill Kurthy ran the Union Pacific-Southern Pacific's *Forty-Niner,* and Dan Healey the *Pioneer Limited.* All claimed they were as tony and posh as the Fred Harvey trains. But did they have his exuberant stubborn sense of taste? After the turn of the century Fred Harvey, almost until the death of the early crack steam trains, would present Beluga caviar at $1.50 a portion, and larded Tenderloin of Beef at 95 cents a cut. Gone are those days, to be replaced by the sly impudence of poor food at fancy prices.

Many a newly rich citizen of the Coast got his first taste of real luxury on the fast limited trains whirling past country crossings, bells ringing, the train climbing up out of California into the Rockies, rolling past the huts and shacks of obscure towns peopled by pioneers who never made it big. The passenger train was a treat that many a town used for entertainment. Going down to the depot

Dinner.

Blue Points on Shell

Cream of Barley

Boiled Fresh Salmon, Shrimp Sauce
Sliced Cucumbers

Boiled Ox Tongue, Sauce Piquante

Roast Beef, au Jus   **Loin of Veal, Stuffed**
Young Turkey, Cranberry Sauce

Mashed Potatoes   *Browned Sweet Potatoes*   *New Beets*
Spinach   *Asparagus on Toast.*

Sweetbreads Saute, Petits Pois
Minced Ham, with Eggs
Queen Fritters, Madeira Sauce

Roast Spring Lamb, Mint Sauce

Fresh Lobster   **Chicken Salad, au Mayonnaise**   **Cold Ham**

Sliced Tomatoes   *Dressed Lettuce*

Apple Pie   **Peach Pie**
Rice Pudding, Vanilla Sauce

Assorted Fruit   **Batger's Orange Jelly**   **Assorted Cake**
New York Ice Cream

Edam and Roquefort Cheese
Bent's Water Crackers   **French Coffee**

Meals 75 Cents.

CAR CORONADO LEAVING CHICAGO
FRIDAY MARCH 15. 1889.

to "watch the Limited go by" was a tradition—to see the well-dressed people seated behind plate glass windows at white damask-covered tables, looking at tall vellum menus while a herd of waiters play-acting at Uncle Tom bent over, adjusting, replenishing, waiting for the order. Mostly it was steak—rare, well done or medium. Then to the village watchers the train was gone, hooting for the next crossing, streaking to meet the horizon. Many a boy and girl decided then that some day they'd sit there in the glossy dining car and casually order all the rich Fred Harvey fare they could only imagine. From Willa Cather to Sinclair Lewis we hear of this dream.

Years later when they could really taste it all, to these children and youths it was never *that* good, and somehow the thrill of desiring and waiting had been better than the actual sitting down to Harvey silver and crystal and food cooked at eighty miles an hour.

Fred Harvey himself was mortal for all his deeds—he died in 1901, happily before the railroad train passed from glory into shabby freight hauling, and the dismal super-service of airlines dumped food tasting of the paper it was reheated in on too crowded laps. He was sixty-seven, and when he entered heaven he had served thirty dining cars, fifteen hotels, forty-seven restaurants and the seagull spattered ferryboats crossing San Francisco Bay.

The dining cars of today are old and crumbling; the food dull and overpriced, and little better than the iron-hard uneatable stuff first served to those early hard-rushed travelers at depot counters. The silver shows wear and the waiters no longer enjoying serving Mr. Charlie; for the age of service is past and to get what one pays for is pretty much gone with the great steam engines, rushing in the night, spewing flames and steam, headed for a wilder coast.

Today the Harvey sign merely means the usual bland and taste-less food of the usual American motel, hotel or cafeteria. There is a legend that as Fred Harvey lay dying he called in a group of Harvey Girls and his last words were reported to be: "Cut the ham thin, girls."

When citizens of San Francisco traveled out to the back of be-yond, as the territory land was called, there were hotels that offered a kind of frontier version of the city. The Desert Hotel issued a broadside, in the middle seventies, that is a prime example of the advertising style of Western copywriting. It brags:

This hotel has been built and arranged for the special comfort and convenience of summer boarders. On arrival, each guest will be asked how he likes the situation; and, if he says the hotel ought to have been placed up upon a knoll or further down towards the village, the location of the house will be immediately changed. Corner front rooms, up only one flight, for every guest. Baths, gas, hot and cold water, laundry, telegraph, restaurant, fire-alarm, bar-room, billiard-table, daily papers, coupe, sewing-machine, grand piano, and all other modern conveniences, in every room.

A discreet waiter, who belongs to the Masons, Odd Fellows, Knights of Pythias, and who was never known to even tell the time of day, has been employed to carry milk punches and hot toddies to ladies' rooms in the evening. Every lady will be considered the belle of the house.

Dogs allowed in any room in the house, including the w(h)ine room. The proprietor will always be happy to hear that some other hotel is "the best house in the country." Special attention given to parties who can give information as to "how these things are done in Yewrup." The proprietor will take it a personal affront if any guest on leaving should fail to dispute the bill, tell him he is a swindler, the house a barn, the table wretched, the wines vile, and that he (the guest) "was never so imposed upon in his life, will never stop there again, and means to warn his friends."

In the middle of the 1850s there arrived in San Francisco—no one today knows how—a most strikingly beautiful girl of about sixteen with a new baby and an alcoholic, skirt-chasing husband. The latter was always too drunk to practice medicine, but always able to lift a bottle or a skirt, though little interested in the support of his wife and child.

The girl was Victoria Claflin Woodhull, born in 1838 of a worthless father (frontier loafer, innkeeper, arsonist, medicine show man) and a German inn servant mother (religious fanatic, camp meeting singer and table-rapping organizer). Victoria ended as an English lady (leaving a daughter named Zulu). In between she became famous as the first woman candidate for the President of the United States (the People's Party). She and her sister Tennessee were the first women brokers on Wall Street, netting nearly a million dollars a year, but not for long. Victoria worked hard exposing the adulterous secret sex life of the great clergyman Henry Ward Beecher (his sister wrote *Uncle Tom's Cabin*). But that was all in the future.

The San Francisco that Victoria met was still stained with miners' muddy jeans, still busty and bawdy with gold rush boom times, hard and wild and no place for a child-wife and mother. Because of her beauty she had no trouble getting a job in a Barbary Coast saloon in a skimpy outfit as a cigar girl ("Sell 'em and light 'em"). Although raised on the frontier to her father's rough ways, still she claimed later she was shocked at the language and habits of the rowdy cigar buyers. She was gently fired by the saloon owner, she explained, because "I was too fine for the work." She also claimed he slipped a twenty dollar gold coin into her hand and escorted her back to her hotel. Certainly she also failed next as a seamstress, while her husband did little but cadge drinks at the town's bars boasting that he came from a fine Boston family (true) and a good medical school (?). Why Victoria stood him as long as she did is not known, for he was a chaser of other women. He must have had great charm.

It was an actress, Anna Cogswell, who rescued Victoria from needle and thread and buttons by the dozens. She put her in some small parts on the stage in her repertory company. Victoria felt that the stage was a fine place to be seen, but the memorizing of parts in gaudy melodramas, the false chatter of primitive drawing room comedy, even the ranting of frontier Shakespeare, was not for her. In Victoria, as her later life showed, there burned an enigmatic core; she belonged with spiritualists, she claimed to have second sight and was even ready to predict the future. She and her sister, Tennessee, claimed they could communicate with each other without speaking and even when out of sight.

One night during a loud and bloody scene in the popular thriller *The Corsican Brothers,* the spirit voice of her sister came to her crying out, "Victoria, come home!" A vision of her mother appeared over the footlights, then Tennessee herself was visible, arms flung out, beckoning. Victoria with a cry left the stage in mid-play and still in stage dress and slippers ran through the mire-filled streets, a sea fog from the Golden Gate flaring in the lamps. To her sodden husband she insisted they leave San Francisco at once. The next morning the strange group was on a steamer making for the Horn, bound for New York. No more is known of that venture.

The Victoria Claflin Woodhull that San Francisco knew, the cigar girl, the seamstress, the actress, admired for her great beauty and shape, pitied for her alcoholic parasite of a husband, was to change and become notorious on the national scene. Soon gone and forgotten were the psalm-shrieking mother, the medicine show father, the years of healing through the spirits and the clairvoyance she practiced with her sister in many towns and cities. (There were also villages that ran them out as common whores.)

Such were the beginnings of famous careers that led to many marriages for the sisters, their own newspaper, *Woodhull & Claflin Weekly.* Victoria became loud and flamboyant for women's rights on public platforms, advocating free love and more sexual pleasures. She was called the "Terrible Siren" and "Mrs. Satan" when she exposed the bedroom peccadillos of the pious, Bible-thumping Dr. Beecher. People who remembered her from her San Francisco days added to her notorious reputation by tales, mostly invented, of her life there during the fifties.

In 1872, after trying to organize a woman's party, she stood on the stage of the Apollo Hall and shouted, "Who will dare to attempt to unlock the luminous portals of the future with the rusty keys of the past!" thus echoing both her San Francisco stage training and the language of *The Corsican Brothers.*

A ready follower leaped on the stage crying, "I nominate Victoria C. Woodhull for President of the United States. All in favor of the nomination say Aye!"

The Ayes had it—the new People's Party had their candidate. The party nominated the country's most famous Negro, Frederick Douglas, for her running mate. There were cries of "We have the oppressed sex represented by Woodhull, we must have the oppressed race represented by Douglas!" But someone wanted an Indian called Spotted Tail. "Indians ought to have a voice before Negroes." Mr. Douglas won out in the end, but not being present and not knowing of the honor he did not express an opinion of a woman in the White House.

No records exist as to how many votes Victoria got, or on what ballots she was listed. . . . She died after a very full life the year Charles Lindbergh (1927) flew the Atlantic solo. She died comfortably seated in a chair, for she had a spirit warning that to lie down was to invite death. Victoria was a pioneer fighter for women's rights in home and bed, and is the only American female who has to date run for the office of the President of the United States.

San Francisco was always turning up odd girls. There was Isadora Duncan, of course, whose hungry family roamed the town near the turn of the century, before Isadora went on to reforming the modern dance in her own way. It is claimed she often stole fruit to feed the hungry Duncan brood from the orchard of the Stein family. The Steins were respectable Jews of San Francisco. The father became one of the directors of the famous cable car company, and one son spent his life as a jolly somewhat talky and boozy motorman on the cable car platforms in all weather, working his bell and brake up and down the steep grades, a town character. His sister was Gertrude Stein ("a rose is a rose is a rose") growing up in a San Francisco she was to leave, when grown, for college in the East. Also growing up was a dark and small girl who practiced the piano and was named Alice Toklas. Ernest Hemingway, much later, in conversation at a café bar was to say: "The two ugliest women God and San Francisco ever produced were Gertrude and Alice."

The two women met in Paris, made up a ménage (with a poodle added) and addressed each other as "Lovey" and "Pussy."

Alice (to quote Hemingway again) "looks like a kosher Apache Indian mummy." She was Pussy. In the love affair Gertrude, who was only five feet two, seems monumental in a man's panama hat and square cut clothes that looked tailored by a stevedore. She also cut her hair short and smoked cigars. The Steins, who remained in San Francisco, and there were a lot of them, in time acquired many Picassos and Matisses under the direction of Gertrude and another brother, Leo (who holds the world's public record for treatment in psychoanalysis—twenty-seven years). Today many of these great paintings are in San Francisco, divided among the surviving clan. Lovey's other famous line: "Pigeons in the grass, alas . . ." she once said was her girlhood memory of the busy birds around the town's Ferry Tower.

37. *A sailor's shanghaier and his bait waiting for a jolly tar.*

17

GOING 'ROUND "THE HORN"

She had some hair on her back;
Some was orange and some was black.
She had two teeth in her mouth;
One went north and the other went south.

The sailors in most demand by sea captains were those who had come around the dangerous Horn. One crimp, Mike Conners of the Chain Locker Saloon and Boarding House, was a pious Catholic, who attended mass, spattered himself with holy water and had his sordid soul put in a state of grace from time to time. When the demand for sailors who had come around the Horn was greatest, he'd salve his fears of hell-fire by having a cow's horn put on the floor near the entrance and seeing to it that the victim about to be shanghaied walked around it. Mike could then swear on a stack of holy relics that the men he sold had all been around the Horn. ("Holy Mary, would a man have that kind of a lie on his soul now?")

Shanghaiing was also used to get rid of persons who would be better out of town, or so their relatives, employers, wives or mistresses thought. Before the jet age the far corners of the world were mysterious unknown areas. For a fee Shanghai Kelly would lure the nephew mentioned in the will, the honest bookkeeper who had just discovered some embezzlement, a husband who came home at the wrong time or lover whose charms were turning to demands for cash; Kelly would have these social blunderers visit him on some pretext and give them the house special; booze-and-opium, or the Chinatown Shanghai Smoke—a cigar made by a Chinese tobacconist that contained a heavy mixture of opium. A few sips, a few draws of impure Havana and the unwanted citizen was ready to depart for a long sea trip. Often, because of an "accident" at sea they never came back; but that cost extra, a special service charge. In an age before telephone, cable, radio, TV, fingerprinting or aircraft, the earth could swallow up an unwanted person.

Shanghai Kelly became a legend himself with his great *coup* in the seventies when ships were demanding sailors and getting none. Kelly publicly announced it was his birthday; he had hired the old paddle-wheeler *Goliah,* and it was all on him: a stag picnic trip, food, drink and fun for men only. Kegs of drugged whisky and beer were proudly exhibited on deck and the Barbary Coast loafers, town moochers and freeloaders came on board to celebrate. Kelly cast off when nearly a hundred men had walked up the gangplank. The boys were soon at the wet goods, drinking toasts to Kelly for a long and fruitful life. When the drugged alcohol had dulled his guests' senses, Kelly sailed the paddle-wheeler out to the Bay and sold the picnickers to three ships awaiting crews. On the way back to the wharf Kelly picked up some sailors wrecked off Point Conception and brought them to port in place of the others—and somehow the missing men were not mentioned much. It was a self-immersed society in those days.

Shanghaiing was not a one-string business. It had sidelines. The Shanghai Chicken or Johnny Devine (himself shanghaied from New York in 1859) got to the Coast and set up as a pickpocket, footpad, second story man, prizefighter (he lost too many fights) and worker of prostitutes. He had a half dozen girls on the streets or in the rooms where he brought the mark to be plucked. The Chicken was not a man who demanded high prices for any of his skills. He offered to work over a victim for a modest sum with a blackjack, bare fists or brass knuckles. He did not draw the line at murder. In one year he was arrested thirty times, but because of political protection he was jailed only once and that for fifty days. A man had to be predatory and reconnoiter all the time to make crime pay.

The Shanghai Chicken did not invent highjacking, but he used it more than most. His game was the stealing of sailors away from other runners and crimps instead of hunting his own prey. His habit was to knock out the sailor with a blackjack and then pull a pistol and shoot the accompanying runner if he didn't make tracks. The Chicken was notorious for his lasting powers as a boozer and for the violence he did with knife and pistol. Out with a pal one night on the Coast, knifing and firing his pistol into saloon ceilings, he came up against a saloon fighter named Billy Maitland. The Shanghai Chicken faced him with a pistol, but Billy had a knife he had just taken from the Chicken's drinking buddy. The Chicken was too slow in pulling the trigger and Billy lunged and severed the Chicken's left hand at the wrist. The member dropped off into the sawdust on the bar floor. Billy, vociferous and mean, then threw the Chicken and his friend out into the street. The Chicken got up and howled, "Billy, you no good dirty bastard, throw me out me fin!"

Billy felt this was only fair, and threw the gruesome severed hand out to its owner. Weak from loss of blood, the Chicken managed to reach Doc Simpson's Drugstore at Pacific Avenue and Davis Street. He offered the hand to Doc, who hardly believed what he saw.

"Doc, you gotta stick this back on for me, will you, huh?"

The Chicken collapsed, and no wonder. He was taken away to have his stump tied off and sewed up. In time he had an iron hook attached to the stump, kept needle sharp. But the loss of the hand marked his downfall into drink and mere petty theft. He lost his girls, he served time for stealing so miserly an item as three pickled pigs feet. In 1871 he murdered a sailor, tried to get away on a ship, and was arrested at Meigg's Wharf. "I'm afraid you guys will have to hang me," he told the arresting officer. The state accommodated the Shanghai Chicken. Such was the grim outline of a worthless cruel life of piled up atrocities.

When in time reform had its moments, or seamen grew smarter and captains protected their crews, the Coast still held them by its whores, dance places, concert saloons and the general desire to show them a good time in exchange for their money. They came from many lands; the Sourwegians or Swenskies (Scandinavians), and Mister Peters (Negroes, so called because of the legend of the size of their genitalia), Krauts (Germans), Froggies (French), Limies (British), assorted wogs, wops, dagos, bohunks, burr-heads, Fuzzy-Wuzzies, gooks, spiks (the lesser breeds as Mr. Kipling called them). All had their favorite bars and places of entertainment. The Bella Union got a lot of the trade and the hoochy-koochy dancers wriggled themselves into breakdowns. Bottle Koenig's joint kept to liquor and dirty shows with revolting tableaus. In the dance halls known as rub joints the gestures on the floor could hardly be called dancing, but were satisfactory to the sailors.

Various desires for perverted debauchery could be satisfied in the stalls, cribs or in the alleys under terms that have entered slang dictionaries. Only a few of them will be listed here: frenching, seafood mama, wick dipping, in the kip (an early version of shacking up), getting one's ashes hauled, changing one's luck (sexually engaging with a Negro, believed in as gospel by most gamblers), and copping a cherry (losing one's virginity). Naturally most of the thousands of terms can hardly be printed, consisting of good old Anglo-Saxon jargon going back as far as Chaucer, and expressing vital anatomy in detail, also actions, and dreams. It was amazing how much of the desires of the sailors, the miners and railroaders was pure fantasy, and was hardly satisfied by the drinking, brutal fornicating—sex à la paresseuse, au bord du lit, and dismal hangovers.

Venereal diseases were common, of course, and quacks treated them as "no worse than a bad cold." Seldom, before the age of penicillin, was a sailor (or many famous statesmen and artists and writers) left uninfected by Big Casino or Little Casino, the major and minor diseases of Venus. It was also called the Old Rale, Big Charlie. Death on land was labeled the Deep Six. At sea it was the Needle Through the Nose (from the ritual of sewing the dead sailor into his hammock, and the sailmaker passing the needle and thread through the nose of the corpse with his last stitches to protect him in King Neptune's world (as with much ritual, no reasonable explanation of the Needle Through the Nose exists).

The drinkers, who in many cases had little desire for women, made for the popular bars such as the Bowhead, the Foam, the Whale. The Whale was dangerous at times because Tip Thornton, a polite little thief, hung out there. In a fight he'd pull out his knife and reaching for his rival's nose slice it off. Many ears were also lost to his knife work. Tip was protected from the police by the bar bums and the owner of the place. But an Officer Cleary invaded the Whale after the loss of a nose by a protesting patron, and fighting off a dozen barroom toughs, he carried off Tip in handcuffs on his way to prison. These ruffians and swaggerers were not often amusing people, their humor was too black and macabre.

Cowboy Maggie of the pendulous breasts ran the Cowboy's Rest and had a reputation as an unencumbered woman of passion, aching for love. Her saloon, and hotel rooms to rent, day or hour, she controlled with fist and blackjack. Yet her weakness was a desire, a naiveté, for true love. Her record shows she shot a lover, shot a husband, beat up various men in her love life and thrashed half a dozen women who tried to lure her great love of the moment away with gyrating hip and buttocks. Cowboy Maggie, for all her quality of exuberance was hardly a raving beauty. Surviving pictures of her show a hard-faced, solid-jawed woman, with a drab bun of hair hoisted under an unbecoming hat.

During the Spanish-American War, when we were shipping Negro regiments to Manila to cure the native population of their own ideas of freedom, R.J. notes in his daybook: "Cowboy Maggie, Queen of the Barbary Coast—there are actually at least three Queens—in trouble again for standing in front of her place with a big .45 Colt in her fist, howling: 'Hate niggahs! Shoot the goddamn head off any niggah tries to come into this here place.' I gather she must have been a true Southern lady at one time. Went to the Exchange for a drink and to see the new paintings. Had Professor Nichol show me how to make his Pisco Punch. Made of Peruvian brandy, La Roas del Peru grape as a base."

The daybook does not give the recipe for the true Pisco Punch. The modern version mixed today in San Francisco is a fake. Professor Nichol was Duncan Nichol, a master barman who died with his secret for the punch. The Exchange mentioned above was the Bank Exchange, a fancy saloon for the gentry that claimed its oil paintings were worth a fortune. Art collectors and Pisco Punch buffs would gather to sip and admire in the Exchange's marble setting. Thomas W. Knox gives us an idea of the fabulous taste of the punch in his book, *Underground, or Life Below the Surface.*

The drink, the author claimed, "perfectly colourless, quite fragrant, very seductive, terribly strong, and has a flavour somewhat resembling that of Scotch whiskey, but much more delicate, with a marked fruity taste. It comes in earthen jars, broad at the top and tapering down to a point, holding about five gallons each. We had some hot, with a bit of lemon and a dash of nutmeg in it. . . . The first glass satisfied me that San Francisco was, and is, a nice place to visit. . . . The second glass was sufficient, and I felt that I could face small-pox, all the fevers known to the faculty, and the Asiatic cholera."

Peru brandy also was the base for the Button Punch, which a visitor, Rudyard Kipling, touring America, took to swooning over: "I have a theory it is compounded of cherubs' wings, the glory of a tropical dawn, the red clouds of sunset, and fragments of lost epics by dead masters." Rudyard, one suspects, was a beer and ale man.

Street preachers, the Salvation Army, the Praying Band, and other folk, each had the secret of the *one* true God, tried to save the souls and bodies of the sailors, the Pretty Waitress Girls, the dancers, singers and whores. Most were splendidly earnest in their efforts. There was public confession, much banging on drums. There were also independent street messiahs and soul grabbers like the one called Old Orthodox, and his rival hell painter, Hallelujah Cox. They both calmed their dry throats with many a beer. All faiths were reached for; all creeds and rituals offered as the final answer. There was even a bony preacher called Old Despair, who wandered about the Coast, quoting from St. Augustine a warning that easy converts could not be too sure of salvation.

"Do not despair," he would thunder in front of the Cobweb Palace, at Meiggs Wharf, or the Martin and Horton Saloon on Clay Street. "One of the thieves was saved. Do not presume, one of the thieves was damned."

Ambrose Bierce had different ideas on theology and related subjects. "PRAY. To ask that the laws of the universe be annulled in behalf of a single petitioner confessedly unworthy. . . ." "CHRISTIAN. One who believes that the New Testament is a divinely inspired book admirably suited to the spiritual needs of his neighbor. One who follows the teaching in so far as they are not inconsistent with a life of sin." Bierce was San Francisco's only cynic who could be witty. To this interest in the city's morality and its support of prostitution he gave historic study at many bars. "ON THE OFFER OF A WOMAN'S BODY. A custom as a sacrifice of virginity, to earn dowry, or as religious service, a religious duty."

Among the Jews, he'd lecture at a bar to R.J., one found the object of Mosaic law was to preserve the race, the religion. Prostitution was not forbidden if confined to foreign women. Jewish fathers were forbidden to turn daughters into prostitutes (Leviticus 19:29); the daughters of Israel forbidden to become prostitutes (Deuteronomy 23:17). In the Old Testament prostitution prevailed. The Reformation brought a change in sexual morality; an insistence on celibacy had deprived clergymen of licit outlet for sex. Now the Christian condemnation of non-martial lust was emphasized. The Protestant Reformers' attitude toward chastity was echoed by the Catholics Counter-Reformation . . . aware of the harm done to the Church by licentious conduct.

Many statutes to control prostitutes were hardly enforced. . . . Certainly not in Bierce's San Francisco. In the nineteenth century the usual solution was to force prostitutes to segregated districts. Here they would be least embarrassing to respectable society. Houses of prostitution were numerous but disappeared after the policy shifted from segregation to suppression. Anti-vice campaigns were launched. Red light districts and brothels in major cities across the country went. The brothels disappeared; prostitution didn't. The prostitutes forced out of segregated districts became streetwalkers, bar whores and call girls. San Francisco retained the wide-open brothel longer than most American cities.

18

LIFE UP ON THE HILLS

Life in the best parts of San Francisco, while not all lucidity and sobriety, hardly vied with scenes in Petronius' *Satyricon*. The world of Mrs. Charles Mackay, Mrs. Ogden Mills, Mrs. Mark Hopkins and other ladies of grandiose gestures and lots of money was hopefully turning East—toward the gleam of the great balls, fetes, galas and dinners on the Eastern seacoast, so different to them from the lives their husbands led in the parlor houses and sporting bordellos. On the surface the men attended to the demands of the forces of reform and morality. But the world in the evening often went visiting Nell Kimball's place, or sporting with R.J. as he showed off the town to visitors. For all their infidelities and weakening kidneys the sons of the forty-niners resented being dragged East; they had no wish to merge with true society, the *haut monde*.

("You don't get me into a monkey suit to kiss the ass of no duchess.")

It was no easy task the wives had set for themselves based on the buying power of the fortunes their menfolk had piled up. The East could perhaps teach them fine living under the Welsbach gas mantles or Mr. Edison's mazdas. Husbands and sons would refine their vices away from the Belshazzar's feasts of West Coast venison-and-turtle at Cliff House, and tone down their dependence on people of no impeccable character. Many did seem to forget the days of the washing of grandfather's one shirt in a mine shaft bucket, the long road they had traveled to the society columns.

The Mills, the Mackays, Huntingtons, Stanfords, Hearsts, other Western status seekers really saw a pattern set. Some were present as guests attending the great New York ball of the Bradley-Martins on a February night in 1897. It was the turning point in the social entertainment patterns of San Francisco life. No party from then on, no affair could have the proper exclusive flavor that didn't begin where the Bradley-Martin innovations left off. High echelon vulgarity at great cost dates from the year B-M 1.

The Bradley-Martins were of no great importance. A social historian has called them "well heeled parvenus from Troy, New York, who moved to town and perpetuated the slow growth of an imaginary hyphen." But revolutions are made by parvenus; old families don't man the barricades.

The Bradley-Martin ball excited society because of its extravagant cost, its maddening costumes, the notorious coverage given it by the mud-slinging yellow journals of Joseph Pulitzer, and William Randolph Hearst (neither were invited). It cost—this one bust-up hoot-and-holler of an evening at the old old Waldorf—the sum of $360,000 in nineteenth century dollars (to get today's value multiply by four and whistle).

An early stone-age press agent for the Bradley-Martins released certain items of the decor of the coming ball to alert the town. The Western millionaire guests began to design costumes and jewels to fit. "There are to be five mirrors on the north side of the ballroom richly but not heavily garlanded in curtain effect by mauve orchids and the feathery plemusa vine; garlands will be hung irregularly across the mirrors to loop onto the capitals of the columns separating the mirrors; the chandeliers on each column will be decorated with orchids and suspended from each chandelier will be a Rosalindlike pocket filled with Louis XVI roses and ferns. Roses will fall in showers over the balcony and will festoon the columns; not a space on the balcony, wall or column that will not be festooned, banked, showered with bride, American beauty and pink roses, or lilies of the valley or orchids. The profusion of mauve orchids will stream carelessly to the floor, like the untied bonnet strings of a thoughtless child."

38. One of the grand parties that could cause great talk.

Mrs. Bradley-Martin ordered four hundred two-horse carriages from O'Toole's livery stables so her guests would not keep their own coachmen up. Scores of police patrolled Fifth Avenue under the supervision of Theodore Roosevelt, Assistant New York Police Commissioner; detectives scrutinized the guests as if hunting bomb throwers. Inside was regal splendor: six thousand orchids in clusters illuminated by concealed electric bulbs. The 22nd Regiment Band of fifty musicians was only one of several orchestras. Supper from twelve to two-thirty was served by waiters in livery, knee breeches, powdered wigs. The feast included whole roast English suckling pig with trimmings. An ample buffet held tons of other goodies, and in an age of vast girths, the eating was a Byzantine fete, no calories barred. Rome in its decline, the press claimed, never guzzled more.

The newspapers of the world had a field day over all this luxury and it was termed in the press as "the depravity of the rich." Some samples: "The guests freely used cosmetics in making up for the ball. An estimate of the material so used ran to more than 500 pounds of rouge and blanc de perle, impalpable powder two and one half flour barrels, powder puffs that would make a bouquet ten feet high and six feet wide. The sermons that will be preached, the morals to be pointed . . . would fill many pages. . . ."

The *Herald* and the *Times* gave front pages to the ball. The *Herald's* account was cabled at James Gordon Bennett's order to the Paris edition. "It seemed exactly like a stately court function in one of the capitals of Europe, even to the liveried lackey who stood at the foot of Mrs. Bradley-Martin's dais and announced every guest by name, character represented and historical period in a loud tone."

The London *Daily Mail* announced: "Mrs. Bradley-Martin, we have every reason to believe, is dressed at this very moment in a train of black velvet lined with cerise satin, and a petticoat, if it is not indiscreet to say so, of white satin embroidered with flowers and arabesques of silver." The London *Chronicle* grew moral: "We congratulate . . . society on its triumph. It has cut out Belshazzar's feast and Wardour Street and Mme. Tussaud's and the Bank of England."

Ministers could scarcely wait to express their moral wrath. The Reverend Madison Peters preached a sermon: "The Use and Misuse of Wealth." "Sedition is born in the lap of luxury—so fell Rome, Thebes, Babylon and Carthage." Another pulpit in Brooklyn cried out: "God pity the shivering, starving poor these days and send a cyclone of justice upon the ball of selfishness." The guests from the West could hardly get back fast enough to San Francisco to do a little Bradley-Martining on their own.

The men whose newspapers blasted the party and its hosts most of all were Mr. Pulitzer and Mr. Hearst. Both were notorious party-givers. Hearst began and ended his gaudy, wonderful and slightly supercilious career with California party-giving. William Randolph Hearst, laconic and precise for pleasure, was the only son of Senator Hearst of silver mine fortunes. The Senator permitted Willie to have his own newspaper in San Francisco after he was bounced from Yale for painting the picture of the college president on the bottom of chamber pots. This gay life, never touched by austerity, was continued when he moved back West to settle in at the fabulous fairyland castle below San Francisco, San Simeon. He represented the last will to exalt among the heirs of the forty-niners and the Edwardians, the desire to live the very good life as a grandee, as a latter-day Magnifico.

For a full lifetime he sported a mistress as casually, indifferently and publicly as George IV or Francis I. Hearst collected overripe art by the warehouse; armor, Cellini gold work, importing whole castles and monasteries brick by brick and stone by stone, numbered and boxed and still unassembled to this day. His vast estate on the California coast, reached from San Francisco in those early days by boat, was the dream of many a railroad builder, gold and silver miner, real estate shark, land grabber, sly political hustler—the symbol of *how* to live well. Few had Hearst's courage, the splash and drive to follow him into the flamboyant, iridescent dream world of visible personal empire among the piñon pines and Pacific salt winds. Shrill-voiced as a tenor, petulant, lizard-eyed, and often bored, he tried everything—in the end even death, for which he found no price tag.

At the turn of the century San Francisco parties, while modeled on the best and biggest of the Eastern doings in New York City, Newport and Saratoga, had a Western flair and flavor all their own. They were less rigid; and one was never sure the hostess's mother hadn't come from a parlor house.

The parlor house was the accepted place for male pleasure (gloried in song and rather bad prose); establishments like the popular brothels of San Francisco caused no man any shame. A parlor house whore felt she had arrived in her trade. And if, as legend had it, she sent money home to her folks in Pittsburgh or Boston, bragging she had a good job, her little brothers proudly spread the news: "Sis is a whore in San Francisco!" Such was one American Dream.

Parlor girls were good-lookers, young, fresh, at ease in their specific environment. Most of them were farm girls, small-town misfits. Nell Kimball gives us some idea of how they entered the trade.

"I never liked procurers but used them when I had to. I liked a girl to be recommended to me by some madame I knew in Cleveland or Chicago or St. Louis. And I'd pay the girl's way out and see to her gowns and underwear. But that wasn't always possible in San Francisco. The people who saw to the collecting of the young stock from the surrounding towns all along the peninsula had to be watched. I didn't take or want drugged girls, heavy drinkers, or girls with bruises all over them. A good whore has to want to be a whore, or she's no credit to the place. The trouble with forced girls is they usually lead to trouble. Besides there was never any real shortage of willing girls who wanted to be whores. The whole white slave story-telling is very much the malarky. It's true the Italians and the Eastern European ponces have an underground railroad to bring in girls attracted by promises of stage work or governess jobs and so are lured into the trade, but I never dealt much with them. At least not until the rage for red-headed Jew girls took on in the town. Most of the Jew girls were snappy but willing and a great many of them soon became madames. They learned quickly, and they gave a john the act he was impressing them, driving them mad with his abilities as a man. Jews I found always deliver what they promise.

"Most of the girls who went into the parlor houses had found themselves in the city, hungry, no job, no rent money, clothes getting tattered. There might be some mack talking to them, seducing them, but not as often as you'd think. The girls would soon get the truth about working in a parlor house. There never was much problem in getting them to see the advantages of a good house and a square deal. All the rest is bleeding heart sentimentality by people who don't know whores.

"I don't say—never did—that whoring is the best way of life, but it's sure better than going blind in a sweat shop sewing, or twenty hours work as a kitchen drudge, or housemaid, with the old man and the sons always laying for you in the hallways. Wages were low for women in the town, and no one had much respect for a girl who had to work. Believe me, it's the Good People who exploit poor girls who make a lot of whores. So in many ways the parlor house did have a good side for the girls; seeing and enjoying things different from their mothers bent over a hot stove all day, a half dozen dirty-nosed kids dragging at her skirts, and a husband who never bathed, treating her like a breeding sow till he often began eyeing his daughters. I don't know if this kind of talk by me is shocking, but I've lived a coon's age by these ideas, and if it hasn't been a life bedded down in roses, I'm hale and hearty, not on my way to the poor house or dead in some city hospital charity ward before my time. Or living the brutal life my three sisters had, who married mean farmers back home and were physical wrecks before thirty, old toothless hags at forty.

"A lot of the parlor girls were once singers, dancers, entertainers, who didn't have the real touch of talent for that work; and so it was easy for them to drift into a house, kidding themselves all the way they'd be out of it as soon as they put by a bit of cold cash and could buy new costumes and music. But few did. They were lazy, dreamy, and failures they knew on the stage. So they treated their lives as a kind of play and never admitted they were full time whores. As a whore is acting almost all the time with a client, they were in their own business in some way.

"Love didn't have much to do with becoming a whore. Some find it a sentimental way to look at it—a girl ruined for love of a stud—but mostly it was a desire for an easy lazy life, an outlaw feeling too of being against the snide smug society outside. Usually it all comes down to economics; a place to earn food and clothing and a little on the side for a bit of luxury. I wouldn't say they had much schooling; I didn't. A lot were knotheads, chowder brains, who had to take their shoes off to add up anything over ten. But I've seen educated whores too, who read books and played opera on the victrola and could talk to a john about painting and things like Greece and Japanese prints or Caruso or John Drew. These intelligent women were usually very unhappy, and very much in fear of the world outside. They liked being isolated, crossing the bar as it were of their respectability. They drank more too, some sniffed snow [cocaine], some went in for Lesbian games. I didn't much like that, but if they were quiet and didn't ruin the other girl as a tart I had to accept it. In my world you never feel you're any better or less a mess than the next person. Smarter, sure, that's all."

"A girl who wasn't a fool and didn't keep a ponce or pimp who beat her and got her into drugs, who didn't drink too much, could last a half dozen years in a good parlor house. I had a fine Polish girl, Reba, who was with me twelve years and in the end ran the best and biggest house in Easton in Pennsylvania after she left me.

"But the whore who led a happy normal life, so called, after some years in the trade was the rare exception. Only two girls in my house in the years I was in S.F.—and I suppose I had about two hundred girls coming and going—really made a good life for themselves on the other side of my double oak doors.

"Mollie was the daughter of a railroad track layer, and at first so much a country goose when she walked in cold she had to be taught not to look for corn husks to wipe her ass. She learned fast. The rich college boys were always asking for her and she liked them. After two years Mollie told me: 'I'm going to get married. I'm going to make something of my Goddamn shanty life.' I told her once a girl gets used nicely by a rich john young or old, it's not easy to go out and marry some smelly longshoreman or gandy dancer [railroad worker]. Mollie would dress in her best duds on her day off, neat, not too flashy—she did have a weakness for feathers and she'd 'lose' her gloves six or seven times a day in the lobby of the plushiest downtown vaudeville theatres. This way, through the finders, she met several actors and orchestra men. But she knew the type and didn't googoo-eye them. One day she came to me, blue eyes so wide open they'd hold silver dollars. 'I've met him. Rich, handsome, and it's the ring, parson and all, believe you me.'

"I said to be sure he wasn't on the con, a get-rich-quick gold brick seller, or recruiting for South American brothels. He turned out to be as Mollie said, in shipping, lumber, green houses and fruit groves. They eloped—didn't try to make it a big event in his church in Pasadena, as who knew how many of the deacons had come to S.F. to frolic with Mollie and get joint-copped. Mollie did fine in society; served tea without lifting her pinkie, had a raft of kids. Her husband was a political power behind the dummies who got into California public office. In time what was the real hoi poiloi society in Pasadena was led by my Mollie."

(I have edited Nell Kimball's text here as she fully identified Mollie's husband's family. Today Mollie's grandchildren are the top society leaders of the coast, grand patrons of art museums, music centers, public events, charity foundations.)

"The other whore who did well for herself was a small wirey kid who always looked hungry—she was a lunger—[TB] looked more like a boy than a girl and for that reason I suppose she appealed to the shy johns and those who wanted to warm up to the idea they were protecting and loving a child, both at the same time. Emma wasn't even a good looker, but she had her steady trade of clients who came only to take her upstairs. She saved her money, bought lots and land in Oakland, was always looking at the stock market reports, and I know in three years she had savings bank books she told me she kept in a wop bank on Montgomery Street, not in a carpet bag or suitcase as most of the girls did. She left me giving me a carved cameo broach of some Roman heads set in a gold pin with pearls round it. Emma married an old man who was in the Panamint silver mine strikes with Senators William Stewart and John Percival Jones, and he died leaving her some few million dollars. Off went Emma, stylish as at a lodge funeral, to Europe, owning by then several big downtown business buildings. She never did come back to America. I heard now and then from her; she didn't drop out of my life like all the others did. I'd get cards and it would read Egypt or Lisbon, or Oslo or London on the postmark. She had no family—had no use for the human race. I suppose cats and dogs got those millions. You find people who over-love animals, see life as a lot of kennel turds.

"Two girls out of maybe two hundred making something of themselves is not a good average. Most girls after six years in a house have to become street hookers, grabbing elbows, whispering spicy offers. A parlor house girl could be an earner and saver, but usually wasn't. I liked to pay a girl a percentage of her earnings—one half of all the cash the john paid for his ride. Some houses paid less and some charged up to forty, fifty dollars a week for food, room, laundry, and the girl kept the rest. It was easy to cheat them either way. A lot did. I liked my system best. Some low houses just paid a girl a salary of say twenty-five dollars a week. You couldn't get a really good whore for that kind of pay. You're just buying meat— and that's what the client is most likely getting away from at home.

"Some houses had a cash register in the hall, and the customer paid, and had it rung up in advance, and the girl got a brass check to be turned in at the end of the week to show how many tricks [clients] she'd turned. Not in my place. I asked for payment in advance—it avoids scenes and bargaining—but I'd simply pin a bit of blue ribbon on the girl's kimona or robe, like a little flower, for a one shot, a yellow ribbon for a guest staying the night and a green

39. *Waiting at a fashionable brothel for the guests to come in.*

one if he was hiring the third floor for an exotic show for himself or some friends. It was dainty and decorative and no girl could match the ribbons and beat me as I imported them from Hamburg. What a girl really sells is an illusion; the idea the john is *some* guy and she's just crackers for his kind of kip work. I tell them the ribbons are like gold stars for effort and improvement.

"The real trouble in the life of the girls were the men they loved, the mack or loafer they kept in belted jackets and brown derbys, in cigars, whisky, gambling joints or drugs. The girl had a day off each week and she'd be off in a breeze of bath powder and her perfume to drink and cavort with the bum. It didn't do her any good and she often got a mouse hung on her [black-eye] or had a tooth knocked loose. Physical violence is a form of love, I suppose. We proved it nightly on the third floor. But their day off was their affair.

"Most houses worked the girl from noon till morning. But I kept a house that didn't open till nine at night unless some favorite customer called and wanted to drop over after dinner (as lunch was called in those days) or had some men friends in tow and wanted a quiet place to drink and look at pretty things. Otherwise Harry, my house man and strong arm, didn't open the doors till nine. Then Teeny, the nigrah maid, put on her cap to answer the knocker. I had no red light, no bell, and unless you came with someone I knew, no dice.

"A good house girl could make from a hundred and fifty to two hundred and fifty a week. And be broke the next week, if as usual she was mooched on by her guy. Most were. The girls were sentimental slobs; most whores are in their private lives. They get the hump hung on them over being lonely and not wanted if they have no man of their own. Usually too, they are undersexed, or have lost any real feeling except for some tin horn pimp."

> Serene indifferent of Fate
> Thou sittest at the Golden Gate.
> *Bret Harte*

San Francisco—as it sittest or not—tried hard for respectability, but liveliness kept breaking through. The days of the *caballeros* were gone, the *meriendas* (picnics) no longer included horsemanship and roping wildcat and coyote. On the hills called Telegraph, Russian (after a group of Russian sailors who died of scurvy in port and were buried there), Twin Peaks, Lone Mountain, a society had been breeding itself away from the washtubs, brothels and miners' shacks ever since the forty-niners of that miserable song married the Barbary Coast whores.

Actually there were many families there of a much swankier origin. The escapades of Lily Hitchcock are still remembered and two monuments she left behind are still there for all to see. Lily came to San Francisco at the age of eight in 1851. She was the daughter of an eminent army doctor and the family became socially important. Lily grew into a strikingly handsome and what in those days was called a *dashing* girl and today perhaps is called delinquent. She was a firehouse buff, as familiar in the Knickerbocker Fire Company Number Five as the spotted coach dog and the great horses that pulled the belching steam-fed pumper. She was always attending fires on the run when she should have been at a ball or some local social affair. She did appear at one ball in her red fireman's shirt and helmet, wearing the red and black colors of Company Number Five, having been made an honorary member of the Knickerbockers long after the dreams of an adolescent usually had faded. Before she was twenty years of age Lily had been engaged to twenty men. Dressed in men's clothes she was seen at cockfights shouting for some feathered champion chicken. She played poker with noted gamblers and had a keen eye for an inside draw and a royal flush. Historians give only skimpy details of her romantic involvements or impetuous moments, and so we can only guess, and feel we had better not, beyond saying she craved emotional stimulus all her life.

As the 1860s passed and she still followed the fire bells there did seem to be one man who felt he could marry the ecstatic, irrational fun lover. His name was Howard Coit. After Lily became Mrs. Coit the bets were down in the city as to how long it would last. It didn't last long; she had an incurable side to her existence. And so Lily was off to Europe to lead a life a little less polite and dull than Henry James was writing about Americans living abroad. Many regretted her leaving, remembering the balls she had given which featured the best people *and* prizefighters and firemen friends. Lily came back from time to time to a suite in the Palace Hotel, surviving into middle age on vitality and the idea that the extreme is a true expression of universal significance. She was sixty years of age when one day a shot rang out in her suite and a man named McClung stepped out, mortally wounded. He had shielded Lily from an Alexander Garnett, who had come at her with a pistol, and Mr. McClung (who had survived the Civil War on the rebel side) had neatly caught the bullet, intended for Lily, with his chest. He died and Lily took another trip to Europe. No clear explanation of the reason for the shooting was ever given. Lily returned to San Francisco in her eighties and died in the Palace Hotel, leaving a fund of one hundred thousand dollars to build the Coit Tower, which dominates San Francisco—as R.J. put it—"like a phallic mockery at Lily's city." She also left funds to erect in Columbus Square a statue to her true love, the fire laddies of her youth. The statue depicts a group—firemen rescuing a little child. Some think the child's features are modeled on Lily Hitchcock Coit's own features, when perhaps she realized that moments of snatched happiness are the only true happiness.

Lily accented the fashion for imported clothes. But if the madams or girls of the Coast bought cloth and had dresses made at the town's two best shops. City of Paris and the White House (in those simple days they were still called *dry goods stores*), they would do so after hours, for the two shops were the places for the best people to pick out the silks and satins, the buttons and bangles, and have the dressmaking departments of the store run them up. Some of the railroad kings' wives might import a gown or frock or coat of fur from abroad like Lily, but most of them used the two local *bon tons*.

The wife of Ambrose Bierce was seen at the City of Paris fingering heavy silk while her husband (whose life she made a hell) was often away in some country inn, claiming the fog of the city was bad for his asthma. The wit and cynic had a hard load to bear besides the shrew at home—he mourned his son, shot to death in a low saloon brawl. Like the society at the top of the fashionable hills, even Bierce could not escape the infection from the Coast.

One runs across little footnotes to the scenes that bring the old town and its active citizens back to life. A Mr. Lankman was killed by a heavy beer schooner flung at him by Ellen Londaine in 1875, resulting in a city ordinance barring women from saloons after dark. A horse car ran over a Mary Ann Whalen, which hardly seems hit-and-run driving, for the horses pulled the cars at a steady three miles an hour.

The better hotels did their best to tame society with decor, music and Mr. Edison's lights: The Lock House, Occidental, Russ House, the Commercial, Lucky Baldwin's Baldwin, which was both hotel and theater. (Anna Held played there in 1898 in *The Gay Deceiver*, and a theater critic on the *Examiner* raved: "A rare bit of feminine bric-a-brac.")

Ned Greenway's Friday Night Cotillions were famous at twenty dollars a couple for five balls, music by the Fourth Artillery Band. Ned was the town's social dictator and he sneered at rival ball givers: Mrs. Monroe Salisbury's Friday Fortnightly, and Ynez Shorb White's New Cotillion Club. But the young sparks and the daughters of the house, in dimity and silk with Gibson Girl piled-up curls, escaped to what were called "chippy balls" at public dance halls and met people from the Tenderloin and the Coast; at times society's long-suffering countenance sagged. By 1903 it could be reported—with a bit of shock—two ladies were seen smoking cigarettes in public in the lobby of the Palace. Worldly and celebrated visitors were coming to the city. Sarah Bernhardt came from France to an eight room suite with her pet parrot, which cursed in elegant French (*"en flagrant delit!"*), and a baby tiger, which she led on a leash. She starred in Sardou's *Fédora* and denied to the press she had kicked a loaded tray out of the hands of a waiter. She came back twice more to San Francisco, but kicked no more trays, having had to have a leg amputated. A local showman cabled her asking at what price she'd let him exhibit the leg; and Sarah cabled back, "Which leg?"

Trixie Friganza came bubbling into town showing both her legs and her best points and singing a ditty to the town:

> Still an armful, all that a man can hold!
> There's no danger of anyone catching cold
> From a girl in San Francisco!

The city did have a reputation of producing wild girls from good families, Isadora Duncan and her family went hungry in their cheesecloth Greek underwear costumes and invented dances that were soon to be the shocking sensation of Europe. But the town, though ignoring Isadora Duncan, had a big welcome for Lillian Russell, who by the turn of the century had taken on weight and more delightful curves in Gargantuan eating contests with Diamond Jim Brady and other millionaires who liked to see a girl eat her fill. When she appeared with a Weber and Fields show a local critic called her "Airy Fairy Lillian," which was hardly true in her hearty eating stage. She carried a Japanese terrier which she claimed was worth ten thousand dollars, and shrugged her shoulders at her stage career: "Swinging cheap music is hell." And asked where she could get a real *rare* steak.

The city retained a perceptiveness, a cocky self-reliance. There was never any iron curtain drawn between the San Franciscans trying to create a society and the low life of the Tenderloin and the Coast. There was seepage *both* ways. The husbands and sons would drift down to the waterfront with male guests to visit the cabarets, the Bella Union, or a favorite brothel. And a bright girl working for Nell Kimball with the right dash and endearing charms could marry a millionaire not too far removed from his hard days, and end up on Nob Hill.

THE BIG BIG FOUR

You got to cross that lonesome valley,
You got to cross hit by yo'self,
They hain't no one goin' cross hit for you.

No greater human circus was ever lived out on the coast than the lives and doings of the four men who began as shopkeepers and ended up as the railroad kings of San Francisco. They built the great mansions on Nob Hill, and through their control of the Central Pacific Railroad empire, ranches, vineyards and much else they were the town and the state and often the nation in that last half of a turbulent century. They were sinners in their own way, and certainly spenders of vast sums beyond the dreams of earlier robber barons.

Collis P. Huntington was the giant among them, smarter, harder, meaner, more alert to the chance of the moment, the sense of what was to be exploited and how to grab it. But all had the gift.

The most public figure was the partner called Leland Stanford. Of him one adoring historian of the period said: "At an earlier era he would have been a Christ or a Confucius." Another let it go merely as: "The greatest man in the world today." To balance all this partner Huntington called Stanford "a damned old fool" and his own lawyer said Stanford had "the spite of a peanut vendor." At least he came with labels even if they were in conflict.

He was big and bulky, slow-voiced, and he never made his mind up quickly as to what he had to say, so speaking with him was like drawing teeth. He built a huge redwood mansion on Nob Hill. Of the four partners he was the only one who wanted to be loved; he was always running for public office, beginning with justice of the peace in a tent camp of miners, on to alderman, state treasurer, governor and senator. Usually he bought the office, and when a friend was asked the cost of the senator's office he replied, "Not a cent less than a hundred thousand."

Stanford saw God through the eyes of a Unitarian Methodist and paid a bribe of ten thousand a year to an editor to get kind words said about himself. At twenty-eight he was in San Francisco, married to the daughter of another storekeeper. He began his life there with a love of display he never outgrew. Often stupid and ruthless, he was always full of self-justification.

Stanford's mansion had high marble steps, a circle-shaped hallway seventy feet high with black marble signs of the zodiac set in the floor. There was the usual hothouse conservatory of the newly rich who were awed at seeing a pineapple grow; an East Indies room where hymns and waltzes were celebrated in a misty Victorian elegance, aided by birds brought in from the aviary. Cotillions, mahogany escritoires, vases (pronounced with a soft a). None of the fun of the Tenderloin or the wildness of the Barbary Coast invaded the house. The Stanfords hardly went in for any light touch in living and were far from being connoisseurs or bon vivants.

Leland Stanford called himself a horse breeder rather than a railroad man and he felt every home should have copies of famous paintings. He didn't bother with originals if cleaner copies were at hand. However he did insist on a private railroad car, all gold and silver trim, with teak and stained glass and marble washbasins. When he toured the line in it, at all crossings the working staff, road menders, yardmen, engine drivers and clerks had to stand at attention and salute as the special ran by carrying Mr. Leland Stanford along the right of way.

He had extravagant drives toward limitless spending, building the California Street Cable Railway up to his hilltop home so guests could get off at his front door from a cable car. But his most fantastic money outlay was his Palo Alto Farm, 9,000 acres

40. *A Stanford horse always got the best of care.*

with two racetracks on it, 60 acres of trotting park, 150 hired hands, 60 stallions always at stud or ready for it, 250 brood mares, 250 colts and fillies for whom he grew 60 acres of carrots for their nibbling.

He paid thirty thousand dollars for his horse Piedmont, and from the father of Franklin D. Roosevelt he bought a horse named Gloster that was killed in a train wreck (causing some talk of how badly the rail lines were kept in repair, "Not even fit for a horse, let alone human beings").

Stanford's interest in horses resulted in his hiring a camera expert named Eadweard Muybridge to try to discover if a horse kept all its feet off the ground at a certain time in its running pace. With a series of cameras set off by trip cords, Muybridge proved that at a certain moment it did. And in doing so he practically invented the motion picture. Muybridge published the results in a book called *The Horse in Motion.* . . . There were certain delays, however, in Muybridge's work for Stanford. The cameraman murdered his wife's lover but he was set free on the old cry of being a husband betrayed, protecting his honor and his home—in that order. Muybridge also photographed a series of nude girls in motion, but not for Stanford, who preferred fillies with four legs. The very rich with no deep-seated vices had a difficult time to keep from being bored.

Stanford had a deep adherence to a formal order and he poured millions into planting three million rare French grapevines at Vina, California, a town he built. He also imported Gallic vintners who promised wines as good as anything bottled in France. The Stanford brandy was sealed in oak kegs and sent on four year sea voyages around the world in sailing ships; the cradling swish of the sea was to age the liquor properly. However the whole scheme collapsed because the climate and the soil were wrong for good wines. It was all inspired audacity with no common sense behind it.

The four partners were not breeders of dynasties. Two were to remain childless, and only one, Crocker, to spawn a surviving brood. The Stanfords seemed barren, then after twenty years of marriage they suddenly produced Leland, Jr., in 1868. He was at once marked for educating in art, music, languages, and actually did turn out to be an expert wood carver of planks. The family traveled to give the child an ardent and idyllic interest in the better things. But the wry role of destiny, unimpressed with rich hopes, killed the boy at sixteen by typhoid in Florence, Italy, a city deadly and unhomogenized in those days with no British and American germ-destroyers. It was a cruel blow and unsettled the parents' minds.

All hopes of a dynasty shattered, the Stanfords turned to table-rapping as a means of reaching the dead. It was a spiritualist, Maude Lord Drake, who claimed divine origin, and who suggested the Stanfords found a college as a memorial to their dead son. Maude Lord Drake was later exposed as a fraud during a table-tapping session, and the college today doesn't care to talk about its founding spirit, claiming it's all a legend. It isn't. Stanford University was opened in October of 1891 and present was a young man named Herbert Hoover, not deficient in hopes of great wealth himself.

Someone suggested the college gates be marked with the words: WITH APOLOGIES TO GOD. The dedication song was "We Give Thee but Thine Own." Ambrose Bierce was not impressed and as usual spelled the donor's name as £eland $tanford.

Stanford spent most of his old age playing with his big toy, a mechanical orchestra for guests, or tuning on his tin birds, whose clockwork insides produced bird songs. It all suggests a life situated in stability, saturated in tedious pomposity.

All three Stanfords lie buried together today on the campus of Stanford University, as if keeping watch on the doings of students and officials. The beat and hip student generation calls it "The Tomb of the Holy Family" and drops gum wrappers in homage. The dead hardly deserve this; their natures were generous even if grim.

"Uncle" Mark Hopkins was the frugal partner. He didn't drink, didn't smoke, and having a tender gut lived off vegetables which he grew and hoed himself in a little garden while living in a thirty dollar a month cottage even after he was worth twenty million dollars. He was lean, long, cautious, yet a man who ran with wild speculators. He was called "the stubbornest man alive." It was bet-

ter, some said, than having no reputation at all. Hopkins hated
waste and was a string saver, an old paper hoarder, and around the
railroad shops was always picking up bolts, nails and other junk.
He lit his cottage with a coal oil lamp and never frittered away his
time or his money.

At forty-one Hopkins married his cousin Mary. She was twenty
and they never produced a child. It was she who began to spend
the millions on the then bleak Nob Hill, which she saw as a place
for mansions. Railroad crews built huge stone walls to hold the
land in place and an inventor of San Francisco, a Mr. Hallidie
and his wire cables, which he saw pulling cars up San Francisco's
steep hills, made the place livable. The California Street Cable Railway was up there by 1876 and was of very practical use to the
partners and their mansions.

Mary Hopkins was what used to be called a "constant reader."
She was floating in a romantic sea of bad novels, and no doubt the
prose of Bulwer-Lytton and Ouida affected her view of life. Totally
immersed in their mushy world she designed herself a castle on Nob
Hill, all towers, gables, steeples, bumps and medieval doohickies.
Uncle Mark chewed his vegetables and said little, as if observing
secret obscenities. He got for his money a Palace of the Doges drawing room, carved English oak dining room (to hold sixty guests),
a master bedroom of ebony, ivory and inset jewels. Also a library for
the reading of poetry, where Browning and Tennyson could be
heard by the fastidious and worthy, looking out over the San
Francisco rooftops. Mockers called the monstrosity the Hotel de
Hopkins. Old Uncle Mark, rheumatic, wispy as an apparition, sipped
his vegetable juices and decided it was too grandiose a place to die
in. He passed on in a train in his sleep and was interred in a rose
marble mausoleum costing $150,000. He was a man—someone said
at the grave site—who liked to know the price of things.

His widow became "America's Richest Widow" and she kicked
up her sensible heels and liked the title. She was fifty and still reading novels when she began to build romantic houses all over the
country. A château modeled on Chamboard at East Barrington cost
her two million, and how San Francisco's society boggled its eyes

at that. Mary Hopkins didn't flinch. She was imperious and dictatorial and had a burlesque set of eccentricities that the town enjoyed all through her addled widowhood. After all it already had Emperor Norton, and here was a woman who alone owned a quarter interest in a great railroad system and was acting like the Red Queen in *Alice*.

One day a young man called on her. He was twenty-eight and he asked to see Mary Hopkins' furniture. He was simply *mad* about wood and form. His name was Edward T. Searles, by love and profession an interior decorator. The two hit it off at once in a spontaneity of delight and spent the day caressing chairs and fingering draperies. Mary Hopkins and Searles shared three pleasant years of courting furniture, eyeing cabinets and unrolling rugs. Then they were married in 1882. And didn't that tie San Francisco society into knots of laughter at the happy couple! But it was a successful marriage and the pleased wife watched her young husband move the furniture around and change it back again the next day, adjusting bric-a-brac in scented sweat and wondering if the sofa would not look better *there* and the drapes perhaps in a more puce tone of orange? Happiness is after all the avoidance of the formidable obstacle of boredom.

After nearly ten years of contented marriage among furniture polish and Louis XII chairs Mary Hopkins Searles died, leaving her vast railroad fortune to her husband, Edward Searles.

An adopted son of Mark Hopkins at once took the will to court, and Searles on the stand had to admit he had married as the result of "no love match." In a later statement he gallantly changed it to "for love and riches." The case was settled out of court for eight or ten million dollars, and Edward T. Searles retired to peace among the Chippendale. As for the Hopkins mansion, in time it was torn down and the Mark Hopkins Hotel arose; the Top of the Mark, which became known as "The Swinging Mark." No ghost— as far as we know—arose from the pink marble tomb to ask them to cool it, man, cool the scene.

Charles Crocker was the angry man of the railroad combine, the outdoor man who spent his time on horseback and in labor camps and on work trains getting the actual railroad built. At his best he weighed more than 230 pounds, and he didn't mind being known as a crude fellow. He and his partners had divergent designs for living.

When it came his turn to build a mansion on Nob Hill, he knew damn well what he wanted; something called "Early Renaissance," which in San Francisco turned out to be a woodworkers' heaven, a debauch of intricate scrollwork never seen before in such size and profusion. It cost a million and a half to saw and put together. It had a 76 foot tower in which gossips said there were outlets for pouring down hot lead on any mob that dared storm it. It certainly had a fantastic panoramic view, and the opening of its 172 foot facade in 1876 to selected guests was a city event. It was also the host's silver wedding anniversary.

Crocker was like most self-made rich men, illiterate and aching for social status as an art collector. (The art game has now moved down to Los Angeles.) He owned "*the* Crocker Meissonier on the coast!" Actually the Americans were buying the wrong French dwarf (Meissonier could walk under a tall table). The other dwarf of real genius, Toulouse Lautrec, they couldn't see for beans, until San Francisco's Stein family (Gertrude among them) got to Paris.

Crocker overate, overworked, overshouted, and in a sloughing collapse he died in a diabetic coma. His name is remembered today as half the title of a bank. Like most of his partners he lived in an immediate urgency, with a formidable vitality that ran out on him.

With Collis P. Huntington, he of the inexhaustible copiousness— we come to the true giant of the combine, even if the historian Arthur McEwen recorded that Huntington had "no more soul than a shark." Another insisted Collis P. Huntington *did* have principles . . . "he was scrupulously dishonest." This didn't bother Huntington; he had his goals and he had his ideas of what the world was and how one tamed it. Huntington was a grim New Englander who had no use for what he noted as the imbecilities of philanthropy, politics, high society. He would chuckle and say, "I'll never be remembered for the money I give away. . . . You can't follow me through life by the quarters I've dropped."

Impressive by his coldness and a sly dishonesty on principle, yet he had a weakness against seeing birds shot at as a sport. He had bursts of profanity, usually let loose against rich fools who lived it up in the Tenderloin and even descended to the Barbary Coast for kicks. He was "bald as an American eagle on our dollar . . . with the paunch of a marsupial . . ." Indoors he wore a black tight-fitting cap, and in public he seldom took off his hat. He collected very bad paintings and it was said, "his view on architecture was that of a Digger Indian."

Huntington used his brains early and kept them alert until old age. He was born a Connecticut tinker and pot mender's son in 1821. As a hired hand and petty dealer he saved money and made it to California in 1850, aged twenty-nine, and already a merchant skilled by trade along the way. He had started out—a non-drinker— with a few kegs of whisky and was soon setting up stores for the miners' trade. His whole idea was "quick turnover, large profits." No cost study system, sales charting, computer figures, have yet improved on the Huntington money machine.

He was a strong healthy man and from two hundred pounds in youth he went to over two hundred and fifty in old age with the paunch the cartoonists made even bigger. He began by cornering the shovel market in a mining country, in time the blasting powder kegs, the bar iron. He spent no time in melancholy contemplation on ethics. Waste raised his hackles.

If the four partners lacked anything it was a sensual desire for women, whisky, gambling at tables, the delights of orgy, the spending of time in sinful passions. Their lack of children in almost all cases may show they didn't much indulge in the one common domestic sport. ("Sex is the poor man's polo.") Huntington insisted that his clerks lead a pious celibate life. He permitted no whoring or drinking by his young men, and dismissal was instant for anyone seen in a gambling house or brothel. He accepted the business of the sporting houses but he would not let his clerks deliver late hour orders at a knocking shop; perhaps he sensed any male might be tempted by the cry, "Liberty Hall! Company girls!" He impressed on his young men his belief that a formal education was wasted and friendship could be a dangerous thing. "I ran in a crowd by myself." Like Prometheus's fire, for Huntington life must be stolen.

He had a certain powerful tenacity and native shrewdness and failed only in his taste for sleazy *objets d'art* and embalming-house decor. He was a trashy connoisseur of paintings—as most rich are who "know what they like." But he knew he believed in Collis P. Huntington against the world, and if it came to that he'd even bargain with God. "I know I shall reach 110." (One can almost hear Jehovah chuckling.)

He married at age twenty-three, and later when he asked his wife to join him in California, he was sure Elizabeth was his kind of mate. What he wanted from a woman was full self-effacement. She was good at that; never was able to give him children.

Huntington felt sad about not starting a direct line of heirs; he marked out as his crown prince another hard case, his nephew, Henry Edward Huntington. Henry was perhaps too showy, and old Huntington wondered about that. For himself he simply sat among his innocuous paintings, hundreds of them, proud they hadn't cost more than half a million. No French chef for him; he kept a low-paid Chinese cook, as he said, "who didn't waste a thing."

When Elizabeth died, not attracting attention to her going, but being missed enough to be pronounced dead, a few months later, in 1884, Huntington married at the age of sixty-three an ambitious matron from Alabama, complete with a fearful magnolia-scented accent and a stepson who at sixteen weighed two hundred and twenty pounds and was growing.

Huntington still ran the railroads, the business enterprise his partners should have helped with. But they were high society now, just lazy old men. He hated Stanford, the political slob. Although Huntington gave money to educate Negroes as blacksmiths and tool workers, he insisted Negro education was folly. "What will they do with the education after they get it? No place for them to use it." All social theory he considered *philosophique merdeure*.

Collis P. Huntington outlived the public exposure of his famous letters about the bribing of courts of justice and government, as they were read out in a court case that he felt should not have come to trial. He should never have trusted in writing a man he thought was his friend, and who was asked to destroy the so-revealing texts.

Huntington died in 1901 and the obituary column of the San Francisco *Examiner* stated he was as "ruthless as a crocodile," unaware perhaps that the crocodile was worshiped in Egypt once as a very wise god.

The widow Huntington was not left unconsoled. Collis's nephew, Henry Edward, married her. He was sixty-three and a maniac collector of old paper and old paintings, hopelessly infected with the collector's disease. He simply had to have *every* great book ever printed, vital letters, documents, maps and prints, drawings and paintings that went with historic events. There was no real reason for all this. It was hardly even social status seeking; he didn't give a damn about that. It was a colossal greed to possess what others couldn't afford—to pile up things he would never read, in many cases items he'd never see. It was some guilt-haunted ambition to stem a seepage of self-confidence by plugging it with the paper of greater minds.

Where his uncle had looted the nation, built rail lines, bribed and bought law and government, Henry Edward looted castles, libraries, seized collections with his checkbook and made those pirates called book and art dealers grow richer and greedier than ever; sneering at him from a safe distance.

Henry Edward, fleeing San Francisco, bought the San Marino Ranch at the Pasadena city limits, and from here, in a marble library and art gallery, he gutted the markets of the world for yellowing paper, vellum, parchment and canvas. No hereditary collection was safe from the power of his purse. In those cheap days when prices were a fraction of what they are now, in time he paid out thirty million dollars. He knew, it was said, "the brute force of money." The last stage of maniac collecting is moral and spiritual bankruptcy. . . . Midden building is all. Higher grew the piles of

41. *Growing up rich in California was a splendid thing—nobody hated money.*

incunabula, Elizabethan editions, documents, paintings by minor society schools of art, second-rate Gainsboroughs, black Reynoldses, lesser lights, a few samples of Turner, Hogarth, but best known are the insipid "Blue Boy" and the banal "Pinkie."

Henry Edward Huntington did not use his old age as Collis had for billiards and whist, and even (horrors, for the principles of his youth) for cigars and snorts of strong brandy. Nor did Henry Edward plan for himself a quarter million dollar mausoleum into which his uncle's remains had gone to dust like any ordinary mortal. Henry Edward made his pack rat collections of rare items over into a trust, for the public to be able to walk his grounds, stare at the items kept for view under thick glass. And he endowed it all with eight million dollars.

The gardens are still lovely, but the hired hands who run the enterprise are not too helpful if one really wants to see the collection. One runs into excuses: *that* section not hung just yet; *those* are still in sortage; *that* is not for examination or display. One senses in the snide atmosphere a kind of distaste at the idea that Henry Edward should have let the damned rabble in to see costly things a multi-millionaire ought to keep only for his own pleasure in the massing of incunabula he could not read or care for.

Joe Duveen, the sly pope of art dealers to the forty-niners and their heirs, peddler to the descendants of men who drove the Central and Union Pacific to the sea, never let up selling status fantasies, the value of positions money could buy by embracing Art. Most of what he sold is now considered second rate. When Huntington first saw the "Blue Boy," he felt it was "too green." Duveen said that was the light, and when next it was shown it had a fine new blue glaze on it.

As Henry Edward Huntington lay dying in his California palace, Duveen had a model made of a fantastic tomb for the old collector. He had it carried in on the shoulders of four men to show Huntington how a Pacific Coast Medici should properly be laid away. But Huntington was too far gone to complete this final deal—God was driving for the jugular, and accepting no bribes.

Book Five

THE BEST PEOPLE AND THE WORST PEOPLE

20

MORALS AND MANNERS

Come live with me and be my Love,
And we will all the pleasures prove.
Marlowe

The decadence of this inexhaustible city in the years of which we write had a unique sexual rhythm. Fluid yet chaotic in its pleasures —a great deal of this was the result of the prominence of the whore and the prodigious appetites of the port visitors and its citizens for her favors. While there were susceptible women in the town's own social hierarchy, the harlot seemed to get most of the trade in unchanneled sensibility and the desire for the satisfaction of away-from-home emotional *and* physical drives.

Looking back at the times our modern writers and film makers cast a glow of romance, some kind of irrelevant provocativeness over the prostitute on the American frontier, and the early years of our Western cities. Perhaps Mr. Greeley should have said, "Go West, young harlot." Many today submit to the myth that the heroic ages are always in the past, our own times disintegrate beneath our feet—*only* our fathers knew heroes, or their fathers before them. San Francisco is very prone to this kind of grotesque thinking, dreaming of the pathos of perished beauty, even if only of a crib whore or a parlor house slut.

It is hard to convince anyone of the anomalies and miseries of these girls; self-depreciating women peddling reciprocal love on a cash-in-hand basis, ready to satisfy at any time what society called—in those days—"perverse human impulses."

Let us try to look at the true cadence and color of the Bay city whore in the nineteenth century, at the cocotte, the Chinese slave, the false Parisian gamine, and in most cases just some native well-set-together girl, neither forced nor beaten into her life but propelled by some lack of will, an adolescent assertiveness, a unmoral insensitivity. As one old madam put it, making a sales point, "Every woman is sitting on a fortune if she only knew it." Hardly a fortune as a girl found out—in what is after all a morbid degrading trade in our guilt-ridden social order.

Yet San Francisco, being further away from the New England morality of the puritan past, took its tolerance of the strumpet and the sporting house from a more historic view. Say from the Middle Ages when prostitution was tolerated, "the caprice of the passions" being recognized as a necessary evil. There was even Saint Augustine: "Suppress prostitution and capricious lusts will overthrow society." Saint Thomas Aquinas in his *Summa Theologica* wrote: "Prostitution in the towns is like the cesspool in the palace. Do away with the cesspool, and the palace will become an unclean place."

Not that the bordello madams or the city fathers were given to reading Augustine or Aquinas. They were closer to the Early American philosophy of founding fathers Benjamin Franklin and Thomas Jefferson, both of whom accepted prostitution as a natural part of society. Jefferson added a house of prostitution in his plan for the new University of Virginia. (Of course it was not made a part of the final school.)

Even today San Francisco is in advance of the nation—or lacking in moral shame—it's all in one's point of view. One can still find the sound of sexual rebellion in the San Francisco *Chronicle*:

PROSTITUTES DEMAND EQUAL RIGHTS.

"Two Oakland women have appealed to the Alameda County Superior Court to reverse their conviction on prostitution charges on grounds their Constitutional rights were violated. The women contend that the men who were with them when they were arrested

*should also have been prosecuted and that they were thereby denied
equal protection under the law. In an appeal brief filed by their attorney, the women charge that they were discriminated against because they are women. The document argues that the law under
which they were convicted last July in municipal court makes it
just as illegal for a man to solicit a prostitute as it does for a prostitute to solicit a man."*

San Francisco could be the direct heir of the morality of eighteenth
century England and France—the wild rakehell world of the novel
Tom Jones, of Hogarth's "Harlot's Progress" and "Rake's Progress."
As historians have noted: "In the 18th Century, particularly in
France and England, whores enjoyed a popularity such as on any
large scale had not been theirs since the Italian Renaissance." Some
called it the "Golden Age of Prostitution. The 18th Century . . .
was the century of the prostitute. The prostitute was idolized and
idealized. The more vice and pleasure she knew, the higher she
stood over respectable women."

So San Francisco from the Gold Rush until the Great Fire was
either a free-living city, not bowing to the pious cant of hypocrites—
or a throwback to a cruder, wilder eighteenth century—again it is
which point of view one accepts.

Of authentic documents most likely the best account we have of
the half shadowy world of the San Francisco whore, the madam and
their customs and customers was set down in the manuscript of Nell
Kimball in her unpublished memoirs of San Francisco brothel-
keeping. Her regular occupation—a life's work—was running a New
Orleans sporting house. But because of a crime committed there
(not by her), Nell Kimball was advised "to leave town for just a
few years to get beyond the range of being asked questions." One
of her girls, tormented beyond reason, murdered a sadistic client
in Nell's bordello in New Orleans, and as the murdered man came
from "one of the best and richest families in the city the matter
was hushed up. The police captain I paid the protection money to
and the city fathers who took a cut off my earnings agreed it was
best for all. A fair and square decision for everybody. I decided
on San Francisco because I had friends there in the trade and the

town was wide open. I was given letters of introduction by a judge and a shipping man to those politicians on the Coast who would give me protection and see I operated a fine place with no interference from the law or the hoodlums.

"For three years, 1898 to 1901, I ran a high class house for the top hat trade in the Uptown Tenderloin and never had a bit of trouble, but for the usual breakage, three heart attacks by over eager older customers, the passing on of two girls from lung trouble. And then the time the railroad builder's nephew set fire to my place one New Year's night. That fire didn't amount to a row of pins and his family paid for the drapes, the wallpaper and Monica's dress. The girls and myself traveled on a free railroad pass all the time.

"To run a good high class house you have to be sure of your girls—agreeable, active, inventive but not nuthouse crazy—your location—respectable but not conspicuous. But first of all your protection. Every city that caters to after dark pleasure has a whorehouse. And on a much more discreet street or streets the best run bordellos in town are giving the leading families and the richest sports and the most important studs in politics, law and business a great deal of fun and girly activity. I never looked into the church-made morals of these things, but if nature hadn't meant the males to go down the line and frolic with the tarts, then nature shouldn't have made the johns so well-hung and active most of the time—up to 70 and beyond—trying to prove it. As I saw it I served a vital natural need. I always felt I offered a good product, kept everybody's secrets, and saw to the health and well being of every one concerned. And charged all the customer could pay. He got damn good whisky—for like in New Orleans I insisted on the best Kentucky bourbon, good wines for those who knew wines. The furniture and surroundings of any house I ran was as good, or better usually than the client had at home. The beds were real mahogany, none of your jewed-down cheap veneers, and the china wash basins, mirrors and fixtures and fittings later were sold as antiques on California Street.

"But first the protection had to be arranged and paid for. I ponied up to the police lieutenant who came around to say hello, to the health inspector, to the lawyers of the pious family that

42. *The prostitute was a town fixture and often in the news.*

owned the building. My grouch bag was nearly empty by that time [a bag on a string worn around the neck of actors and others, containing emergency cash].

"Before I unlatched the big double fumed oak doors, I studied the history of the town and the trade. Old Sugar Mary, pearl diving for a living [dish washing], who had come here early with the first gold rush, and run dives and hook shops [whorehouses], she said to me, 'Maybe made the fortune of five thousand girls.' You gave her a pint of gin and a good cigar and she'd talk of the first sporting house life on the coast. I myself figured out each town has its own habits and patterns after dark and San Francisco had one that was alike in some ways to all towns and different in some ways. I had begun in the trade casual and easy in St. Louis, just a young gay girl of fourteen, and later had run a fine place in New Orleans. San Francisco was unlike any of the other towns in one way— it was younger, real young. It had more spunk, sparks and sports for that reason, and the spenders were freer with their china [money] and wilder in the kip [bed]. 'They'd come off Jack Lloyd's Panamint and Lone Pine Stage,' the old whores said, 'steam coming from their ears' loaded with silver bank warrants.

"Old Sugar Mary said she remembered back to the first days of whoring on any impressive scale; it was in the tents and shacks of the Mexican and South American whores called *Chilenos*. They worked the waterfront and the long climb up Telegraph Hill. The demand was steady and the work rewarding as the competition was only nigrahs and squaws. Then the boom time rush got wilder and land values rose and Yerba Buena Cove itself was filled in, Sugar Mary swearing, 'They just cut off the masts of ships and covered them with goddamn dirt and extended the harbor.' The trade moved over to Portsmouth Square, but that didn't last either as a working place.

"It wasn't my kind of living and never would be. You're only as low as you set your goal. I never ran a house on the Barbary Coast, it being too mean a life and cheap for the kind of place I ran. Sugar Mary knew a madame named Labrodet who ran a good house in the seventies, over on Turk and Steiner streets, and I wanted

43. *Ragtime music on the Tenderloin.*

something special like that as to an address myself. I didn't want anything like the gut-busting House of Blazes that a biddy named Johanna Schrifin ran on Chestnut Street near Mason, with three or four houses working at the same time and street girls could bring their trick [patron] right into the place and rent a hot sheet room. The wrong crowd hung out there—lags and pete men, paper kiters, carny grifters. Old Sugar Mary remembered a police officer who went into the Blazes to bring out some wanted character and the lawman got his hogleg [pistol], hat, handcuffs and blackjack stolen.

"As for me, after a lot of hack fares and walking and talking I decided to open a class house in the Uptown Tenderloin, away from the Coast. This district had fine gambling houses, flashy goods in the saloon trade and the cabarets with music. All on Mason, Larkin, O'Farrell, Turk and other good streets below Market. There were fine theatres, splendid eating places where the quality and the gentry and their women came to enjoy themselves. The night life was not dangerous, not infected with the low types that flocked to the Coast. It was class, money people, or people who wanted to pass for money people, and you soon learn the last kind often pay more than the first, just to keep up the impression they were the Four Hundred, just like Mrs. Astor's horse.

"The three story uptown house I ran [Nell Kimball does not give its address or the name she used in San Francisco] was among the posh places in the district. I had an eye for furniture and fittings, like a nice bit of wood, and there was a small hotel going out of business because they were knocking it down for a newer building, and I got some fine things you didn't even see in those days any more, except in the gyp decorating places. Comfort isn't enough in a first class house—luxury is what the johns must feel all the time.

"I didn't take any Coast girls but sent to St. Louis and New Orleans and began with eight girls, my old cook Lacy Belle, and Harry the houseman and order keeper—with a hard hand to keep the girls in line. The girls knew they were high class, working so near Market Street. You've got to give a whore a pride in herself and her surroundings and you'll have a happier girl and one who's

44. *Crib girls never worked for the madam Nell Kimball.*

pleasant to the johns. The girls are miserable enough at times as it is. A lot crack up and go low down blue, and some even take the deep six [suicide]. I never knew any always cheerful, golden hearted, always laughing whore; except in the plays and later in the flickers—and when the actresses are made to appear as hookers in those things, it would make a cat laugh—they're that far away from the real article. I never saw a gold tooth in the play-acting—most whores like one or two in their head.

"I kept the girls up to snuff, insisted on great cleanness of body, hair (not too many combs) and dress. I saw they appeared in fine gowns or scant outfits designed to appeal to specialists. I catered to what people called 'plain old fashioned fucking'—sometimes with trimmings to please the special customer. Like in New Orleans I didn't go in much for perverted acts. There was a half Spanish girl—Nina—who had a hard rump and could take or use the whip, and there was a top floor room where the girls put on various spicy acts for some rich man giving a party. But I didn't go in for dyke [Lesbian] or freakish [homosexual] mixed games. Old Sugar Mary said I lost a lot of trade by not going in for the sissy byplay, as there were places in town that did a land office business in it. By the time I opened up I suppose some of the 49ers were jaded and seeking more *outré* things. I continued to produce a fairly honest article in rich fine surroundings and I didn't hanker for things that pleased Arabs and Englishmen."

We shall return again to Nell Kimball's perceptions and reflections. Her memoirs are laconic and precise and show her to be fully aware of the trenchant rationalism with which she ran her business. ("I'd run a tea shop the same way but I didn't see any percentage in tea.")

There was some part of the gay scene she did not care for and that too was part of the town's recurrent obsessive desire for pleasures. There was a small huddle of homosexuals who worked out of a certain Turkish bath, hardly noticed by others, sly and secret. The trial and jailing of Oscar Wilde drove them even deeper into the shadows. There is almost no documentation of any of this. Even R.J. in his daybook has little to say beyond: "W.C., sherry dealer in town from London. Wanted a boy today. Revolted at idea. Got doorman at Fairmont to arrange meeting at Sutro's Turkish Baths. . . ."

Around the time of the great fire there was a two story house called Aunt Josie's on Mason Street which kept a dozen photographs of handsome male youths on hand for viewing by the town ladies, those who might want a house of prostitution of their very own. Aunt Josie, a Negress, would show the veiled ladies who came in for servicing the photographs of the available men whores; there were notes on their height, eye and hair colors, special physical skills and attainments. When a client had picked a partner, he was brought over to Auntie's by a phone call to meet a lady usually masked (mask furnished by the management). The two then proceeded upstairs to a discreet bedroom. The project—perhaps for some excessive prudence—was a failure.

Various other reasons have been given. "Normal women, so called, don't go to male whores." Hardly true, for such places did exist in New Orleans, and of course in "wicked London, Paris and Rome" (only European cities were called wicked nests of decadence). It was also the fact that some of the town's most popular harlots came to Aunt Josie's to pay for services that *they* were usually paid for, and so spoiled it for the uptown ladies. And lastly there was labor-management trouble; the town pimps and whore masters made a great racket and threats against the establishment, claiming their girls were spending too much money for the games available at Josie's and neglecting their own trade. We shall never know all the matters of economics and competition that caused Aunt Josie to go out of business. Nevertheless she is certainly a prime pioneer figure to be installed in any Hall of Fame that *Fortune* magazine erects to Prime Movers of Big Business in America. For Aunt Josie perhaps invented and perfected the call house. From her early use of the phone came the modern call girl (and indirectly the end of the whore or sporting house as it once was in the land). Progress and Alexander Graham Bell were to establish the well-heeled call girl. (The presentable prostitute at one end of a phone answering service for the gentleman to plug in on her— often at the insistence of some friendly giant corporation who has the girl under lease, along with Hertz and Avis, to aid the national economy by pleasuring the horny raunchy businessman. The Internal Revenue approves the cost.)

The true owner of Aunt Josie's was supposed to be the town's vice boss in the early part of the century—one Jere McGland, usually called Jerome Bassity, whom the San Francisco *Bulletin* insisted "possessed a moral intelligence scarcely higher than that of a trained chimpanzee; look at the low, cunning lights in the small rapacious, vulture-like eyes; look at that low, dull-comprehending brow; the small sensual mouth; the soft puffy fingers with the weak thumb, indicating how he seeks ever his own comfort before others. . . ."

Bassity was an early version of Al Capone, self-assertive, perverse, sadistic, running the town's vice through the use of political corruption. He was "hand in glove" with the cynical political boss, a master of firm despotism, Abe Ruef, and his stooge mayor, Eugene Schmitz. Abe Ruef, sowing anarchy and doubt, seized power by organizing the workers along strong-arm lines like the later James Hoffa. Through powers at the polls, Abe bought the state lawmakers and City Hall. When he could, he also bribed newspapers. Everyone did. The railroad monopolists once paid a powerful Los Angeles newspaper publisher a hundred and fifty thousand dollar bribe to slant the news in their favor, and the man took the money and added: "The sonsofbitches should of known I'd have supported their interests anyway, without the money."

A grand triumvirate of thieves and rascals ruled San Francisco, protected vice while they looted the city of its utility rights and transportation facilities. The three were Ruef, Bassity and Police Commissioner Harry P. Flannery ("The Irish in America were the first to make politics worth corrupting on a very grand scale, as masters of happy deceit and the sly stealing of votes and money." So R.J. reports Jack London as saying.)

The top cop, Flannery, was the owner of the Richelieu Bar on Geary and Kearny streets. Years later his ten thousand dollar mahogany bar came up for sale; it brought a mere one hundred twenty-seven dollars, for Prohibition was just around the corner and the bar was too big for a private home.

Bassity cut in on every moneymaking scheme from tamale peddling to lewd dance halls and obscene stage shows. Years in advance of the Theater of the Absurd he was producing ideas common to Genet, Unesco and other uninhibited dramatists under the impression he was creating filth and not *avant-garde* art.

Bassity controlled over two hundred San Francisco whores from whom he took shares of their earnings. For those simpler days his take or income was enormous, often ten thousand dollars a month. If Bassity had been born only a quarter of a century later, he would have been able to bring to flower the Chicago crime system he perhaps invented, and could have earned the millions of dollars a week the Capone mob took in (and its heirs still take in, many experts in the field believe, uniquely immune from the law it corrupts).

21

POLITICS AND THE UNDERWORLD

Jerome Bassity with his multi-faceted appetites and habits is worth some further study. Bassity was a mean fellow; he carried a revolver and a huge roll of money at all times, and usually he was encased in one of his fifty waistcoats embroidered as fox hunts, stag drives or blushing flowers. He was given to diamonds as his lucky stone, loading his fingers with half a dozen rings, and rumor had it he wore some on his toes. His consuming vice was women, whom he pursued without prudence, not in his own houses but usually in rival sporting houses. And as he was a heavy drinker his orgies were indeed those of an ape in an ape house, with the ape having a Colt .45, lots of tainted money and a gang of deadly hoodlums to do his will, or worse, his whim. "A mean-eyed, no good bastard," was the best said about him.

Bassity had the ape's simple ideas of pleasure. He was also, like the novelist Nabakov, morbidly interested in Lolitas, nymphets, in child virgins, but unlike authors he made his dreams come true. After a night of orgy he would pull out his revolver and have target practice with the brothel's ceiling, shooting out gas and early electric light fixtures as release of some recurrent and obsessive rages.

In 1906 Mayor Schmitz and Abe Ruef were under indictment for debauchery of city funds and other high-level stealings, yet Bassity announced the opening, with a Madam Marcelle, of a brand-new modern whorehouse accommodating a hundred prostitutes on Commercial Street (an apt name). At once the underworld stock market quotes on available harlots went up; procurers were hard put to find the needed human element for such bold enterprising.

On hearing of this the Grand Jury insisted that the police keep the place from opening. But Bassity had no fears, for he had cut in the mayor's backers and Ruef on his enterprise. "I don't give a good goddamn for any Grand Jury. I'm going to open and they can't close me." They didn't, at least not until a reform city administration came in, and he reopened the place soon again, remaining Jerome Bassity, Mr. Big Shot, for many years.

His final flare-out from the scene is ironic. (The poet Heine said, "There is no irony like God's irony.") Years later, Bassity, still in a gaudy waistcoat, was arrested for swindling a seventeen-year-old boy out of seven hundred dollars at the 33rd Assembly District Club on Turk Street (the tainted partnership between politics and crime as usual scheming under one roof and philosophy). The case never came to trial, but from then on Bassity fades from the public eye.

Best remembered of the Upper Tenderloin neighbors of Nell Kimball was Tessie Wall, usually called Miss Tessie. She was a beautiful wino with a stomach said to hold a gallon of wine at a time. Miss Tessie, blond by nature or science, was full-figured as a Reubens painting come to animated vulgar life; obsessed with an external reality and greed. Before the fire she was just a girl in the houses on the Barbary Coast, but after the great blaze she appeared with some very young, very beautiful girls in tow on Larkin Street between Eddy and Ellis and opened a bordello.

R.J. notes of her establishment: "Best place for really special guests: Miss Tessie's. Trouble is guests may run into their sons up from Stanford, or into visiting Yale and Harvard house guests. Miss Tessie is plumper than ever. Send her free wine by the case twice a year. Can't serve her entire intake, still good advertising for brands I import, Miss Tessie imbibing them one after the other. Prodigious drinker.

"Young H. told me he was present when Miss Tessie, dining with

45. *Ragtime music at Miss Tessie's was loud and clear.*

her lover, the sporting gambler Frankie Daroux, drank twenty-two bottles of wine and didn't once get up from the table."

The gambler and the lady wino were married and at the wedding at which over a hundred guests gathered, R.J., who was present as a wine provider, proudly records "82 cases champagne gulped down. Bride gay, bridegroom polite. Predict a stormy married life. A.B. says, 'You can sometimes domesticate a whore, but never housebreak a madame.'"

Miss Tessie certainly did not domesticate. Frankie insisted she give up her brothel; as man in the family he wanted to keep her in style, with his own vice-supported income, on his fine place in the country out in San Mateo County.

Miss Tessie is said to have replied to the offer: "Listen, I'd rather be an electric light pole on Powell Street than own all the goddamn land in the sticks."

Divided in his love between the country and Tessie, the gambler walked out on her. When Frankie refused to return to her ample bossom Tessie got herself a revolver and sent out word she would take proper aim and see to it no other woman would find him of much use *if* Tessie couldn't have him. During a street meeting with Frankie she whipped out her .22 and fired at him three times, not taking aim but hitting each time. When the police found her she was standing weeping over her fallen Frankie and was heard to exclaim, "I shot the sonofabitch because I love him, goddamn him. . . ."

Frankie recovered—the extent of his damage unknown—and moved on to New York. Miss Tessie too in time retired from an active business career in vice, hauling away to her apartment on 18th Street the huge golden bed in which, as madam, she had run her main command post at her O'Farrell Street bordello. When she died—at a good old age for such a wino—the ornate golden bed (gilded actually) went to an odd buyer. It was sold for $105 to Sheriff Ellis W. Jones of Sacramento. Rumors have persisted up to modern times, though without much proof, that the great gold bed of Miss Tessie Wall is still active in the service of Venus, and that the imprints of many a judge, governor, state legislator, law-

maker, lobbyist, actor and publicity man have been made on its
specially overstuffed mattress and reinforced springs.

The Uptown Tenderloin was for the gentry and the socially
blessed, the big spender, the demanding client who could pay
any price. The Barbary Coast was a democratic district, mean,
colorful, often dangerous, gay, loud and ready for anything: "You
name it." Here no perception nor reflection reigned; even the
prematurely decrepit or diseased whore could find some beast to
couple with her. Nor was there an excessive fastidiousness, no vice
refined to a point of mere pretense. The Coast was not for those
who were prone to dare too little, or for a life lived much too
cautiously.

In later years the district has been so much romanticized by
journalists looking for color, and films glamorizing the past, that for
a true picture of the Coast we can again turn to Nell Kimball.

"I liked to bring in my house girls from the middle west and the
south. I had connections with the organization that brought them
over from England, France, Italy, or collected them from the country
towns and middle west cities. I liked them hungry, eager and free
to come and go. I rarely went to the Coast for a girl, but sometimes conditions were such that I was short a girl or two, and with
the holidays coming along or some war in the offing—that always
sent men in droves to the sporting houses—I had to recruit on the
Coast. Old Mary was wise to the Coast and I learned lots from her,
and I was no dumb bunny. But soon I figured the way of doing
things there and didn't much care for what I saw. I'm not talking
of morals, that's for Holy Joes—I mean conditions.

"It was animal on the Coast, and not in any barnyard animal
way—as a farm girl myself things were natural on a farm and things
happened because that was the way it was. On the Coast it was
unnatural and mean. Low and blue. A whore is maybe dumb,
morbid and sad, but she's human. I don't mean any of that *There*
but for the grace of God goes Nell Kimball guff either—a smart
girl can figure her odds.

"On the Coast there was the cow-yard whore, the crib whore,
and the parlor house whore. A cow-yard could be a three or four

floored building about ready to fall in on itself, with long halls and off the hall as many small cubes of closets you could crowd in. Each closet held a woman, and I've visited cow-yards where there were two hundred and fifty to three hundred whores at work. The noise, stink, talk, cursing, all thick as smoke.

"The Chinese slave girls worked in cribs, and so did nigrahs, and white women who had come down from cow-yard and parlor houses. A crib was just a small mean shack, the display room in front and in back the work room. In front there'd be a chair, and if it was a Mexican whore or mick, an altar with a glass of burning olive oil and the Holy Virgin, head turned away from the work room by the whore. Whores deep down are drawn to religion with a naked man as a god on a cross. The work room had just place enough for a small brass or iron bed and washstand, a tin basin, sometimes a real marble top on the stand. A coal-oil stove and a pot of hot water on it, a flask of carbolic for sanitation, some towels, and a chest for the whore's clothes. All around were hung calendars, ragtime sheet music, colored postal cards, and over the bed in a nest of printed roses or other flowers the name: Ruthie, Mamie, Sadie, Dot, Daisy, Millie. It wasn't the cleanest bed in the world and there was always a strip of red or yellow oil cloth across the foot of it. For the two bit and four bit crib customer didn't take his boots off. He was not allowed to take off anything but his hat to show, as Mary said, "he has some respect for the whore."

"I could find a crib almost any place—on Pacific, Washington, Montgomery, Commercial streets, along Broadway and Grant Avenue. You could smell the home country of the place a crib girl came from by the eating places or cooking around them. Old Mary said on Stockton she could tell the nigrah cribs by the smell of Brunswick stew and chittlings, and the Spanish-Mex cribs on Grant by the chili, the French whores on Commercial by their perfume. 'They don't bathe,' Mary said, 'just swish on the scent.'

"The girls did their own pandering from the padded window sills. All claimed to be French. Bacon and Belden Place was always solid with cribs. Up to fifty sometimes, and they rented to the girl for four dollars a day. The places were sometimes raided by some society for the prevention of vice, or by a church group. But the poor whore, run out one day, always came back, and the cribs were again ready for them. The landlords were often respectable people who supported the anti-vice work out loud and made a good thing of renting cribs to the whores. I never claimed to be respectable, so I don't know how the owners really felt.

"Old Sugar Mary remembers when Mouton Street was the lowest you could get in a crib, working two years there 'when all my teeth fell out. It was really —— and ——, for the worst kind of miserable swine hunting odd tricks. The most brutal kookoo johns with crazy ideas they wanted to try out. You couldn't get a policeman in there to protect a —— unless somebody was dead or cut open by a ripper.'

"It was a fearful street, Mary said, the red lamps lit and the drunken men and the half naked whores at their windows—a wrapper on and nothing else. Cursing and yelling in a dozen spick languages, the screaming whores and drunk men jumped by other drunks, the whores exposing their tits and navels in the windows, all yelling their tricks and offers. All in sight of Nob Hill. The macks would follow a mark and try and pull him back to a window for a *looksee* or *feelee*, to get him to come in for a *doee*. It was a dime a *touchee*, twice for an added jit. A crib girl on a weekend night could take on a hundred studs or they'd say she wasn't trying. There was a color line—cost for a Mexican two bits; a nigrah whore, Chinese or Japanese asked fifty cents. All those who claimed they were French, seventy-five. A Yankee girl cost a dollar.

"I don't know who started the yarn red-headed girls were wilder and more tearing around in their loving, crazy for a man and couldn't hardly hold back. So red heads could get more than the going rate, 'from screaming like they were out of their heads with love.' A lot of heads were dyed red, the damndest orange and scarlet ever seen on the Coast. And a red-headed Jew-girl was supposed to be just pure fire and smoke. Actually few whores let themselves get any reactions while turning a trick."

The Jewish invasion, Nell Kimball tells of, was really the work of a madam, Iodoform Kate, a whore herself in the nineties in the Coast cribs. In time she ran nearly twenty cribs herself, each one with a "genuine Jewish redhead." She swore the hair was natural as gold and each girl a pious Godfearing Jewess, saving to bring her future husband, her mother and father and sisters and brothers over to the Golden Land. From Romania, Hungary, Poland, the Tzar's cruel Russia.

Then there was Rotary Rosie, who moved clockwise and counter clockwise while in horizontal action. She was respected as an intellectual, a reader of books, an educated whore with a vast knowledge of any subject—beyond the dream books, newspaper headlines and vaudeville jests most whores knew. A University of California student saw Rosie, bought, and said he was in love with her. To show off her book reading he brought over the men of his Greek letter fraternity. Rotary Rosie spun in ecstasy, serving her lover's frat brothers at no money charge, while they paid by reading romantic verse to her: Swinburne, Shelley, Keats, Byron. Rosie anounced she was going to go to college and turn as virginal as the college girls. (Hardly a step to put her in gear with the state of affairs she would find today among the coeds.) However Rosie's lover graduated and left town, the frat brothers changed with the seasons, and Rotary Rosie, no nearer her Ph.D., is said to have killed herself, debauched by education and the better English poets. Somehow an inviolable dignity remains in her story.

A crib girl considered her station in life above the cow-yard girl, but dreamed of becoming a parlor girl. The cow-yard barracks they feared were huge supermarkets in low-priced, hastily handled goods. The best-known cow-yards were the Marsicicania near Broadway, the Nymphia on Pacific, and the one the political bosses protected most of all (most likely many of them owned a bit of it) so that it got a near official title, the Municipal Brothel, on Jackson Street. It was a pre-Golden Gate Bridge monument.

The Catholic Church, knowing the weakness of human flesh, tolerated the whorehouse scene, until the Reverend Terence Caraher of the St. Francis Church came along. Before that, as R.J. reports:

46. *A dance floor was a sin place—and even roller skating was evil to some.*

"Talk is the Bishop insists the pious whores be permitted a state of grace and be given Sunday morning off to go to Mass. No fornicating the night before, *after* midnight."

Father Caraher fought to change all this. From 1885 to 1900 he fought a losing battle. He sent shock troops as volunteers to picket the whorehouses on the Coast (never the well-protected Uptown places). Several pickets—weak vessels of lust—succumbed to the girls' offers. The father found the names of the respectable people who owned the cow-yards and cribs and he took the managers, madams, pimps and girls into court. But the earnest father got nowhere as his Irish parishioners were often the ward heelers who owned or protected the vice and exploited the district between Holy Marys and dips of holy water. Besides the good father, lost in vanity and pride, saw himself as a man who could reform everything wrong with life on earth. In the end he made a laughingstock of himself. Poor dear honest man, he preached against ballroom dancing, found foul vice and the return of Sodom and Gomorrah in the nickelodeon early movies. He insisted most of the town's trolley cars were dance halls on wheels, full of lewd women and beastly men. Why men even waited for a show of a girl's stocking when mounting a cable car.

The father saw the devil, Old Scratch, Beelzebub himself, in family card games, even in riding a bicycle (the church games and gambling he overlooked). He came out with fire and brimstone against roller skating: "I have only words of condemnation to utter against skating rinks. I condemn public skating because it is dangerous both to body and soul. Many receive injuries at the skating rinks from which they never recover. In skating the bones are oftentimes broken, limbs twisted, and the body severely bruised. While the danger to the body in the skating rink is great, the danger to the soul is greater. . . . Skating rinks are frequented by the worst elements of society. Some of the male skaters speak to one another afterwards of their experiences and their conquests of young women in the rinks, and where do the skaters go after they leave the rinks? I answer, some of them go to perdition! Skating is not only a foolish, silly exercise, but it is most dangerous to body and soul. I request you avoid the skating rinks."

The father's wrath was also red hot against the Nymphia cow-yard, first called Hotel Nymphomania by its owners and the Kehrlein brothers. Even the police insisted that was a bit *too* much. The brothers said they had a panting nympho on *every* floor who was always stripped bare of confining clothes. Any male of any creed or color would be served by these sex maniacs. To make sure of this—to show the game, a dime dropped into a slot would automatically raise a window curtain exposing the activity going on in the cubicle. The novelty of this peep show was popular, but it was soon discontinued when it was discovered that dishonest viewers were inserting homemade brass slugs in the slot, even though two policemen were provided by the city to act as doormen to the Palace of Nymphomaniacs. Father Caraher had the place raided eventually and thirty-three girls were arrested out of three hundred or more who were usually there. The owners in the end paid some small fines, and under its own or other names the place remained open.

Underneath all this is what one critic has called our Calvinistic fear of the exotic, an opulent frontier hedonism that rarely breaks out in public print, as did a recent headline in a daily newspaper. The editorial page answered protests:

ETHEL LAMARR, 70, KEEPER OF BAWDYHOUSES DIES.
Ministerial indignation, after a long silence in the face of harsh and sordid activities going on, finally boils up—not about those activities, BUT BECAUSE WE MEN-TIONED THEM . . .
If some do not like to face facts, we can't help it.
If some cannot get indignant over acts of degradation—but only over being unpleasantly reminded of them—we can't help it.
We can't turn our backs on the realities in the name of "good taste." The bad taste of too many nasty truths is in our mouths. We don't make the record. We just report it as best we can.

A letter to the editor was closer to reality—and indicated that the city officials and police protected Madam Lamarr's business in return for a share of her income.

Dear Editor:

Mrs. Lamarr . . . took in the poor, saw that they existed as human beings when they were down and out. Also, if you would be brave enough, I can name prominent people who availed themselves of her profession. Maybe yourself.

The good in Ethel Lamarr, God rest her soul, you did not care to print, because it was not in your police files. . . . But many, many people will confirm that she, over a period of 30 to 40 years, contributed to the police benevolent fund for an estimated sum of $10,000.

A Reader

22

GUIDE TO ENTERTAINMENT

Nell Kimball wrote of a profitable sideline in running a brothel; alcohol. "I always made a huge percentage on the cases of beer I sold, on the Bourbon and the wine too, but with wine I had to go by labels and wasn't always sure. I didn't lush like some madames. I'd have coffee on duty—a small brandy with some steady older trick.

"Later in New Orleans we had the early jazz players in, before that a piano man, usually white in the early years, with ragtime and sad sweet songs of Stephen Foster, but later the coon things and the nigrah sounds were it. In S.F. I had a player piano in one parlor fed by half dollars (the cheaper houses had one that ate quarters). In the special parlor for the top private trade I had a big black piano that came off a German ship that went aground near Seal Rock; one customer said it was once owned by a man named Brahms, but I was never sure of that even if I looked up Brahms. I had a little professor on the keys who used to play in the vaudeville houses downtown till—honest—some acrobat fell on him and injured the professor's back and he took to fearing the muscle acts on stage and began to attend spiritual meetings and tap tables and go into trances so no one would hire him but me. He knew everything any client would ask for, and the private parlor had some grand concerts. My favorites were 'The Turkish Patrol' and some of the Chopin. When the professor played the 'Minute Waltz,' the clients would time him, and if he did it in record time they brought him a brandy.

"I didn't do as well as I should have in S.F. Not that I'm crying. I was in the business to do well and I got by with a hefty bank balance and a few good city lots put by. But the police and politicians were pressing the houses hard all the time for the boodle and the graft. The payoffs got very heavy. I paid a fixed grift for each girl I had working. I gave City Hall a cut in the likker sales. And at one time (till I cured a political boss's son of the clap caught from a college girl by sending him to the right doc) I had to let the police take *all* the coins from the player piano. I didn't blame them—everybody has his hand in the till in big cities.

"However I knew how to get top protection from judges and city and state capitol members; so while I paid out heavy, I didn't pay as much as some to inspectors, cops, ward heelers, night court judges, reporters (a few go for a free ride) and firemen. I'm used to human greed, to the dirty use people in power make of their office, their official position. I never knew anyone in politics—and I've seen them all from Vice President on down in my places—who didn't want power, money and the right to push people around. I never knew one that was simon pure and just working for the good of the city or state or country. Don't say that I only got the wrong 'uns. I could give you a list of lily white reformers, law makers with the habits of zoo apes. Lots of those who made the eagle scream with their love of country at picnics and Fourth of July rallies—yet they wanted their nookie on an *Annie* [free of charge: from Annie Oakley the circus sharpshooter who shot holes in things, so a punched ticket was a sign to admit the bearer without a fee].

"Mr. Huntington could pay a half million dollars to bribe the United States Senate, but the hook shops of San Francisco made that seem like a piker's price compared to the millions the police and the fat cats in office took for themselves from us madames."

Nell Kimball, in another part of her memoirs, does list some historic Americans who patronized her houses, but that is hardly part of this social history of a city. After Nell Kimball left to return to her sporting house in New Orleans the city officials began to put an illegal and of course unofficial tax on each and every musical instrument in a house. Or sell a so-called license on a law

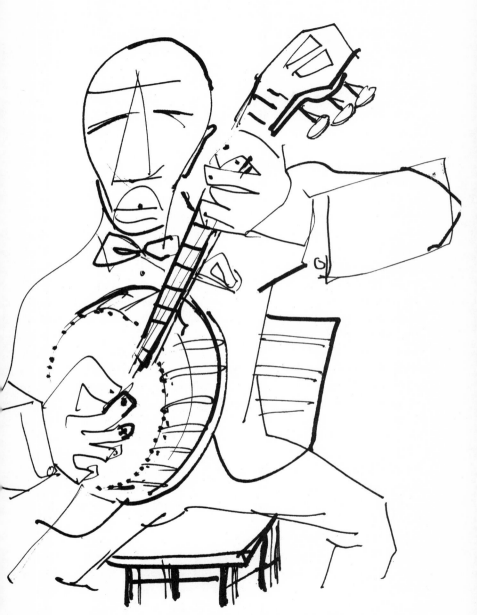

47. *Music was always important to a sporting house.*

never passed, and the money collected certainly never going to city or state. No wonder anarchy and doubt often were around the corner.

Later still the police passed down an order to all madams to have every musical tool removed from the houses. It seemed the music was too noisy for respectable ears. Then a hint was dropped around that the house might use music if it were played on a new mechanical harp. No one had ever heard or seen such an instrument, but naturally who should soon show up in the red light district but a dapper salesman selling just such a harp, made in a Cincinnati music factory. Price: $750. And the salesman's credentials were not from any classical school of music, or from an orchestra conductor, or even Victor Herbert, a gay time musical master. No, they were from the city fathers, the political bosses. Private citizens could, if they desired, buy the same harp for about a hundred and fifty dollars from a catalogue, but the bordello owners and madams felt it would be wiser to buy from the dapper salesman who reported and split commissions in the right quarters.

Only houses like Nell Kimball's, patronized in great number by the males of the best families, could appeal from the local ward pressure and the street police. Pleas for mercy by the madams were usually contemptuously rejected, and in their flamboyant business they could hardly appeal to the courts (which were usually bought and bribed by the railroads and run by the political bosses).

As the West began to feel some of the refining influences of the East, the bordellos also began to move forward more in keeping with their client's idea of good taste. But only outside the Barbary Coast. The men with their gold pince-nez, fur collars, weighted malacca canes liked to enter an atmosphere of fine furniture, undisturbed by obstreperous customers and drunks. R.J. writes in his daybook near the end of the century: "Affluence and boredom seem overtaking the town. People who think of themselves as the *bon ton* are spoiling the better restaurants by their demands for 'French' cooking. Wiser ones still prefer the Scotch grouse, terrapin, canvasbacks, pheasant and soufflés that pleased their fathers.

"Great talk of having the harlots take down their red lights, the lamps with the ruby shade in the window being in bad taste as is the token of a disk with a carpenter's screw attached for those unsatisfied customers—and lettered GOOD FOR ONE—

"Took some visitors to see Madame Gabrielle's Dupont Street sign, *The Lively Flea*, the damn bug spread out in a bed with little Gods of Love floating around. *The Sign of the Red Rooster* had a tin red bird with a light in his beak advertising the Parisian Mansion. Smaller version of the sign indoors lettered *Sign of the Red Cock*. Couldn't show my guests Madame Lucy's sign as the police had it taken down when they saw the quaint lettering: *Ye Olde Whore Shoppe*.

"Visitors think us an evil city where all keep a seraglio of immodest girls and life here carried on with a wild gusto of sensual delights. Had to impress my guests that most of the citizens of the town lead dull respectable lives, never come down to the Coast, or the Tenderloin unless they're going to the theatre. For the most part we are really a town of impeccable character. The champagne magnums I sell do not go into every home. Money and social position are the true goal. But few read Balzac here. Depravity is not generally the dream of most of the city. Frankly I think the interest shown in vice by slummers and visitors points to the fact that this is all outside their imagination or experience. Just as most dogs don't wear diamond collars like their mistresses' tiaras on Russian Hill, yet one or two do."

Few, however, were able, as R.J. was, to see vice as an attraction to a special group, and to sailors and visitors. So the city under a political spoils system remained in the whispered talk of most of the nation as a place where no virgin was safe and no youth not in danger of the pollution existing in this Babylon of the Pacific.

The lowest form of pleasure one could find in the city was in the wino cellars on the Barbary Coast. There was no catering to the customer. Plain planks on wooden horses, crates or kegs served as a bar. The wine, and vile stuff it was—made from the last pressings or just alcohol colored and given a tart taste, was four to five cents a pint, eight to ten cents a quart.

Humanity was at low ebb in the wino caves; sawdust on the

floors and a few benches for the ragged, bleary-eyed bums, the scabby drifters, panhandlers, old whores lost in memory and young thieves who had not yet made a connection. The badger game was worked on the Coast often from the dives and saloons, as well as the panel game, the selling of keys. In the badger game the girl picked up a customer, tried to appear not as a whore but rather like a wife or sweetheart just earning a few dollars on the side to buy some needed gift. Once the chump was in the hotel room shedding his clothes, the door would burst open and a pimp, playing father or husband, would level a pistol at the victim's head and shout he'd kill the *both* of them—the foul betrayers of his honor! The woman would plead for forgiveness, saying the chump was ready to pay for his life, and usually the victim would offer his wallet and run, buttoning his clothes as he left. The panel game was almost the same, but the victim was drugged by a drink and during the night a panel would open in the rooming house wall where he usually was taken, and the pimp would steal wallet, watch and in some cases even clothes. In the early days the victim was also often in danger of being shanghaied aboard a ship, sold by a crimp to whom the panel workers had peddled him.

The key game was a hasty sales talk to a raunchy male by an attractive girl in some hotel lobby. She promised she'd meet the customer later at her place, but she didn't want to be seen leaving with him. She'd ask anything from five to twenty dollars for the key to her flat, the latter price if she were working the Palace or Uptown Tenderloin. A good quick girl working in several parts of the town in one night could sell six to a dozen keys, with an address that led nowheres—to a room number that didn't exist.

As the city progressed and the waterfront grew more and more out into the Bay, as business and politics settled down, even taking on a pride in the city, the Coast became a sort of tourists' trap, a slumming game. After the fire it was to become mostly a false facade of its past. What ended it was the fire. The swing back and forth of corruption and reform politics all helped to change the inner reality so that in the final decline only the legend, the tourist pitch and the false opium dens remained.

The nation's dances of the new century were often invented and popularized on the Coast. There had been the original French import, the cancan, then came the hoochy-koochy. The dance halls of San Francisco had first presented many bedazzling steps. Paul Whiteman, who played there before World War I, saw many dance steps that later went on to become a national frenzy. The dancers moving over glossy dance floors stepped out San Francisco's own Turkey Trot, Chicken Glide, Bunny Hug, Texas Tommy, Pony Boy Ponce and the Grizzly Bear. Some say a version of the Cakewalk began here, but that has been traced to New Orleans and Atlantic City.

And let us not forget Lola Montez's "Spider Dance," which certainly could be seen as the forerunner of the shimmy, or even the later Charleston—without the rubber spiders. Of course church, school and society always cried out in horror against the frenzy of sexual shaking limbs and torso on the dance floor. The first jazz on the Coast in early New Orleans, Dixieland, even Kansas City styles, was greeted as a welcoming of the jungle into the heart of our civilization, even if in those days it was sometimes spelled JASS.

After the fire there was the flare-up of recovery and then a final decline of vice into its modern version. The last of the dance halls to carry some of the color of the early town was the Thalia. Its opening night was featured by the benediction and honor of the presence on the platform, in person, of City Board of Commissioner Sullivan and Chief County Jailor McCauley.

The San Francisco *Call* described the Thalia in what can hardly be called in Hemingway's term a clean, well-lighted place. "Above the nickel a glass section is the real money getting section of the hall. Here, in half open booths, the women of the dance hall ply their trade. Here are invited the sailors who drift into the place. Here men are plied with liquor and urged to part with their cash. In these booths Thursday night were many sailors, drunk or nearly drunk, each with a woman at his elbow. Others were there too— men showing signs of labor and young fellows in good clothing and bearing evidence of coming from decent homes. Below, in the cheaper section, were many men sprawled asleep or in a drunken

48. *Fight in a dance dive, hard and deadly.*

stupor. On the dance hall floor a few couples cavorted and displayed the fancy steps of the newest tenderloin dances.

"The lobby of the Thalia is a great open space before the bar, and here the women congregate and attempt to entrap every patron who enters. Hesitation means a dozen groping hands and a dozen voices clamoring for drinks. 'Be a sport; buy just one.' The Thalia provided a 'Salome dance' just before one o'clock as the final 'big' attraction of the night. The 'Salomes' danced and strained and twisted, received a faint spattering of applause, and then, throwing coats or loose gowns over their scant costumes, joined the throngs of dancers in the comparatively conservative steps of the Grizzly Bear, the Bunny Hug, and the Texas Tommy.

"Three o'clock in the morning, and the dancing at the Thalia was beginning to lag. An hour later, and the place was half deserted. The few remaining were men and women listless in appearance, with bloodshot eyes and pasty faces."

At North Beach were dance halls—five cents for men, women admitted free. And signs:

Turkey Trots, Couples
With Their Heads
Together, Walking,
Bowerying, Dipping,
Or Gentlemen Introducing
Themselves to Ladies in the Hall
STRICTLY
PROHIBITED!
Introducers on the Floor.

An age was ending—not with a bang, but with an introduction.

49. *Inside a San Francisco opium den—the real thing existed.*

23

THE SONS OF THE DRAGON

In some ways San Francisco is a Chinese city with its own social hierarchy, surrounded on all sides by a white American city of the same name. Within its smelly confines, before the fire, and with its gaudy red dragon style of building after the tremor and blaze, existed a world private, secret, self-assertive and given to the gang war of the tongs, a jockeying for positions of power in the vital and profitable trade in opium, slave girls, the control of vast far-flung business enterprises. Some merchants legitimately imported "antiques" (replicas of Han and T'ang and Sung originals) but mostly trash created for the export trade. Others dealt in strange foods, dried and pickled as mummies, in "jade", herbs, beef-bone-ivory, human hair for wigs, soya oils for industry, pig bristles for brushes, silks and other exotic cloths and all the wonders of those products that Marco Polo knew, as well as a few the frugal Chinese had perfected since to sell to the foolish whites.

In this Chinese city in America, legal, illegal, the tong leaders could look for protection money, blackmail, extortion of ransom for kidnapings. And being allied with drug addicts and prostitutes, this also offered a formidable hostile climate for gang warfare.

Mr. Big of the early Chinese rackets, in partnership with the white political despotism that ran the city, was a perverse Chinese called Little Pete, born Fung Jing Toy in Canton in 1865. He was brought to this country at the age of five and as a child he saw the early tong fights in the streets and was a delivery boy for a Chinese shoemaker. At twenty-one Little Pete was making shoes himself under the Anglo-Saxonized name of J. C. Peters & Co. But it was merely the front of a skilled and wily criminal mind that soon permeated the city. He expanded into gambling dives, opium smoking nests and investments in Chinese slave girls. He knew he had to have an organization and so Little Pete soon seized power in the Sum Yop tong, whose fuhrer he became with a ruthless power, and as full a disregard of personal rights as any Hitler, Stalin or a Texas millionaire. He invented highjacking of assets of other mobs on a grand scale, seizing shipments of slave girls from the Sue Top tong that specialized in the crib trade. This led to bloody gang wars with *boo how doy* hatchet men and other forms of violence.

Little Pete at first worked outside the white man's preserves and society—alone and grotesque. But in 1887 he attempted to bribe a jury, also the D.A. and also the court in which one of his killers was on trial for murder. The White Devils convicted Little Pete for bribery on a grand scale and he was sent to San Quentin prison for five years to think things out. His bribery scheme had failed, *not* because the people he tried to corrupt were honest, but because his huge wholesale attempt to bribe the whole field of local law was too open and it involved too many people who feared each other. He had ruffled the violable dignity of a tainted system.

If he was Mr. Big in Chinatown, then the man to team up with, he realized, to boss crime in the city was the white Mr. Big of San Francisco. That was Christopher A. Buckley, the political king and dictator of the city. Buckley was the most corrupt man in San Francisco and for twenty years held the city in his grip and milked it like "a staked out cow." What was most amazing was that Buckley was a blind man who had lost his sight at the age of thirty. He had come to the Coast in 1862, made himself a sterling expert bartender at the Snug Café of Duncan Nicols, and soon owned the place. In five years with the cunning of a morbid sensibility he *was* the Democratic party, lock, stock, and stolen ballot box. His looting of the city was a masterpiece in chicanery. His ward leaders encompassed all the deserving dishonest and the paying for favors;

selling of influence was efficiently handled by the blind man, seated in the back of his café, and by touch and sound he seemed to know everyone, and also recognize their desires, wants, and the price of a bribe offered or the bribe to offer.

It was to Christopher A. Buckley, the blind city boss, that China-town boss, Little Pete, came from San Quentin prison to arrange to join forces in a crime syndicate that made local history. Buckley and Little Pete—two social monstrosities—shook hands and the sky was the limit. Boundaries of power were drawn up, prices set; Little Pete bowed to the Blind White Devil as he called his partner and proceeded to *his* Chinatown—he owned it now.

Chinatown was Little Pete's by royal Buckley grant. He collected fees from all vice enterprises, all legitimate shops, importers, sellers; gambling, opium, whorehouses, all had to pay a certain percentage of earnings to Little Pete. Those who welched or reneged were at once raided by the police. Buckley saw to that. Usually the raided Chinese lost their entire investments; for Little Pete's organization men moved in, taking over everything. If the opium wasn't as pure as it once was, the Chinese crib girl slaves and parlor house whores were given lead half dollars by Little Pete to palm off as change to men who were not too clear as to what was going on.

Little Pete was a traditionalist, a conservative—as most believers in the status quo are. He wore a long shiny queue and spent hours having it combed, washed, oiled and braided. As a true gang lord he never did any killing himself, but his mob, on his orders, did away with over fifty people who got in Little Pete's way.

He himself led a wholly respectable life as a father and husband, at least at home. He and his family of a wife and two children made their home in a three story house on Washington Street that had been Little Pete's father's. Oddly enough he could not read, it was claimed, or write Chinese, and used translators and interpreters to carry on his city-wide control of his countrymen.

Little Pete was a spick and span dandy, given to showing a dozen large butter-yellow gold watches and diamonds of all sizes. A careful dresser, he changed his jewels and rings several times a day, put on a freshly pressed suit every morning. His wardrobe was bursting with a choice of garments. He was fantastically rich from looting the city with Blindman Buckley, and from his own small and large rackets. Little Pete liked gambling, if the odds favored him. When he turned to horse racing he saw no reason not to expect the running of the nags at Bay District and Ingleside to continue his luck. He averaged in betting eight to nine thousand dollars a day and always seemed to win. In two months he was ahead a hundred thousand dollars. The stewards of the Pacific Coast Jockey Club felt there was a Chinaman somewhere in the tracks' woodpiles. Horses became ill, collapsed; fine jockeys lost easy races in what were called *boat rides*, and somehow odds and breeding and form charts of splendid horses began to mean nothing at the two tracks.

Jockeys were followed by detectives to the offices of J. C. Peters & Co. Soon it was proved that Little Pete bribed riders, trainers and hot walkers to slip drugs or poison to those horses he wanted out of the way in races in which he was betting on a fixed horse with the big odds. Jockeys were ruled off the turf or suspended in the resulting scandal. Lucky Baldwin's own trainer was barred from the tracks. Little Pete, in inviolable dignity, retired from the sport of kings and suckers, a big winner. But his reign was in danger.

The other tongs figured if they couldn't lick Little Pete one by one, they might do a grand assassination by combining forces against his Sum Yop tong. Thirteen tongs came together and sent out the hatchet men, the *boo how doy,* to earn a reward of three thousand dollars, itself a record price for one man's life in China-town. But it was not going to be easy to collect. Little Pete lived and slept in a room without a window, behind a barred steel door with a huge savage dog leashed to each doorknob. Under his fine tailored suit he wore a long coat of chain mail as perfected by Christian Crusaders centuries ago in the Holy Land. Inside his hat Little Pete, anticipated Ian Fleming's James Bond villain called Iron Hat; he had a chapeau lining of a sheet of curved steel.

His person was guarded at all daytime hours by a half dozen Chinese hatchet men, hands up their sleeves, gripping their razor-sharp weapons. *And* an inner guard of three white thugs who de-pended on hard muscle and pistols within reach to keep Little Pete

50. *Chinese gamblers were Little Pete's friends; he also wrote plays.*

safe from harm. The rear of this armored panzer group was made up of Little Pete's valet, carrying a case of the boss's jewelry and his toilet kit of combs, brushes, sprays, powders and other cosmetic needs.

Little Pete was a sort of yellow Great Gatsby, a crime lord dreaming of softer things. He was an expert performer on the Chinese zither, could tune in the night music of his collection of pet crickets. Like Nero he felt inside himself the creative artist stifled by a vulgar world. Little Pete wrote comic plays, and as he owned the Jackson Street Theater, its stage boards were often heavy with the step of Chinese actors performing Little Pete's dramas, in translation, of course, into Chinese. It would need some deep study to discover the true enigma that was Little Pete. One wonders—we lack so much the details of his life—how the killers and drug addicts, perverts and whoremasters whom he invited to his plays reacted.

Chinatown had developed its own versions of later Dillingers, Baby-faced Nelsons and Mad Dog Coles. They stood out as personalities in their own right. Little Pete's glory put them in the shadows but they are worth a glimpse.

There was Yee Toy, called Girl-Face, a dainty, limp-wristed killer, who after each murder liked to leave a neat corpse, adjusting its clothes in place, combing the hair, pressing a smile to dead lips, if it were possible. Sing Dock was called the Scientist Murderer, as he never moved to slaughter without endless research and the perfecting of every step before he struck the final blow.

The only personality that could have matched Little Pete in sensitivity and breadth of interests in crime and the arts was Hong Ah Kay. He too was a student of art and poetry, prose, scrolls, moods and sensations. Kay's own poetry is said to have great merit, but has not been translated into English because of its subtle nuances. He is best remembered for his epic moment of greatness; when cornered in a cellar by seven deadly enemies, Kay whirled his hatchet in so noble a Roland-against-the-Saracens fashion that he killed all seven men with only seven blows, one for each.

Before Hong Ah Kay could challenge Little Pete, the White Devils hanged the poet and art lover and seven-at-one-blow scholar.

But it was none of the trained and merciless *boo how doy* who cornered Little Pete. For months the killers, professional and apprentice, tried to get beyond the guards around Little Pete. All failed. Then as in an epic Western film, down from the cold mountains, in the January of 1897 came two young gold hunters, Lem Jung and Chew Tin Gop, who had filled their pokes with flake gold and were out to celebrate in Chinatown with slave girls, warm wine, the true Peking cooking, before shipping home to China to end their days as rich men who had traveled widely and seen strange places.

Lem and Chew, as members of the Suey Sing tong, listened with interest to the talk of the reward for the killing of a man they had never heard of. Lem, perhaps full of hot wine, proudly boasted, "There is no reason why we should not earn this reward money!"

Chew agreed. They were not hatchet men, gunslingers, nor had they even been in a Chinatown gang brawl. But they had dug gold standing in cold green rains, frozen on mountain trails, faced the white bullies in dry gulch standoffs, lived through dangers and come out rich. They were of a sterner breed—and they decided they wanted this last deed to their credit *and* the Suey Sing before sailing home.

The two young miners made their move on the night of the Chinese New Year, a January 23rd. On Washington Street there was a barbershop on the street level of the place where Little Pete lived. Here, gay with the celebration of New Year's, Little Pete carelessly sent his body guard away to do some errand, feeling very safe in his own building. Little Pete's hair had to be just right for the night's festivities. The barber, who knew his whims, had him bending over a washbasin, the first step in preparing the two hour ritual it took to fit the fine queue for its proper plaiting.

Into the shop walked Lem Jung and Chew Tin Gop. No one was ever sure if they had skillfully planned their move, or had been lucky enough to stumble upon Little Pete, all alone with the barber—his head down under a flow of water, his back to them. Lem moved quickly toward the defenseless man, elbowed the barber aside and gripped Little Pete by his long loose hair. The barber gasped in horror. Chew Tin Gop remained on guard at the door.

Lem pushed the cold nose of a .45 revolver down between Little Pete's naked spine and the coat of mail. Five times he pressed the trigger, five times the barrel exploded its bullet and sent slugs into the backbone of Little Pete. It was that easy. The killers walked out into the noisy New Year's night to collect their reward money. To all the tongs (but one) they were folk heroes. They slipped home to China, and no records appear to be available of their later lives.

With Little Pete dead there was the usual gangster funeral, already it would seem an American tradition. Some say it was the most impressive and sensational cortege for a dead man that was ever held in San Francisco. It was more than a mile long. Three Chinese bands wailed and roared, firecrackers exploded like the blasts of Gatling guns often drowning out the rattles of the mourning priests shuffling along in their soot-black robes. The livery stables had their best hacks and carriages in line, and wagons followed loaded with the baked funeral meats—special rice dishes, crates of prime alcohol, chests of tea. While these viands were for the departed Little Pete symbolically to tuck away a good meal before starting the long climb up toward a special Chinese heaven, in reality the guests were to refresh themselves after the heroic procession and burial of the dead chieftain. However the unruly riffraff, the moochers and tramps that had followed the procession suddenly with a great cry threw themselves on the food and drink, putting the true mourners to the run and making a shambles of the funeral goodies and booze as they did away with it all. Little Pete's conservative orthodox religious soul would have been horrified.

With Mr. Big gone civil war reigned in Chinatown as power plays for the rich booty came into focus. Little Pete's Sum Yops were stomped into the ground and felt the edge of hatchets as rival *boo how doy* began a killing off of all competitors in grand free-for-all choppings in alleys, in the darkness of hallways, in the eating, gambling and sporting places of the tong boys.

In far-off China the Emperor Kwang Hsu called for his wise and worldly diplomat Li Hung Chang. It was this Chang who at a banquet given by him in New York City in 1894, fearing the white

51. *Chinese girls could cause tong wars by a smile.*

guests would not have the delicate civilized palate to appreciate true Chinese cuisine, had his chef throw together a mess of meat, soya bean, vegetables, salt and molasses which had been named then and there, in disdain, *chop suey*. Chang had a head on him. It was more than a hot dish for white devils that troubled the Emperor. The lawyer of the Sum Yops in San Francisco had written to the Emperor asking for royal aid to end the tong war that was destroying so many subjects of the Dragon Kingdom on foreign soil.

Li Hung said simply: "I have attended to the matter, sire. All the relatives of the Sue Yops have been collected and taken to prison. Word has been sent to California that all their heads will be chopped off if another Sum Yop is killed in California."

(Perhaps this was where Nazi agents in America during Hitler's days got the idea to influence some German-Americans by the sinister whisper, "You have maybe relatives in Germany?")

The tong wars ended in San Francisco as soon as Li Hung Chang's message was received. The Sue Yops and the Sum Yops sat down to draw up a permanent treaty of peace, to include all tongs.

Minor tong fracases have broken out. There have been killings, but no great war like the one that followed Little Pete's last shampoo has been repeated. Chinatown was to remain an unsavory, smelling place of alleys and cellars, opium and gambling dens, slave girls and crib whores. But more and more it was becoming a gathering place for outside visitors to eat food never heard of in China, for *chow mein*, too, was invented on American soil. There was a market for shoddy art, fortune-telling, "jade" ashtrays. The growing new Chinese-American population began to replace the vice and the sinister legends of the Chinese in the United States with a respectable blending of two cultures.

What was needed was a cleansing flame, the destruction of the firetraps, the slave shanties, the rotting refuse with which much of Old Chinatown was built. A cleaner, better designed, stronger (and safer) Chinatown would arise. But first would have to come the legendary Fire Dragon as pictured on so many Sung and T'ang screens, flames and soot pouring from flaring nostrils, sending tongues of scarlet flame in all directions.

The Fire Dragon was on his way in the warm spring night of a season of which a later poet would write: "April is the cruelest month."

Book Six

GOING OUT IN A BLAZE OF GLORY

52. 1906.

24

THE FATAL MORNING

At dawn, April 18, 1906, R.J. was awakened in a room of the Fairmont Hotel by a feeling of oppression, an incomprehensible uneasiness. He looked at the old double-lidded gold watch left him by his grandfather. He had difficulty seeing the hands. As he got out of bed he realized he was not alone. He remembered that the night before he and the young actor John Barrymore had attended a late party and had taken two ladies back to the hotel. He saw that Maude was still asleep, and he wondered if Barrymore (he actually did not know the actor very well) still had some man's fiancée in his suite. Walking to the window R.J. drew aside the shade and saw by the watch it was 5:08 A.M. He stood there looking over the streetlights dimming and heard the early cable cars already making their underground groans.

His daybook records what happened *then* (and from the care with which it was detailed and the many sheets of notes, collected by R.J. of his own impressions and vivid details, we can see how he set down a version of the next few days in the 1906 volume of his daybook).

"Had a sense I was at sea, an absolute impassiveness, the street below suddenly seemed to undulate, rippled like a pond, then an ocean. Saw a wall fall, heard behind me Maude cry out. I didn't move, just saw the shiver, the dance on roof tops. Chimneys went over, bricks fell, and I could feel the jar of the shock right to my toes as concentric fury shook the world. Some colossal quake was in progress.

"I said, 'It's a tremor.'

"Maude protested that her mother would worry. Grabbed at her lacies and gear and ran into the bathroom. I timed the shock. Began at 5:12. Ran itself out in one minute four seconds. Wood protesting with excruciating sounds, doors rattling, and outside dust beginning to rise. Was as if something, someone, was punching a great fist up from underneath. Began to dress and heard for the first time the roaring—grinding of the city in shock. Much awed I told Maude to hurry, and hunted my shoes. Head ached but I paid no attention to it. A wind swept by and made tearing sounds some place and the whole hotel seemed to shake. Grinding breaking noises lasted all the minute after the tremor.

"Felt somehow the colossal silence that followed was worse. A last brick falling, then the awful sense I was still drunk, this was only a nightmare; preposterous and still exuberant. Wanted to call on the actor, decided not to. Heard people crying in pain some place and yet I couldn't leave the window. South towards Market Street I seemed to see buildings huddled in bent shapes. Knew the dismal hotels there, Valencia, Brunswick and Cosmopolitan from my younger days. Wondered how the new City Hall had done with its six million dollars' worth of stone and style. Banal thought seemed to push aside the horror outside.

"Maude scurried past me, hair piled up every which way, hat on wrong. Hardly seemed to me anyone could dress that quickly.

"Thought of a drink but had nothing in the room. Dressed and went down. All confusion in the lobby, all over-polite etiquette forgotten. Some clerks beating their hands together, and from the street a pale gray-green light coming along with little puffs of dust; the air seemed thickening. Some desk clerk said: 'All that filled land once under water. Not going to hold, would you say?'

"Wondered why he said it. He added 'Montgomery Street out to the bay, all filled in. Just anything.' Heard water rushing some place and a dark stain seeped across the lobby rugs to my boot soles. 'Is the Ferry Building Tower still up?'

"No one knew if it was still there. Outside I saw twisted shadows. It was really a beautiful day. Now I saw a fine sky, in good April weather, dusting over. I saw people about in the street, animated and worried, in panic. Children still half asleep, rubbing their eyes. Felt silly myself, my shirt tail out, half of my braces down, the bowler hat too far back on my head. I suddenly remembered I hadn't combed my hair. The clerk came out to the sidewalk to join me.

" 'Telephone not working. Central doesn't answer. You think the fire alarm system could be out too?'

"Smoke was rising on Market Street. Wondered if the *Call* Building would burn. Decided to go back in, have a drink, some breakfast and wash. Thirteen minutes after the first shock, at 5:26, felt the first after-shocks and thought it wiser not to go up to the room after all. Never suspected such sanguine sagacity in myself, having always been a fool, prone to trouble."

As R.J. was later to discover and note, the City Hall had come apart with the brutal thrust of the shock, its columns falling like thunderbolts, toppling away with the grim weight of tons of stone, one slashing off the face of a Larkin Street rooming house. The filled land—as the clerk had feared—that once had been part of the Bay, wrinkled like a prune as the earthquake shivered the peninsula and the houses built on the fill sagged and bobbed about in all directions before settling all out of kilter. The market district, not much populated at sunrise, saw millions of bricks separate themselves from their wall positions and holding cement and strike out in all directions. The hill streets seemed to survive best, but plate glass and chimneys shattered, dishes came off shelves, pots banged against each other, art objects dissolved in fragments as they vibrated off their stands. The crash and clatter seemed to gain in volume after the first shock had passed in some capricious whim of balance and counter-balance.

Families came awake groping for each other, children howled and the old-fashioned box water-tanks secured over the toilets splashed out much of their contents. The shock left the city in a debauched condition. But worse was to come.

The wharves held up better, being cushioned in water, but Long Wharf, loaded with railroad coal, tens of thousands of tons of it— was crushed like a stepped-on-fruit by the black fuel in movement. R.J.'s worry over the famed Ferry Tower, a landmark in the city, was valid, for it had snapped itself about in the fury of the shock and gone back and forth observers said like a needle on a compass. But it stood, it still existed. Smoke stacks fell killing a few people. A fireman died before the fires started when he was hit by a section of falling roof. There was little awareness yet of the horror— just shock and disbelief.

It was more than only a San Francisco earthquake. R.J. collected newspaper clippings of the tremor's extent. The shock was estimated as covering thirty to forty miles in its widest part and being two hundred miles long, running from Fort Bragg up north to Salinas in the south. The State San Jose Insane Asylum walls gave way killing a hundred patients and attendants. Santa Rosa lost every brick structure. Hundreds were already dead while R.J. worried about his shirt tail sticking out. Millions in property was destroyed. The shock was deadly also in Berkeley, Oakland, Gilroy and Sebastopol. Its spasm struck redwood trees thousands of years old. They were toppled and broken at Santa Cruz, sixty miles south of the trembling city.

Already the streets were sending up smoke signals. Huntington and partners' railroad lost four thousand feet of steel rails in one gulp—they just slid off the cliffs into the blue Pacific. One train that remained on rails on land had its wheels knocked off by the shock and fell over on its side. But no one here was dead. Nature in places seemed to spare some with a kind of casual dalliance.

R.J. found a bar and had a drink of bourbon and a Denver egg sandwich. He went to see his friend, acting Fire Chief Daugherty. He writes in his daybook:

"Nothing too much known. D. said the units are all out and he thought fifty fires were raging. The alarm system working on wet cell batteries went out, but one had just to look up at the sky to locate a fire. Cable cars, phone services also out. Big columns of smoke settling over the water front. Mission District also sooty.

"General Funston commanded the local Militia; was said to be out inspecting the damage. Grace Church and Old St. Mary's stood the shock and the pious were soon going there to give a prayer. Sansome and Washington streets seemed to have the worst fires. Fire horses and bells went clanging, the grind of wheels loud on the streets, inordinately fearful sounds. No practice runs now, I thought, for a keg of beer at the station house. I felt my skin go taut and I held onto a strangely sensitive feeling of fear and excitement.

"Walked to Bush and Taylor streets to the firehouse of Engine 38. Damaged, but the men had the gear out and also gave me the news that Fire Chief Sullivan was dying in the ruins of his station. Never had a hope. Found the engine crew of 38 fighting a fire on Steuart Street, a sailors' supply shop. Hydrants all useless, just a few muddy drops came from them. Firemen cursed and I had full fear for the city for first time. San Francisco was in grave danger. Driver said, 'Mains all busted to hell. No water no place.' That was true all over the city I found out. Only thing to do was to form human chains and try and get out people trapped in ruins. Fires too strong in many ruins to get to anyone still alive in the rubble and timbers. Broke my cane trying to pry up a granite step beyond which lay a man with a beam across his back. He died yelling, 'Come on, get me. For the mercy of God come and get me.'

No one could. The smoke, greeny-yallery, was choking, the flames bright yellow, with red edges. Wondered how my sisters were doing on Golden Gate Avenue, and also the horse and gig I had stabled in the Hayes Valley district.

"Helped get some laundry wagons done into ambulances—threw out the bundles and began to aid in loading hurt people for the hospitals. Engine driver shook his head. 'Them horsepitals ain't takin'. They're movin' out the sick and dyin' to safer places.'

"Later heard the Central Hospital was a ruin. The shock just tore it apart like paper and it fell back on the doctors and nurses. They had little chance to survive in the dust and fallen ceilings. Happy to hear my friend Dr. McGinty was saved. There was a rough sort

of hospital set up camp style in the Mechanics Pavillion. It was
soon flooded by an army of the hurt, burned and dying. The city
was entirely unprepared, yet we had jested for years on the earth
fault under us.

"Water soon being pumped from the bay and talk of dynamiting
buildings to stop the spreading of fires talked of. But not enough
pumps. Many people fought the idea of blowing up their homes
and businesses. Lost my bowler hat, had one knee burned out on
my trousers. Hurt like the devil.

"9 o'clock before I realized how tired and smudged I was. Went
to our wine warehouse in North Beach where I kept some extra
luggage and clothes and washed up, salved burned knee, and
changed into some hardier clothes than a claw-hammer coat. Put
on a hunting jacket and checked Scot's cap, heavy shoes. Mayor

53. Refugees from fire soon were every place, moving on.

Schmitz had ordered the police to close every saloon and bar. Couldn't get to the *Call* Building, the office space I rented.

"The mayor seized all auto cars to carry messages and a Committee of Fifty was appointed. About that time looting and breaking into saloons going on on the Coast and Tenderloin. The greed and rancor added to the terror of the day. Potent evil there since the 49er days still mean and vehement. Smelled only doom, the reek of burning shacks, soot and carbon in the air every place. Plumes of smoke rising in new places, yet here and there sky was clear. Had a hasty meal of *pasta* and some fish with Angelo, the warehouse man, at his place. Told him to load a handcart and put his *bambinos* and Bianca on top and start for his brother's farm if the fire came near. Said to him if the city's men wanted to use the barreled wine to put out fires they could. But asked Angelo to bury the good brandy under wet earth and damp sacks in the deepest cellar where I kept some tins of Malossol cariar. I felt disconsolate and lonely."

R.J. knew things would get worse. The looting of pawnshops and breaking into houses was proceeding from the Barbary Coast into the more respectable parts of the city, the fires growing and the smoke making an oily choking darkness over the streets.

The mayor wrote out telegrams: SEND FIRE ENGINES, HOSE, DYNAMITE IMMEDIATELY. The governor telegraphed Los Angeles: FOR GOD'S SAKE SEND FOOD. Fire engines with steam up and chomping gray horses came over from Oakland across the Bay on ferryboats. They fought off the flames approaching the Appraiser's Office at Washington Street. Now everyone knew it was a full disaster. General Funston ordered all troops in the district to assemble at the Hall of Justice. Lawlessness was primed to take over the city, for the sons and grandsons of the Sydney Ducks, the thieves, second story workers, pickpockets and ponces of the dives were out to see what they could take away from the fire. Army H.Q. was stationed in the Phelan Building on Market Street and the gray quilt of smoke bannered across the city as in a Chinese painting from already burning Chinatown.

R.J. the next morning at 7 A.M. (he does not tell us where he slept) saw the troops armed with bayonets on their rifles marching down Market Street. The Presidio Army detachments reached the city an hour later, made up of horses, guns, batteries, infantry and stubborn army mules. Seventeen hundred men were ordered out to patrol on the streets with orders "to shoot on sight anyone looting or committing a misdemeanor."

"The crowds," R.J. wrote, "still felt this a sort of bad dream ending, and cheered the soldier boys. Thomi, the young fruit peddler, with his empty barrow was watching the fire and passing around some vile red wine he brewed himself. He was singing his favorite song:

> *Voi; chi sapete*
> *Che cosa e amor!*

"A group were gathered in the Palace Hotel, old companions. We had been young men together in the city. There was the sad gray look on our faces I saw, of our awareness of youth gone and the city going. Suppose it was because we were drinking, against the mayor's orders, rye whisky from kitchen glasses in a passage by a pantry. Sensed how much I had loved the city, had accepted it and always hurried back to it when away. Now it was burning and nobody talked much. Among us the manager of a Wells-Fargo office, the chief accountant from the Central Pacific, the lumberman who had six barges of Douglas fir timbers at Long Pier and no crews to move them from the fire.

"Felt the pioneers had it easier in disaster. They had no burdens of the responsibilities that had followed. We had a city. Thought of my grandfather, a young rebel fleeing the failure of the Revolution of '48 in Germany. Suddenly he was a student no longer but one of those who came here, he used to say—to change himself rather than the rules of the world. Made a fortune cutting railroad ties, lost a fortune speculating in silver, but lived well. He laughed a lot, said the city was something a man could be proud of. Now, no water. The whole crowded way of life a fiasco because no one had thought the water mains would be broken, snapped by an earth tremor. All that water in the Bay, but not enough pumps or lines to carry it to the fires.

"Went out to the lobby. What was amazing was the absolute impassiveness of some of the watchers, just staring stonefaced. Then the twitching uneasiness of so many others as if feeling guilty, shaking their heads as if begging your goddamn pardon for all this. A pantry-man passed and said the flag was still flying over the hotel. Some man, very drunk, cheered. No one joined in."

Already there were voices crying out San Francisco was a city of sinners and God was punishing it.

Quoted was Saint Augustine, who could point to himself in his youth as an evil fellow wallowing in the pleasures of the act: "And what was it that I delighted in, but to love, and be beloved? but I kept not the measure of love, of mind to mind, friendship's bright boundary; but out of the muddy concupiscence of the flesh, and the bubblings of youth, mists fumed up which beclouded and overcast my heart. . . . I was tossed about, and wasted, and dissipated, and I boiled over in my fornications."

Some found other early church writers on the subject more deeply outraged against women as sinners: "In the woman wantonly adorned to capture souls, the garland upon her head is as a single coal or firebrand of Hell to kindle men with that fire. . . . In a single day, by her dancing or her perambulation through the town, she inflames with the fire of her lust perhaps twenty of those who behold her, damning the souls God has created and redeemed at such a cost."

And the man who felt safe in his own marriage, legally blessed by the church, sporting with his own wife, had a shock coming from the preachers who found texts as the flames spread: "It is disgraceful to love another man's wife at all, or one's own too much. A wise man ought to love his wife with judgment, not with passion. Let a man govern his voluptuous impulses, and not rush headlong into intercourse. . . . He who too ardently loves his own wife is an adulterer."

25

TRUE AND FALSE

A mighty fountain momently was forced,
Amid whose swift half-intermitted burst
Huge fragments vaulted like rebounding hail,
Or chaffy grain beneath the thresher's flail;
And 'mid these dancing rocks at once and ever
It flung up momently the sacred river.

"Cynicism, prayer, candor and lewdness," R.J. wrote, "held the city as the fire spread. . . . The *Slocum*, the army tug, is bringing in the 22nd Infantry. Commanders have been alerted as far away as Fort Baker, also Vancouver Barracks, near Canada, the Presidio in Monterey. Also Alcatraz on the island in the Bay. Got a copy of the mayor's poster (pasted in daybook).

PROCLAMATION

BY THE MAYOR

The Federal Troops, the members of the Regular Police Force and all Special Police Officers have been authorized by me to KILL any and all persons found engaged in Looting or in the Commission of Any Other Crime.

I have directed all the Gas and Electric Lighting Co.'s not to turn on Gas or Electricity until I order them to do so. You may therefore expect the city to remain in darkness for an indefinite time.

I request all Citizens to remain at home from darkness until daylight every night until order is restored.

I WARN all Citizens of the danger of Fire from Damaged or Destroyed Chimneys, Broken or Leaking Gas Pipes or Fixtures, or any like cause.

E. E. SCHMITZ, Mayor
Dated, *April 18, 1906*
Altvater Print . . . Mission & 22d Sts

"Spreading fires are fearful sights. By noon everything south of Market Street seems gone. Merrill & Stetson, The Emporium, Willie Hearst's building.

"Meanwhile a woman in the Hayes Valley district, attempting to cook a meal, set the house on fire because of a damaged flue; and the fire was let loose in a new place and it spread a fury of destruction. The Ham-n-Egg fire, as it came to be called, one of the largest if not the largest let loose on the city."

Headlines in the Oakland newspapers: PALACE HOTEL ON FIRE. Yes, the dream place of so much planning, so much plush social doings, was going—with the imported toilet seats, the fine spittoons, all destined to end up in smoke.

CLIFF HOUSE TOPPLES INTO THE OCEAN. It seemed a sad ending for all the discreet private rooms, such an easy meeting place of lovers, the town's concupiscence and love of life, the garter snapping joy of courtesans and actresses, memories of a thousand mock seductions orchestrated to the soft tap of a waiter bringing in the coffee with averted eyes. (But actually Cliff House was unharmed.)

FERRY TRAFFIC STOPPED. (Private boats charged all the traffic could bear.) The city seemed isolated from the mainland beyond Berkeley and Oakland, from all California massing behind its dun-colored hills.

ST. IGNATIUS CHURCH AND COLLEGE OF JESUIT OR-DER BURNS.

So Old China, the Chinatown of fake opium dens (and real ones), the nest of shacks and cellars of slave girls: all gone. Afterward there was talk of not permitting a new Chinatown to be erected in the city which was to come out of the flame. *The Over-land Monthly* was smugly to write: "Fire has reclaimed to civilization and cleanliness the Chinese ghetto, and no Chinatown will be permitted in the borders of the city. Some other provision will be made for the caring of the orientals." But owners of land know no bigotry—see only income. It was to be rebuilt right where it had burned out. No one ever knew how many girl slaves were lost or how many escaped the fire. They were too cowed and morally destroyed to run away—and where to?

Before the last flames of San Francisco's fire died out nearly thirty thousand buildings would be destroyed, from shacks to the great mansions of the merchants and railroad kings. Four square miles of city would go—522 blocks would be lost. And human loss? Between those persons who were reported dead and those *missing* and never seen again nearly seven hundred people were dead.

HORRIBLE CRIME OF A REGULAR SOLDIER!

A United States soldier, a sentinel on duty, last night outraged a young woman in San Francisco, using his gun to enforce his demands and to intimidate her terror-stricken relatives.

It was amazing to some moralists how cleansing the fire had been in the vice districts. Parlor houses, sporting dens, cribs, crimp saloons, deadfalls, wino cellars, tong hideouts; almost all were gone. On Grant Avenue, Morton Street, on Telegraph Hill—most were just black-burned carbon, crisp brick, broken glass. The smell of stale bedding singed and burned out was every place. Sorry weeping and cursing whores on the run gave a heightened irrelevance to the damage.

Here and there a whorehouse had managed to survive, and soon reopened to business but when the Army stepped in with the police they cut short the cries of "Company Girls! Liberty Hall!" However the demand was there (as soldier rapists proved) and across the Bay the brothels were kept open. The chief of police of Oakland put it squarely man to man to a reporter:

"It seemed a proper thing to do to calm the nerves of the sufferers with a little fun and girls." (R.J. once reported Ambrose

Bierce, the critic of social morality, as saying: "It's the duty of every Christian to offer a drowning man a cup of water.")

The daybook gives some interesting sidelights on the dramatic turbulence of the fire. R.J., as a man who regularly gave cases of wine and brandies to police, to fire department balls, had a special pass and the run of the ruins, and he seemed to possess an inexhaustible energy.

"Oddest sight, the Chinese, hands up their sleeves, a derby called an iron hat on their heads. Many herding Chinese children, calmly marching them out to parks—as the women carry bundles, and behind them their homes burn. On Morton Street met Charlie J. carrying a huge metal letter file. Charlie, a noted pickpocket and visiters tout, is an amusing clown. Said to Charlie, 'You'll be shot for looting.' 'Lor, gov, ain't nuthin' 'ere but me life's savings. Can't carry it much further.'

"Charlie, an old Sydney Duck, set down his burden, got some iron railing and mashed open the metal box. Inside a collection of Indian seed corn, some faded red hair ribbons. Charlie looked at it, kicked it into the gutter, raised his hand as if in benediction: 'Bloody well diddled, warn't I?'

"Many of the water mains burst, broken by the tremor. Already there is a stink in the air. Yet saw several young boys calmly playing at paper boats in a puddle made by water pumped from the bay to fight the fire. In an empty lot among rusty discards and weeds sat a little old lady eating ship's biscuits out of a bag and weeping. It seems her dog Nig is lost. 'He was such a comfort, such a bright animal, you know.'

"Told her he'd be found, but doubt it. Several dogs had been bayoneted by the soldiers when they went wild among the ruins or appeared fearfully burned. Went down to Kearny Street where I was amazed to find that Mother C——'s place was still standing, singed but there, the perceptible vitality of the iron horse tie (a jockey figure) still cleanly painted at the curb. I didn't get an answer to my first knock, but then Bitsy the colored maid opened the door, her face stained with tears. Inside the parlor a great noise. Mother shouted for me to get out of the g.d. door—was I raised in a barn?—and I found her in the yellow silk parlor with two men, both of them drunk. Mother seemed wider than ever, her usual cheroot shorter but lit, and her massive neckless head resting on her breasts, legs crossed before her. 'The damn girls all run off. Wouldn't you know. Take my linen, take my towels, and leave me to handle the boys.'

"One of the drunks smiled, had the good color of an open air dweller. 'We come a far bit, been delivering riding stock down the coast aways. Come here to jolly the girls. Get our ashes hauled. Been on the range six, seven months. Not a damn thing to shag.'

"Mother threw up her hands and shrugged her big shoulders. 'Now they want to take *me* upstairs.'

"The talkative one said, 'Yes mam [sic], we'd deem it a pleasure, mam.' [sic]

"Suggested to them the fire might come back. Mother was worried only about the towels and linen the girls had carried off in their flight. 'Hand-hemmed sheets, you don't see that no more.'

"I left them—very *en famille*, unreal in the fire, the two cowboys and the madame drinking and meantime they trying to coax her to take them upstairs. It hardly seemed possible at Mother's to feel that the whole city was burning, hundreds were dead, soldiers patrolling the peninsula against looters, plague a threat. No, not at Mother C——'s fire-circled bordello.

"Saw a sign chalked up on a board as I left the street: EAT, DRINK, AND BE MERRY, FOR TOMORROW WE MAY HAVE TO GO TO OAKLAND. Never was much love among the people for those who live across the bay. Bank tellers carting negotiable bonds and bags of silver down Market Street in wheelbarrels, a million dollars at a time, they say. Tom Crowley on the water is working his motorboat over time carrying passengers to safety. Fifty cents a head over to Oakland from foot of Vallejo Street. One woman was left behind because she wanted to take two huge cages, each containing a parrot, refused to pay four bits for each bird; cursing; and the parrots, I must say joined her and were as talented as she was. Some woman almost got burned alive rescuing plants, rare ones, from the California Academy of Science.

The uniqueness of what people want to save at near cost of life is baffling to me.

"Got back to the Palace Hotel—everything deep in fallen debris. Enrico Caruso, the opera singer—he fell out of bed on the first shock, I hear, covered with falling plaster. He got away today by train, saying he'd rather take Vesuvius. Delightful fellow and a great feeder. It's hard to live in a city with no newspaper. The most dreadful rumors go about: hundreds shot as looters, rapists active, wide cracks swallowing up dogs and ponies. Stories of criminal men and women out from the Coast dives cutting off ring fingers and ears with earrings from the dead and injured. Later General Funston told me, 'Oh, just two or three on the spot shootings.' Reporters insist between fifty and a hundred were shot, mostly by the militia.

"Homeless people are gathered in Mission Park, Lafayette Square, the Presidio, Golden Gate Park. Everybody carries something. Birds, dogs, bundles, trunks, banjos, plants in pots, frying pans, rolled rugs. Exodus of the new Jews into the flaming wilderness. Whatever is saved seemed doubly precious.

"Saw Jim the waiter from Cliff House—famous for his answer to Hearst's 'I do openly what others do behind doors.' Jim's answer, 'Sir, that is what doors are for.' Jim says Cliff House did not fall into sea.

"Reports are the dynamite wasn't doing much good. Rocked the Hearst and Call buildings but structures too well built to be blown to dust. There is a lot of talk the whole business of blowing up buildings is stupid and does little to stop the fire.

"Old man comes to me carrying a Civil War sword and Michigan regiment battle flag, a buffalo-hide trunk on the sidewalk. Curses the draymen. 'Twenty dollars I'll give them, but seventy-five I'd rather burn to the effing ground here with all my things! Seventy-five dollars to haul me away! Why, sir, they'd kiss your ass in good times for a dollar.'

"Irish drayman passing shouts, 'Foxey Grandpa! Today you kin kiss *my* arse, *and* for free.'

54. *The San Francisco fire out of control.*

"Police are being killed by badly fused dynamite charges. I knew
Lt. Pulis, who was blown to bits by an explosion that went off too
soon on Van Ness Avenue. Poppa Coppa's place is saved, and he
fed a few old patrons through the side door as long as he could.
Myself I'd rather have lost the Mint than Poppa's, but Mint is saved
too. Later was told a gang of about twenty men tried to attack the
Mint at the height of the fire to get at the coin and gold bars
stored there. Some say 50 million, some 200 million in gold is
there. Troops are rumored to have killed the entire gang on the steps
of the Mint as they attacked.

"Added note: Although the Mint attack never took place, people
swear they witnessed the robbery attempt and the battle. I myself
was sure I saw an uncle of mine, dead ten years, drinking a bottle
of wine and waving at me from the windows of the Palace Hotel,
its flag flying. I clearly saw my uncle's ribbon of the Legion
d'Honneur. Knew it was an illusion of too much smoke, too much
excitement, frayed nerves, drinks. Uncle had been a calm lazy man

who when he got back from the Klondike and was asked how were conditions up on the Yukon answered, 'Cold.'

"It is about 3:40 when the flag on the Palace Hotel is burned off. By late afternoon the marvelous hotel is gone. The whole center went up first, a red inferno, a great flaming monstrosity, disquieting to us who loved it—who feel a part of ourselves is gone.

"I hear that Jack London has come down from his crazy ranch place up in Sonoma to write a report of the fire. . . . Saw it in print later and I figured Jack must have gone to some bar, gotten slowly drunk and made up the report. J.L. has a fundamental incompatibility of temperament."

The Jack London report of the fire R.J. writes about can be found in a book called *Current Literature*. In part London wrote: "I saw not one woman who wept, not one man who was excited, not one person who was in the slightest degree panic stricken." R.J. may well have been right when he suspected Jack London made up his report, at least that part, and the lines, "Never, in all San Francisco's history were her people so kind and courteous as on the night of terror." Hardly in key with press reports and R.J.'s daybook.

The newspapers, when they got editions onto the street, all imported from Oakland, used the biggest type on April 19.

PEOPLE SHOT DOWN BY SOLDIERS
IN STREETS OF SAN FRANCISCO

PEOPLE BURNED ALIVE!

TODAY IS DECLARED A LEGAL HOLIDAY.

The last item remains a puzzlement, unless it referred to court cases and bank loans, which, on a non-holiday date might have been the cause of some legal claptrap later on. No other reason for declaring a holiday unless someone was celebrating the anniversary of the burning of Rome by Nero.

The Big Four mansions, some already public institutions, went up with a roar. Mark Hopkins' towered, gingerbreaded Victorian fruitcake architecture burned as did all that Central Pacific loot used for the mansions of Stanford, Huntington, Crocker; all were soon ash. The elegant Fairmont Hotel of rare marbles and loaded with art and splendid furniture was not spared.

R.J. records: "Chinatown, all gone. Thousands of Chinese have left it, many with rarely or never seen wives on tiny bound feet. Nob Hill, Russian Hill devastated, everyone sooty, everyone looking for water, something to eat. Children crying, women weeping, men looking numb, or drinking warm beer salvaged from ruins. U. S. Navy is landing men of the Pacific Fleet rushed here from base at San Diego. Stupidity takes no holiday, small minds in power causing trouble. Military most of all.

"Hell to raise with the soldiers who are ordering thousands from their homes and give them no time to pack or carry off more than the barest necessities. People cursing now the boys in blue they had been cheering the day before. Great fears the prisoners in the jail at Hall of Justice would break out and cause terror. Went down there, found most of the prisoners and the bodies from the temporary morgue deposited there have been moved elsewhere. The desperate, hard case prisoners handcuffed, to Alcatraz; the hobos, vags, street walkers, pickpockets, drunks sent on to Fort Mason.

As the fire advances to Portsmouth Square the bodies of victims from the morgue are being buried in shallow scooped out graves that will not protect them from the advancing fire. Dreadful, horrible idea, even if they are dead. Strange sight of a dazed man looking at a corpse of a child. 'No, no, she isn't dead. She just sleeps hard. No, I tell you she isn't dead.' Man led off dry-eyed, still insisting, by National Guards.

"Slept the night in Jefferson Square, a kind of picnic atmosphere. Lots of whisky around and lots of nips taken. Saw a couple of tarts seated on a piano in the street, sipping whisky and singing 'A Hot Time in the Old Town Tonight.' Strange sense of humor. Men eager as satyrs for the whores. Tents and blankets being given out by the soldiers. Young hoodlums and the gay girls laughing and carrying on.

"Hay is being spread around to sleep on and feed the thousands of horses who have no stables for shelter, no one to care for them. Everybody writing messages and trying to send them out through some kind of makeshift post office. Have no word of my sisters, but I'm sure they got away to the farm. Lots of stories of babies, prime and premature, being born all over the place, but I've seen no new babies. Supplies coming in; there's no hunger. No gourmet dishes either—bread, beans, corned beef, and vile it is too; rumors it's from the War with Spain. The bakeries are busy on 24 hour shifts. Grocer I knew at North Beach sold me canned lobster, French peas, six pounds of dried mixed fruit—at only three times usual price. The water supply doesn't exist. No one is allowed to use the toilets or plumbing indoors. Army is giving lessons in how to dig latrines. Went back to Mother C——'s but the place was burnt down to a malodorous ruin. Asked some Naval person on patrol if they had found three bodies in the ruins, but they didn't know. Red-eyed and drunk. Very young soldiers. Treated me with a sort of fastidious shyness."

R.J. need not have worried over Mother C——, the whorehouse madam, wherever she was. Three months after the great fire it seemed most of the brothels were back in business, concert saloons blaring, the dancing more shameless than ever. Yet it was different. Moral bankruptcy would continue, but the old patterns would be radically changed.

R.J. was aware that neither the Coast nor the new city to come would ever be the same as it had been. The great raunchy days of the Gold Rush had to subside into the historic past; old buildings, the rats' nests, even the solid stone of the robber barons were gone. What would come would still make room for laughter, the cavorting and carrying on. But San Francisco belonged now to another era; as if the twentieth century had come to it just a little late—in 1906.

The local poets were soon at work. Larry Harris dashed off an echo of Rudyard Kipling, Robert Service and Eddie Guest.

THE DAMNDEST FINEST RUINS
Put me somewheres west of East Street where there's nothing left
    but dust,
And the boys are all abustling and everything's gone bust;
And where the buildings that are standing sort of blink and blindly
    stare
At the damndest finest ruins ever gazed on anywhere . . .

And a professional gambler wrote a letter to his brother in St.
Louis: "The damn truth is the sports are so busy trying to figure
out how to get enough cash and men and lumber to rebuild you
can't get a card game going in this burg unless you like solitaire.
As for the can houses, Maude Smith told me herself the husbands
are staying so close to their wives like they were first married, and
the girls in her place are eating their heads off and it's hardly worth
opening the parlor and getting the piano player in. But she says
once the excitement of the fire goes skiddoo, they'll all be back, eyes
out on stems for a bit of fun."

Citizens still talk of "the swine among the insurance companies,"
the German ones. "The Rhine and Moselle Fire Insurance Company" just refused to pay the nearly five million dollars it owed
burned-out householders and businessmen; refused with that firm
Teutonic indifference to decency and law for other people. One
insured citizen, Edward F. Braunschweiger III saw his warehouses of
wine, whisky and brandy go exploding in smoke and flame. The
just claim he had was for $38,000. The Germans merely sneered.
Since 1906 Mr. Braunschweiger has been trying to collect. Congress
and the federal courts after World War II heard his pleas that since
the U.S.A. then controlled the funds of the German insurance
companies, the Alien Property Custodian should pay him from their
rich hoard. With interest and legal fees he was owed $700,000. The
Kennedy brothers, who seemed to favor the Germans against American interests (as *Fortune* magazine revealed in a big story), killed
all hopes of just payment. The *Congressional Record* shows Mr. B.
is still trying to collect. One of his splendid moves was to ask that

55. *The city recovered from the fire quickly.*

the final peace treaty with Germany be delayed until he was paid
—a gesture in the true San Francisco manner of *la belle époque.*
Few people remember the chicanery of the German insurance
companies. But almost any modern citizen will repeat untruths as
published in a San Francisco newspaper in 1956: "Fourteen men
were shot, picked off like birds, trying to loot the United States
Mint. Fourteen soldiers, caught by other soldiers in the act of looting
a saloon, were hanged."

And proud is the native who will take you to the main post office
and point to the crawling cracks—like demonological writing—in
the terrazzo floor that date to the morning of April 18, 1906.
It all fits Coleridge's lines:

> But oh! that deep romantic chasm which slanted
> Down the green hill athwart a cedarn cover!
> A savage place! as holy and enchanted
> As e'er beneath a waning moon was haunted
> By woman wailing for her demon-lover!
> And from this chasm, with ceaseless turmoil seething,
> As if this earth in fast thick pants were breathing . . .

R.J. writes very little of how he survived, but two weeks after
the fire he sent out a small personal notice that he was back in
business.

FINE IMPORTED WINES AND SPIRITS

Some rare Vintages have Survived.

Listings taken for New Shipments ordered by cable.

"A little fire is quickly trodden out."

Shakespeare, *Henry VI*

We shall leave R.J. for good with the entry in his daybook of
Saturday, April 21. "All over now. Smoke smell remains in hair and
clothes—in the water, the food. But all fires are out. Last rush of

fire was down south ridge of Telegraph Hill last night. The Waterfront warehouses are safe. Beginning to rain. Rain hard. Bierce said
it also rained after Waterloo, after Gettysburg."

> Who shall ascend the mountain of Yahweh?
> And who shall stand in his holy place?
> The clean of hands and pure of heart;
> > who has not raised his mind to an idol
> > nor sworn by a fraud.
> He shall receive blessings from Yahweh.